W9-AGT-076

# MY VAST
# FORTUNE

ALSO BY ANDREW TOBIAS

*The Funny Money Game*

*Fire and Ice*

*The Only Investment Guide
You'll Ever Need*

*Getting By on $100,000 a Year
(And Other Sad Tales)*

*The Invisible Bankers*

*Money Angles*

*The Only* Other *Investment Guide
You'll Ever Need*

*Kids Say Don't Smoke*

*Auto Insurance Alert!*

# ANDREW TOBIAS

$$$$$$$$$$$$$$$$$$$$$$$$$$$$$$$$$$$$$$$$$$$$$$$$$$$$$$$$$$$$$$$$$$$$$$$$$$$$$$$$$$$$$$$$$$$$$$$$$$

# MY VAST FORTUNE

## The Money Adventures of a Quixotic Capitalist

A HARVEST BOOK

HARCOURT BRACE & COMPANY

SAN DIEGO    NEW YORK    LONDON

Copyright © 1997 by Andrew Tobias

All rights reserved. No part of this publication may be reproduced or
transmitted in any form or by any means, electronic or mechanical,
including photocopy, recording, or any information storage and
retrieval system, without permission in writing from the publisher.

Requests for permission to make copies of any part of the work
should be mailed to: Permissions Department, Harcourt Brace &
Company, 6277 Sea Harbor Drive, Orlando, Florida 32887-6777.

---

Caution: Portions of this book have been published
in other forms elsewhere. You are purchasing words that
may have been *previously read*.

---

Portions of this work were originally published in *Worth* magazine and
*Getting By on $100,000 a year* by Andrew Tobias (Simon & Schuster).

Grateful acknowledgement is made to Harcourt Brace & Company for
permission to reprint excerpts from *The Only Investment Guide You'll
Ever Need* by Andrew Tobias. Reprinted by permission of Harcourt
Brace & Company.

*My Vast Fortune* is published by arrangement with Random House, Inc.

Library of Congress Cataloging-in-Publication Data
Tobias, Andrew P.
My vast fortune: the money adventures of a Quixotic capitalist/
Andrew Tobias.
p.    cm.
Reprint. 1st ed. published: New York: Random House, 1997.
Includes index.
ISBN 0-15-600622-7
1. Tobias, Andrew P.    2. Capitalists and financiers—United States—
Biography.    I. Title.
HC102.5.T63A3    1998
332'.092    98-21198
[B]—DC21

Printed in the United States of America

First Harvest edition 1998

ACEFDB

*In memory of Allard K. Lowenstein*

Disclaimer: Any phrase, passage or construction herein that may strike you as "funny" should not be taken as such. Do not be fooled. This is serious business. Thinly cloaked as an appeal to amusement and greed, the real aim of this book is to make knee-jerk liberals (of whom the author basically is one) a little less automatically reflexive; and conservatives (of whom the author claims several as friends) a touch more compassionate. As that old wordsmith George Bush might have phrased it: Bleeding hearts—good. Jerking knees—baaaad.

$$$$$$$$$$$$$$$$$$$$$$$$$$$$$$$$$$$$$$$$$$$$$$$$$$$$$$$$$$$$$$$$$$$$$$$$$$$$$$$$$$$$$$$$$$$$$$$$$$$$$$$$$$

# Acknowledgments

I could be richer, but hardly more fortunate. At every unplanned turn there have been people presenting opportunities I would never even have thought to pursue. Dusty Burke and Chip Filson, at Harvard. Shelly Zalaznick and Clay Felker, at *New York*. John Hawkins and Jerry Rubin, at MECA. Nan Talese, who persuaded me to write about the insurance industry. Bob Hunter, who persuaded me to try to fix a piece of it. Eugene Shirley, who had an idea for a PBS series. Joe Ricketts, who suggested an Internet "column." And more.

With respect to this book, I have Jonathan Karp, my excellent editor, to thank (and Amanda Urban, my pal of thirty years, for hooking us up), as well as my excellent editors at *Worth,* John Koten and Jane Berentson. (Two of my other excellent editors: Walter Anderson and David Currier at *Parade*.) Also, Emmy Award–winning fact checker Nick Pachetti.

With respect to some of the events recounted here, I'm grateful to Spencer Martin, Andy Zaslow, Beth McClain, Chris Schoenwald, Mike Starkey, Gary Cifatte and Bart Barker, among the many who made "my" software so good; Sal Patronaggio, Margaret Tynan, Tino and Luis Flores, Luis Roman, William Galecio, Charlie Duckworth and Mary O'Neil, who put in long hours trying to improve a neighborhood; Alexey Krasnov, Ilya Slutsky and Dmitry Cherneshenko, my esteemed Russian partners (and their esteemed wives, Tanya, Tanya and Tanya); Bob Joost and Angelo Papparella, among the many unsung heroes of the auto insurance wars (others, like Mike Johnson and Tom Proulx, are sung in Chapter 4).

With respect to life in general, where would I be without Jane, Fred and Willy? Murph, Nancy, Tim, Duncan and Kelly? Michael, Susie and Adam? Everyone named Zofnass? Almost everyone named Bortz? Marie and Ernie? John and Chelle? Jesse? Laura? Barry? David? David and Arthur? The Hallers? Andy and Jody? Lisa and Steve? Steve Morgan? Steve Gilbert? Steve Neckman? Steve Sapka? Steve Tobias?

And that's just real life (and incomplete). What about cyberlife? E-pals I've rarely or never met have been incredibly generous with their time and expertise—among them, Don Trivette, Less Antman and Dave Davis.

Thanks to Julie Dorf, Kevin Jennings, Jonathan Rotenberg, Charlie Kaiser, Joy and Herb Kaiser, Phil and Linda Lader, Joe Cherner (and Laurent!), who've shown me what terrific things one or two dedicated people can accomplish. And to Jim and Gayle Halperin, Bob Wilson, Terry Watanabe, Fred Hochberg, Adam R. Rose, Tim Gill and Max Palevsky, among others, for saying yes when so many say no.

Thanks, also, to Larry, Mark, Jimmy, Stewart, Eddy, the Banks, Wallace and Andy B, in Miami; and, in Los Angeles, to Paul and Doug, trapezist Tom Moore, Scrabble champ Richard Fischoff, attorney Mark Katz and indie prod Larry Mark.

Thanks, finally and especially, to Charles, who is in charge, and to Mom and Lew, who set a great example.

You can't have everything. Where would you put it?
—STEVEN WRIGHT

Let everyone sweep in front of his or her own door
and the whole world will be clean.
—GOETHE

$$$$$$$$$$$$$$$$$$$$$$$$$$$$$$$$$$$$$$$$$$$$$$$$$$$$$$$$$$$$$$$$$$$$$$$$$$$$$$$$$$$$$$$$$$$$$$$$$$$$$$$$$$$$$

# Contents

Acknowledgments ix

1. My Vast Fortune 3
2. Never Buy Real Estate Over the Phone 39
3. My Partners' Wives Are All Named Tanya 57
4. Ralph Nader Is a Big Fat Idiot 70
5. Bleeding Hearts Versus Jerking Knees 116
6. Your Vast Fortune 158

Appendices
A. Props 201 and 202 185
B. Michigan: The Exception 188
C. Letters to the Editor 189
D. A Sampling of Historic Document Dealers 195
E. How Not to Fix Social Security (and Why
We Don't Need a Balanced Budget) 196

Index 201

# MY VAST
# FORTUNE

# 1

# MY VAST FORTUNE

## Before You Give It Away,
## You Have to Make It

### 1—First Wad

I'll never forget being interviewed by Werner Erhard—for two hours—on the subject of money. Not how to make it or invest it or any of the ordinary topics but how to *be* with it. I had no idea then what exactly the Est guru meant by this, though I was certainly impressed by dinner on his yacht the night before—*he* knew how to be with money, I figured—and I have equally little idea now. I was even more baffled when viewers told me how much our closed-circuit TV conversation had helped *them* be with money. It had?

But I'll say this. I do like being with money.

I began accumulating my vast fortune in 1952, when my father gave me $5 for my fifth birthday. Five dollars was a lot more in 1952 than it is today (about $29 in today's money), and I would like to tell you I did something unusually precocious with it, or with the $6 I got when I turned six, or the $7 the year after that. Not to mention my allowance, which must have been in the twenty-five-cent range back then, before I learned to negotiate.

Instead, the money got spent, mostly down at Trella's, the local variety store.

One of the things I am famous in my family for having said—not that I have any recollection of having said it, or that it took much to become famous in my family—was uttered when my grandmother asked me where all my money was. "The bank," she was perhaps expecting me to say. Or "the piggy bank." But it was in neither of these. "Right now it's in Trella's," I apparently said.

I had not yet learned to save.

But I did like money. For one thing, I liked numbers. For another, I was competitive, and doubtless saw money for what it is—and practically *all* it is once you have more than you need—a way to keep score. Let others be class president or veep; in high school, treasurer was my political calling. I liked counting the money. I liked the feel of a couple of hundred dollars in small bills in my pocket.

It wasn't about greed—it wasn't *my* money, after all. And it wasn't exactly power. I didn't control how we would spend it. It wasn't even about float—savings accounts all paid 3 percent back then, by law, so there was not a lot one could do with $200 overnight.

I guess it made me feel important?

## 2—Uncle Lou

Growing up in Manhattan, and in Westchester on weekends, we led your basic blessed very-upper-middle-class life. We weren't wealthy— all the money that came in went right back out for orthodontia, tuition, the maid (in the Fifties, you didn't have to be rich to have a maid), the two cars, and on and on. Though I didn't know it at the time, there was a period of years when my mother would cry each month when she did the bills. Income was high, but so were expenses.

Uncle Lou, on the other hand, was wealthy. Short, fat and jolly, with a gold chain from his vest to his pants pocket—I never saw him in anything other than a three-piece suit—he looked like the rich uncle in the Monopoly game. Whenever he came to visit, the coins in his pocket positively jingled—dazzling enough to a little kid, but then he would pull out a huge wad of silent green and hand me a dollar or two.

Loved Uncle Lou.

He also gave my brother and me a few shares of stock—ten shares of GM, twenty shares of General Dynamics—I don't remember them all. (I do remember once, aged twelve, getting a cold call from a Merrill Lynch broker eager to discuss my investment needs.) In total, we must ultimately have sat steward over upwards of $2,000 in blue chips, perhaps half a dozen of them. I remember we would check their prices in the paper and graph them. Once I think we even made a trade. (In those days, the commission charged to trade ten shares of stock was higher than the commission today, if you're smart, to trade a thousand.) One thing for sure: we were no Warren Buffett or Jimmy Rogers or anything like that. But I guess we did get into the habit of seeing the glossy annual reports and receiving the occasional $12 dividend check.

If the idea was to mold little capitalists, it didn't work. My brother, summa cum laude from Harvard, went into academe with a decidedly anticapitalist bent (as what self-respecting Harvard grad of the time did not?). And I—well, I was, at best, conflicted.

Yes, I liked money. And I loved collecting stamps and "first-day covers" and totting up their supposed value.* But at the same time, I became aware that we were privileged, and it embarrassed me. I remember being at the Y for some sort of class (OK, OK, it was a puppetry class), aged ten or so, and the teacher that first day asking where each of us lived. Always wanting to be the first to answer, and this being an easy one, I blurted out: "860 Fifth Avenue." She turned red and spoke to me sharply about being "little Mr. Big Shot" or some such thing. I had no idea what she meant, or how she could possibly be criticizing me for answering her question. I realize now that I should have hesitated, looked down and said something like "Sixty-eighth street, but it's pretty cramped and we have no view, though it's more than anyone deserves." Because while I took Fifth Avenue for granted, that's not where most people in America, or even New York, lived (though it *was* pretty cramped, and—except for a magnificent few months when they tore down the building in front of us to build another—air shafts were our only vista).

That moment stuck with me. I also found myself feeling extremely uncomfortable, as I got a little older, being served dinner by a black maid. What had I done to deserve being waited on by an adult this

---

* *Supposed*, because it was based on the prices listed in the catalog. What you would actually get if you went to *sell* the stamps was an entirely different story.

way? (Nothing.) The Sixties were upon us, Schwerner, Goodman and Chaney, not much older than me, were down in Mississippi getting killed (while I was being offered more pot roast), and my sense of injustice—perhaps honed by the tyranny of my older brother, whom I loved then after a fashion and surely love now, but you know what sibling rivalry can be—had grown robust.

And I'm glad it had, because wherever you looked—South Africa, Siberia, Central America—there was ample grist for outrage. What had I done to deserve being born, white, in the richest city of the richest country in the world, and to live on perhaps its richest street?

### 3—Moses and Lenin

My black eighth-grade math teacher, Robert Moses, was soft-spoken to the point of incomprehensibility back then, the year before he went South to help lead the Student Nonviolent Coordinating Committee. But somehow, confused as I was by Boolean algebra and multiplying in Base-8—and as sheltered as I was from any real injustice—his barely audible passion on the subject of civil rights echoed in my ears. It left a lasting impression. (Not to mention the friendship I would strike up, a decade later, with the not at all quiet Al Lowenstein, the one-term congressman who led the "dump Johnson" movement and may have done more to end the Vietnam War than anyone else. "What are you doing about South Africa?" he asked me once, out of the blue. What am I doing about *South Africa*? Why should *I* be doing anything about it? I wondered. It had just never occurred to me. But of course from then on—and long after Al had been murdered by an acolyte turned paranoid-schizophrenic—I was still looking for ways to do a little something about South Africa.)

So when I stumbled upon Russian as my language in high school, and when that led to a summer behind the Iron Curtain (the summer of the U.S.-Soviet missile treaty, the summer before President Kennedy was assassinated), I was ready. I left New York a sixteen-year-old and returned a socialist.

That lasted about a year.

My parents, memories of the McCarthy era and the Black List still fresh, were horrified it lasted even that long. Sure, they were liberals—

what New Yorker wasn't? And sure, they would be against the Vietnam War (first my mom, later my dad). Indeed, the year *Time* ran a contest for ad agencies—there would be one winner a week for fifty-two weeks—my dad's fledgling agency, of which he was CEO and creative director, was the very first to win. The ad he wrote featured an American flag upside down, with a message about the true meaning of patriotism. In that same era he did ads to help launch Ralph Nader's Public Citizen.

But socialism, let alone a sympathy for communism, was quite another thing. When I flashed the Lenin Library card I had scored in Moscow and joked that it was my "Communist Party card," they weren't even secretly amused.

That all this would lead to my owning controlling interest in a Russian ad agency or doing battle with Ralph Nader is not without irony. But wait, I am sixteen. I have yet to amass my vast fortune.

### 4—Tykoon

Seventeen. Freshman orientation week at Harvard. I am riding my bike, tagging along behind a friend from high school only a little less befuddled than me. He is on his way to the $2-an-hour job at Harvard Student Agencies (HSA) that's been offered to supplement his scholarship. I am not on scholarship, but it was a nice day for a bike ride. You could have led me anywhere.

I soon found myself in the dingy basement that was to be my home for much of the next four years. It was here—HSA—that any number of student enterprises were headquartered, including one that distributed a weekly "Student Calendar" to every door in the university. Only first they had to be collated and stapled. "You!" the upperclassman pointed to my friend: "Collate these." He gestured toward six stacks of five thousand pages each—five thousand covers, and five thousand of each of the pages to be inserted and stapled. "You, too"—he gestured to me.

No, no! I explained. It wasn't that I was a socialist—this seemed like appropriately demeaning and exploitative work to hone one's ideological zeal. No, it was just that I wasn't slated to have a job. I wasn't on scholarship.

"Never mind that," said the upperclassman. He just needed to get the job done, and he was willing to pay $2 to each according to his ability regardless of his need.

My friend and I worked all afternoon, all night and all morning. Of course, even then there were doubtless machines that could have done the whole job in twenty minutes. But that wasn't the point. The point of Harvard Student Agencies was to do things as inefficiently as possible in order to generate student jobs. By the time we had finished collating, stapling (electrically—our one concession to a labor-saving device), and delivering, we had worked seventeen hours, I had climbed every stairway in the university, and I had earned $34. My own money! Soon I would graduate from collating to selling ads and class rings.

So much for socialism.

As with being class treasurer in high school, it wasn't the money, exactly—although this money *was* mine to keep—it was, I think, the *realness* of enterprise itself. I was *doing* something. Not just calculating how long it would take two students to collate five thousand magazines if one worked at the rate of two hundred an hour and the other two hundred fifty an hour—*doing* it.

That's what I loved about HSA. Although I had gotten into Harvard, I was not studious or intellectual in an abstract sort of way. I liked doing things.

So when at the end of my freshman year I was asked to run one of HSA's little businesses myself, it scarcely mattered to me which one it was. Indeed, though I had lucked out, I didn't know it at the time. I had never even heard of it.

"We'd like you to manage *Let's Go*," HSA's student president beamed, knowing I would be overwhelmed.

"What's *Let's Go?*" I asked. (And why would you be offering a manager's job to a kid who's not on scholarship?)

*Let's Go: The Student Guide to Europe* had begun as a mimeographed handout to passengers of HSA charter flights to Europe. In those days, before the airlines were deregulated, flights to Europe cost a million bucks in coach, two million in first class—but special charters could be arranged that wound up allowing students and faculty to fly round-trip for fares like $229. *Let's Go* had grown a little each year, gradually becoming a thin paperback book offered to bookstores. It had even secured advertising sponsorship. But it had always lost money. The job was being offered to me, a nonscholarship student, they said, because they thought maybe I could get it into the black. Otherwise they'd be shutting it down and, with it, quite a few jobs for students who did need the money.

It was enormous fun. Highlights included installing WATS lines and recruiting a crew to phone every bookstore in the country (our book sales soared); inserting a "customer survey" business-reply card so we could prove to advertisers what a great market our readers were (our ad sales soared); getting write-ups in national magazines and a spot on the *Today* show (my ego soared). Apparently, there was something cute about a terrified eighteen-year-old on the *Today* show, so they kept me on for twenty minutes.

*Let's Go* broke into the black. I would skip class and ride my bike down to HSA's basement offices at every opportunity. By senior year we had expanded from publishing one book to three. I had amassed a fortune sufficient to buy a brand-new Acapulco-blue Mustang with sport stripes and a too-da-la-too-da-la horn (at a cost, I will never forget, of precisely $2,411, including tax, tip and delivery). And I had been elected president of HSA. Throughout all this, if you divided the pay and profit share by the number of hours I put into it, it worked out to about the same $2 an hour I had made collating the calendar. But that wasn't the point. It was thrilling. And the fact that we were able to grow the various businesses to provide four hundred student jobs—some of them even fun or interesting—gave it all a higher purpose.

(Today, although the students no longer phone bookstores themselves, nor stuff the books into Jiffy bags, as we did, *Let's Go* is a series of twenty-six travel guides providing part-time work to 180 students. All told, HSA today provides $1.4 million a year in wages to more than 1,000 students.)

In the spring of 1968, my senior year, a company called National Student Marketing Corp. went public at $6 a share. By the time I had graduated a couple of months later and, after a brief detour, gone to work there, the stock was 37. I clearly remember this number, 37, because it was the price at which my options were pegged.

Up until this time, I had made No Real Money. What little I had made at HSA went to the ordinary stuff (roast beef sandwiches, the phone bill); to the purchase of that car (God, how I loved that car, which is odd, because ever since I've bought mostly used clunkers and gloated over all the money it's saved me); and, at $16 a month, to Eloy Velez, my Ecuadorian foster child "adopted" through what was then known as the Foster Parents Plan ($16 a month went a long way for an Ecuadorian family in a toiletless, candle-lit hut).

I had saved essentially nothing.

But here it was the fall of 1968 and I was ensconced in an office on the thirty-fifth floor of the Time Life Building, fresh out of college earning $15,000 a year (like $60,000 today), with options at $37 a share.

Eighteen months later, on the verge of turning twenty-three, I had two secretaries, forty employees and stock options—with just six months to go before I could exercise them—worth $400,000 ($1.6 million today). The stock had hit $140. Every point it rose was $4,000 more for yours truly.

NSMC had moved to even nicer offices in the brand-new Bristol-Myers building at Fifty-first and Park (why were they bothering with that? I wondered, always the penny-pincher), and I was its most junior vice president. The next youngest was twenty-five.

In addition to screening most of the wacky new-venture proposals that came in—we got tons of them, because we were much in the news—I had started and was running a couple of little businesses within the company. The better of the two rented pint-sized dorm-room refrigerators, and in a way that made great sense. Up until then, students typically had been renting refrigerators from the local hardware store for $9 a month, because no one roommate had the full $89 retail price all at once—and if they pooled their money, which roommate would get to own it at the end of the year? And where would he or she store it over the summer? So they just rented. Yet at $9 a month, by the end of the school year they had paid pretty close to retail anyway—nine months at $9 a month. We bought them in huge quantity for about $35 each (including a five-year warranty), rented them five hundred at a time to the student government for $25 each, and provided the posters and other materials to help the student governments rent them one at a time for $35. The students thus wound up paying less than half what they had been paying; the student government picked up $5,000 for the prom; and we were assured $125 over five years on our $35 investment. It was good news for everyone but the local hardware store.

Then again, it was small potatoes. What NSMC was mainly in the business of doing was acquiring other companies with its inflated stock. NSMC's founder and driving force was a dynamic old guy named Cortes Wesley Randall. Well, he seemed old to me. Cort was thirty-two.

While I would work late each night in the home office, Cort and a bevy of lawyers would be flying around the country in his Learjet (I even got to ride in it once), swooping down from time to time to make another acquisition. NSMC sales grew from $3 million the year I joined to $100 million less than two years later. Multiply by four to put it in today's dollars.

It was all rather heady, to say the least. Of course, given my left-wing leanings, while others were planning their town houses and Lamborghinis, I was happily sharing a $365-a-month apartment with a friend, walking to and from work most of the time (subtracting 37 from that day's stock price and multiplying by 4,000 as I went—it's astonishing how many ways I was able to find to count that option money), and thinking of amazing ways to give most of it away once it was mine. Endow a scholarship at Harvard? Adopt an entire *village* of Ecuadorian children? An entire *oblast* of poor little Russians?

Anyway, with six months to go before I could exercise my options, it turned out that the "creative accounting" NSMC had been practicing with the blessing of Peat, Marwick, Mitchell—and I should say that in this era companies were criticized if they *didn't* practice creative accounting—was *so* creative you could really only fairly term it fraudulent accounting. Cort and a guy from Peat, Marwick went to jail. The stock went to practically zero (though NSMC never did go bankrupt—interestingly, if you had bought at the very bottom and held on through the final liquidation ten years later, you'd have made almost as much of a fortune as buying it at 6, when it first went public, and selling at 140). And, my options worthless, I went to Harvard Business School. It would be more than twenty years before I'd be able to endow a Harvard scholarship (though I did adopt quite a coterie of little pen-pal Ecuadorians and Malaysians along the way). I was older, wiser and just wealthy enough to split the cost of B-School with my parents.

## 5—Cover Boy

While I waited for classes to start I wrote an article describing what had happened and sent it to a dozen magazines. One by one the rejections arrived (including a "close but no cigar" from *Esquire* and a rather perplexing "duplicate material already available in our files" from *Signatures*, the Diners Club magazine). I gave up on the article idea and, having some time to kill, decided to expand it into a book. Twelve chapters, a day for each, I figured. Well, I didn't need to do any research—I had lived it. Why should it take any longer than that?

About two weeks later, it was done.

As someone who now can take weeks just to get his shirts to the cleaner, I am the first to want to kill the twenty-three-year-old who wrote a book in two weeks. But such is life.

The phone rang just as I was finishing the book, and a fellow introducing himself as Sheldon Zalaznick, from *New York* magazine— that's right! I forgot! I never got a rejection from *New York* magazine!—called to say that my manuscript had gotten lost in a pile, but wondering whether it was still available and whether I could come down to New York Tuesday to have my picture taken to be on the cover of *New York* magazine. And, incidentally, they would pay $750 for the story.

The week business school started, I was inside a soap bubble about to burst on the cover of *New York*. Thanks to Shelly Zalaznick and Clay Felker at New York, I had an agent. Thanks to him, I had a $6,000 advance for my book, which I had titled *The Funny Money Game*.*

I had one other thing, though I didn't take it seriously: an offer to join the staff of *New York* when I graduated.

Well, please—who makes job offers two years in advance? And what do I know about writing? I'm an entrepreneur!

---

* "Adorable," the reviewers would more or less say when it was published. "I'm sorry, sir, we don't sell games," said the bookstores when I went in to try to find a copy. The ratio of sales to favorable press attention may have hit an all-time low.

## 6—New York, *New York*

I graduated, went to work at *New York*, at $18,000 a year, and made it a practice never to take cabs or do anything else that could stand in the way of my saving money.

OK, I was still sending $16 or $18 a month to a foster child some-place—I may have been up to two of them by then—and I was send-ing my $25 to Public Citizen and Common Cause and all that, but basically I was one of the cheapest guys on the face of the planet.

I was twenty-five. It was time to start saving for retirement. Or *something*. I had really enjoyed the notion of having $400,000 on paper. Now I wanted to have it, or at least be launched on a trajectory to get it, for real.

Clay and Shelly treated me far too well at *New York*, arranging for me to do all sorts of interesting profiles (Sam Lefrak: "It's not hard to make fun of a billionaire builder who can't pronounce 'condo-minium,'—he pronounces it 'condominiun'—but Samuel Jonathan Lefrak . . ."; Paramount Pictures chief Frank Yablans: "Frank Yablans can be very funny, very charming, in a tough sort of way, when he wants to be. With me around, he wants to be. Maybe he should have me around more often. . . .") and allowing me to range from gold bugs to "bank capital adequacy" to the last story I did for *New York:* "The Day They Couldn't Fill the Fortune 500."

That one, written at the end of 1976, was a fantasy set in what seemed the impossibly remote future—March 3, 1998, to be exact—by which time there had been *so* many mergers and conglomerations ("Analysts began to wonder whether strategic planners at Mobil/Marcor/Macmillan had decided, in a moment of corporate whimsy, to go after only *M's*—when without warning the company turned around and acquired Belgium. Why not? The Belgians were a practi-cal people, and Mobil's terms had been good. . . .") that there was really no reasonable way to find five hundred separate large corporate entities to fill *Fortune*'s list. (Sure, there were still millions of tiny enterprises around the world, and even a few thousand fledgling giants—but to put them on a list with $50 billion giants? It would be like putting Rockefeller in a room with the owner of the local Ford dealership.)

The irony in this is that, unbeknownst to me, *New York* magazine within weeks would *itself* be the object of a hostile takeover.

When Rupert Murdoch snatched the magazine, most of us at *New York* picked up our pension plans, rolled them over into IRAs and left. I put mine into an IRA at a mutual fund called Mutual Shares, which Michael Price has dutifully compounded at 19.6 percent ever since, turning each single dollar into thirty-six (past performance is no guarantee of future results), such that now, two decades later, it constitutes its own little six-figure sliver of my vast fortune.

On the heels of the *New York* magazine takeover, I was offered a new gig.

### 7—If They're So Smart, How Come They Gave Me $10,000?

On the surface, it was a most intriguing proposition. Not only was I being offered a column in *Esquire*, a publication I had long admired; but inasmuch as it was to be a column about money, I would be given some to play with.

"Some what?" I asked, blinking. It sounded as though "some" referred to "money," but we have all lived long enough to know that magazines do not give their writers money "to play with." Rich men give it to their wives, Parker Brothers prints it with their games, but . . .

Then, I remembered (with money, as with most things, there's no substitute for having been around a little) that this same editor had, at a different magazine, once conned a different writer, Jon Bradshaw, into writing a delightful story about the New York State Lottery in return for a thousand $1 lottery tickets. Anything he won he could keep. The readers got their vicarious thrill, the magazine got its delightful story and Bradshaw, for his considerable efforts, got $196.

"Ah," I sighed, "the old Bradshaw con."

No, said this editor. I was to be paid a normal columnist's fee for my writing. The $10,000—a substantially larger sum in 1976 than in 1997, I might add—was extra. For me to play with in the stock market. And to report back to the reader on my gains and losses.

"And if there's anything left when I'm done playing? Who gets that?"

"You do. Don't you understand? It's your money. You can do

anything with it you want, and the more you make with it, the more you'll have." Many of you are too young to remember that black-and-white weekly TV classic *The Millionaire*, but here was Michael Anthony dispensing John Beresford Tipton's tax-free million to a disbelieving schnook—so that the audience could enjoy watching it wreck his life. (It was a good show, and the million *always* wrecked their lives.)

Now let me back up to say that having even then been offered quite a few deals and opportunities in my young life, I had already long since come through harsh experience to know that the world is divided into two things: things that are too good to be true, which constitute the vast, overwhelming, wildly disappointing majority of things; and, once in a rare while, things that are simply a very good thing. I was beginning to take this offer for the latter. It was only after mentally furnishing my apartment with the $10,000—about $9,000 more than I had spent on it to date—that I realized, finally, the catch. (There was a catch, after all.) The catch was that what I would *really* have done with $10,000 right about then, were it to have floated in my tightly weather-stripped window back in 1976—my fortune being not nearly vast enough at that moment to indulge in any sort of financial whimsy—was invest it in municipal bonds due to mature in 2004, or some equally boring but eminently prudent thing. Only that would have been the stuff of a column that appeared every twenty-eight years, at purchase and redemption. Or at best every six months, each time I clipped the coupons.

You see, I believed then, as now, that by and large you can't beat the system. It is very hard consistently to do appreciably better than average with investments. In fact, the harder you try, the more (odds are) you lose. The more risk you take, the more likely you are to lose; the more frequently you switch from one thing to another, the more money you give up to the house. Patience, not pizzazz, is rewarded when it comes to money. But patience is boring, and I knew *Esquire* was not hiring me to be boring.

"You're asking me to violate all my investment principles," I said, seeing the trick. "You're asking me to set a poor example," I said.

"I'll take it," I said.

What's more, unbelievably, they sent it. Ten thousand dollars.

All right. I grant you that $10,000 was really not such an extraordinary amount of money even then. In New York, if you were single and earning, say, $26,000 after deductions, as I was, almost $5,500 of any $10,000 windfall went straight to the government (until 1980, the top federal income tax bracket, you may recall, was 70 percent, not today's 39.6 percent, and New York tax rates were higher as well). This gift was not only a hundred times smaller than John Beresford Tipton's, it was fully taxable.

Nonetheless, as one who recurrently dreams of finding loose change in the street (well, in the gutter, if you must know, although I can't imagine there being any significance to that), with those dimes and nickels leading to more dimes and nickels, and *quarters* . . . which really couldn't add up to more than twenty or thirty bucks, tops (although that was a goodly sum in my childhood, when, presumably, the dream was scripted) . . . as one who had already had that dream on and off for twenty-odd years, the idea of finding *$10,000* in the street, $10,000 just *to play with* . . .

I gurgled happily all the way to the bank.

Now it is appropriate that I set forth, as modestly as is possible under the circumstances, my credentials at the time for losing $10,000 in public (apart from the considerable practice I had with smaller sums in private). In other words, If I Was So Smart, How Come I Wasn't Rich?

Here's how smart I was:

A year or two earlier I was sitting next to one of the ten—surely one of the fifty—most powerful men in the world, Walter Wriston. Wriston was chairman of Citicorp, by a country mile the world's leading global megabank back then; no slouch today, either. Citicorp was vastly more powerful than most nations; Wriston ran it; and from my limited dealings with him, I felt that if anyone had to be that powerful, I was glad the board of directors had chosen him.

This was an off-the-record dinner Citicorp hosted each year for the two or three dozen financial writers the bank found least offensive. The food was amazing. But placed neatly under each guest's butter dish was what looked for all the world like a two-page college quiz. With our names already typed for us across the top, no less. This, it was explained for the benefit of first-timers like me, was the annual "Fearless Forecast," in which we, the press, were to make our economic projections for the coming year.

Terror seized me by the lapel. Because if the truth be known, I am only vaguely aware of this year's GNP, let alone capable of knowledgeably projecting its level twelve months out. As for such things as the M family ($M_1$, $M_2$, and the rest), or the way the Fed expands the money supply by buying government bonds, let's just say that I have been known to get these things confused. (At business school, our classrooms had no windows. The joke in accounting class used to be "Debits by the windows, credits by the doors." I still don't understand what they were talking about.)

To my great relief, for each question—GNP, unemployment, Dow Jones industrials, Consumer Price Index and so on—Citicorp had charitably included the statistic from the year just past. So, while they were handing out a gold-plated perpetual-motion clock to the winner of the prior year's forecast, I was busily adding a rough 10 percent to the previous year's statistics, much as a cook might add seasoning to the stew. A little for inflation, a little for growth—and a lot for convenience, as it's a great deal easier to figure 10 percent and round off than to figure 8.3 percent on the dot.

A year later, I was back at the annual dinner, no longer at Wriston's table, and he was up at the podium handing me the gold clock. Not only had I won . . . I had won, he said, by a wider margin than anyone had ever won it before.

All of which I submit to prove to you that I am indeed as smart as the next guy (never mind the fact that to this day I haven't been able to figure out how to get the clock to work) but that the next guy may not be smart enough to predict the economy or the markets either. I had won not because I had a clue what would happen, but because it seemed easiest to add 10 percent to everything.

Anyway, *Esquire*'s $10,000 was mine—could I possibly be so lucky with it as I had been with the clock?—and, having made every conceivable excuse for losing it, I set about investing it. My broker could only marvel at the zest with which I churned my own account. There were the dumb little stereo and electronics companies that nearly went bankrupt, the little oil-field service company stocks that quadrupled (shortly after I sold them), and more. By the time the exercise ended, nine months later, the $10,000 had become $13,992, which was split five ways. The largest share went to the federal government; smaller but significant shares went to New York State and New York City; $1,281 went in brokerage commissions; and I got the rest—more than enough to furnish the hallway outside what was to be my new apartment.

Because, you see, my fortune had indeed begun to swell.

There was the money I got when *New York* magazine was taken over; there was this $10,000 (less taxes); there was my relentless thrift. Slow but steady was beginning to win the race.

And now there were royalties from a book that would become a modest best-seller, *Fire and Ice,* a biography of the wonderfully colorful man who built Revlon, Charles Revson. Such was his mystique, or notoriety, or whatever, in New York, if not in Kansas, that when the book first appeared it was given the entire window of the Madison Avenue Bookshop—a mannequin was placed in the window reading it, surrounded by stacks and stacks of copies—and the Doubleday then at Fifty-seventh Street, two short blocks from the General Motors Building, home to Revlon as well as Estée Lauder, sold five hundred copies the first day.

Not that having a *New York Times* best-seller means quite what people think. A man from the *Times* does *not* come to your door with a check for a million dollars, as I had assumed. You can sell a remarkably few hardcover copies to make that list. It varies from time to time, and from fiction to nonfiction, but it's certainly possible to graze the bottom of the list with a book that sells, say, forty thousand copies in hardcover, which even in today's terms, where books sell for $25 and the author's share approaches 15 percent, might mean $150,000 or so. Yes, there are book-club sales and the paperback; but there are also the agent to pay, research expenses and taxes. Cry not for best-selling authors. But unless they've climbed fairly high up the list, or there's a movie (not a movie *sale*—that's typically $2,500 for an option—but an actual *movie*), don't expect a ride in their limo, either.

So I was hardly rich, but I was definitely launched. And that gave me the luxury of considering homeownership.

## 8—My First Mortgage

I'd been paying $365 in rent for a nice tenth-floor one-bedroom in Chelsea and was thus more than a little skeptical about laying out tens of thousands of dollars for the privilege of paying $600 a month instead—even if much of my monthly maintenance payment would be tax-deductible (namely, my share of the building's mortgage interest and property tax).

I was apartment-hunting partly because I wanted more space, partly because I had a few bucks from *Fire and Ice* burning a hole in my pocket, but mainly, that sunny summer Sunday afternoon, as a way to avoid doing what I was supposed to be doing. I was supposed to be finishing an article on Elaine May, a brilliant, wonderful but slightly crazy director who had just shot a brilliant but problematical little movie called *Mikey and Nicky*. *Mikey and Nicky* was a black-and-white, two-character film (Peter Falk, John Cassavetes), for which Elaine had shot more raw footage than was used to make *Gone With the Wind*. Literally. As the months of editing had stretched into years (with that much footage, the possibilities are endless), Paramount had become increasingly upset. Elaine had hidden the reels of film in her psychiatrist's garage rather than relinquish control of the editing, and I was now on page 25 of my article—almost done (and only a couple of weeks late, which is pretty good for me)—doing whatever I could not to finish.

Enter the Sunday *New York Times* real estate section. I had pretty much decided not to buy a co-op—as I say, why pay tens of thousands of dollars for the privilege of, in effect, upping your monthly rent?—but I was having trouble finding the right ending for this Elaine May piece, so I began looking at the ads . . . began dialing a number or two . . . began walking to the subway for a trip to the Upper West side to meet a real estate agent.

I felt guilty to be avoiding my responsibilities, but that of course only made the adventure more pleasurable. Not that I really expected to buy anything.

The first apartment she showed me was a large studio in a building called the Dakota. You know: where they filmed *Rosemary's Baby*, and in front of which, years later, John Lennon was killed. I had heard of the Dakota—the only West Side building I *had* heard of—but found it, and this apartment, dark and gloomy. Fifty thousand dollars for this?

I could see I would soon be back at my desk struggling with Elaine May, but the real estate agent had a second apartment to show me up the street.

Within two minutes I knew it was for me. No view, low floor, but a huge (by New York standards) pre-War two-bedroom apartment, laid out perfectly for me: office wing, living area, bedroom wing. Right on Central Park, even if I had to risk falling out the window to see it. And $5,000 less than the Dakota.

We went down to the lobby and I told the real estate agent: I want it. She said that though they were asking $45,000, she thought I *might* get it for $37,000. (Real estate agents are morally and legally bound to represent the sellers' interests, in most cases, but I have often found them to be more than a little sympathetic to the buyer.)

I didn't want "might," I told her. All thoughts of Elaine May out of my head, I had suddenly become very serious. I knew I wanted this apartment, and I wanted it "now."

"How much do you think they would sell it for if you just went back upstairs and told them I was ready to make a deal?"

"I don't know—maybe forty-one?"

"OK," I said. "I'll wait here."

Not that I had $41,000 handy, but I figured I was good for a mortgage.

In a few minutes the house phone rang, and the doorman handed me the phone. They wanted me to come up. We had a deal.

As we were leaving the second time, once we were out of earshot of the sellers, the happy real estate agent, congratulating me on my purchase, said, "I suppose you know this is a pretty famous building."

"It is?"

It was called the San Remo, but I had never heard of it. (You see its twin towers in a lot of Woody Allen movies.)

"Oh, yes, you'll have lots of famous neighbors." (I don't want to drop names, but for years I shared an elevator with Mary Tyler Moore.)

"Really?" I said, genuinely curious.

I'm not sure the real estate agent believed me. To a real estate agent, it was all but impossible someone might not have heard of the San Remo. But she played along.

"Well, for one thing," she said, getting ready to tell me about some of the bigger names up in the tower, but wanting to start close to home, I guess, "you'll be sharing a load-bearing wall with a woman—

a very funny writer and director, I don't know if you've heard of her—Elaine May."

Honest to God.

I went home, finished my article (suddenly I had an ending), and have owned that apartment ever since.*

With hindsight, I can't imagine it any other way. But at the time?

The case for New York was clear enough. The city was in the depths of its financial mess, but the Carter administration was pledged to its solvency. Griping and emigration to the suburbs had given way to boosterism and immigration back into town; business in Times Square's colorful theater district was booming (and theater attendance wasn't bad, either); Westway, the billion-dollar West Side beautification project, was about to get rolling (or so it seemed); the immense submerged sludge reef that was creeping mysteriously up the ocean floor toward Long Island beaches that summer would soon be driving shoreline residents back into Manhattan, I theorized; and California's superquake, long predicted as inevitable, would do likewise. Except for a few nettlesome problems—gangs of marauding thirteen-year-olds, an eroding economic base—all the city's indicators back in 1977 were thumbs up.

Still, paying forty grand for the privilege of paying $600-a-month maintenance instead of $365 rent? Why would anyone do this?

*Aha!*

To begin with, I argued gamely in an article at the time, by buying an apartment you get to know the difference between a condominium and a co-op.† Further, you get to borrow a great deal of money from a bank. (In my own case, I scraped together $11,000 in cash and borrowed the remaining $30,000.) And you get to pay a variety of

---

* It would be years before I got up the nerve to say hello to Elaine May. Good sport that she is, all was eventually forgiven. And then, flush with cash from another film, she moved to a higher floor.

† With a co-op, you are buying shares of stock in a corporation owned jointly with the other tenants, and you lease your apartment from that corporation. Technically, you don't own the apartment and thus cannot mortgage it (although you may borrow against the value of your stock); nor can you depreciate whatever portion of it might be used for business. With a condominium, you own the apartment itself and have the right to finance it and rent it out to whomever you please, much as if it were a private home. Given the choice, you'd probably be better off buying a condo. But New York City is an odd bird, and until recently almost all the owner-occupied apartment buildings were co-ops.

imaginative one-time fees, including one to cover appraisal of the apartment and another to cover appraisal of *you*. However, you do not get to *see* either of these appraisals, I learned; you just pay for them. "The appraisal report and credit report are confidential and it is bank policy not to release copies to anyone other than bank personnel."

While your loan application is pending, you get to suffer not only your own traumas—My God, am I doing the right thing? Am I crazy? Am I paying too much? Can I afford it? Will the co-op board approve my application? (They can turn you down for any reason whatsoever, without even being obliged to tell you or the seller why.) What if the Depression comes and other tenants go broke and I have to pay their maintenance, too?—but also the traumas of the sellers, who in my case blew hot and cold. One day I was being adopted as their son; the next, when a competing real estate agent told them he could get them a better price if they broke their deal with me, I was persona non grata.

Finally the deal goes through, and you get to meet New York's not inconsiderable legal community, which shows up en masse at the closing to collect $500. There are your lawyer and their lawyer, your bank's lawyer and their bank's lawyer; the lawyer for the building and the lawyer for the managing agent of the building; the real estate agent's lawyer, if it's gotten sticky enough; and lawyers who, passing in the halls, stop to see why such a crowd has gathered.

The lawyers are seated in a special gallery that the host law firm sets up, with attendants, called paralegals, passing out programs and selling drinks. As each check, waiver, note, proprietary lease or duplicate thereof is signed, initialed, notarized, photocopied or affixed thereto, the lawyers demurely applaud. When all the papers have been dispatched, when it has been established that it is not *your* seller who has a $25 parking ticket outstanding against him in Staten Island but a man of the same or similar name (because *were* it the seller, your bank's lawyer fears the city might come after the seller for the $25 and, in the event they couldn't get it, seize his erstwhile apartment instead, leaving you out on the street and the bank without security for its loan)—when, in short, every conceivable contingency has been considered and protected against, the host law firm announces that it will not consummate the deal until each of the lawyers in the gallery is paid. A cheer goes up from the stands.

Besides getting to throw a closing, by buying your own apartment,

I learned, you get to paint it. When you rent, the landlord sends around a nice Greek man with a latex roller and a six-pack of beer. If you ask what the beer is for, he will smile and indicate, through hand signals, that, well, it's all Greek to him (never mind that he majored in English at Oberlin and only dropped out of grad school when he discovered he could make more money as a painter). One therefore assumes that the beer is used to wash down the walls before the paint is applied. A large apartment takes two days to wash down and roller over. Another half day is required to seal-shut the windows, cabinetry and radiator controls. (In pre-War New York buildings, we have radiators.) The job costs you nothing, and it's a bargain.

However, when you own a co-op, you are responsible for your own painting. (Also your own floors, your own toilet, your own sink, your own outside hall—everything but structural damage to the building, as in the case of a plane crashing into the side of it or the onset of Dutch brick disease.) You get to hire your own Greek, supply him with your own beer (it should be imported) and choose from hundreds of shades of white, at $17.95 a gallon plus tax. It takes weeks. You think one man with one roller can do a so-so job in two days, so two guys with two rollers can do Madonna-with-child in four? It took *three* guys with *three* rollers *three* days just to do the room I set aside as my office. Of course, you can get firm estimates from respectable union painters and be sure in advance just what the job will cost. A man I know was painting his seven-room Park Avenue apartment around the time I was painting mine. He did get estimates. They ranged from $10,000 to $27,000—and that was in 1977 dollars.

I could tell you how, when I took possession of the apartment, only a few forty-watt lightbulbs had been left behind—presumably too high to reach. I could describe the scene I envision having taken place between Mr. Seller, begging her to leave them, and Mrs. Seller, determined to take even the half-depleted rolls of tissue from the two bathrooms (they compromised and left one). I could tell you air-conditioner stories that would freeze your heart. But as it turned out, through dumb luck (and inflation), the $11,000 cash I put into this deal, my own home, was by far the best investment I ever made. Me and forty million other Americans. In 1997 it was appraised upwards of $600,000.

## 9—Mayhem at Citibank Branch 007

New apartment, new neighborhood—time for a new bank branch.
While still down at the old place I had sent a friend a check for $10 million. My vast fortune at that stage was in the vicinity of $20,000, if that, so it wasn't a real check. It was this guy's birthday and, being too lazy to go out and buy a card, I just sent him the check. "Happy Birthday!!!" I wrote in the memo area, with a bunch of multicolored stars and smiley faces. It was a birthday card. He deposited it.

Just what the teller at the Cambridge Trust Company thought when this young Harvard Business School student presented my check, with its stars and faces, I can hardly imagine. I had purposely made it out for ten million rather than one—not that one would have cleared either—so there could not be even the slightest possibility of its being taken seriously. (Ten million was a lot of money in 1975.)

Be that as it may, an electronic hiccup momentarily convulsed the Federal Reserve regional check-processing system; Bankers Trust in New York canceled my checking account and line of credit; Cambridge Trust canceled his; and . . . well, I will never forget the call I got from a vice president from Bankers Trust.

"What about this check," he asked.

"Check . . . check . . ." I repeated, trying to dope out what on earth he was talking about. "*Oh!*"

I fell all over myself with explanation and apology.

Silence.

So then I said, "Gee, Mr. Whatever-His-Name-Was—haven't *you* ever made a mistake?"

It turned out that, no, apparently, he never had. More grim silence.

So finally I just said—what else was there to say?—"Well, if the money's in my account, clear the check; otherwise charge me the five bucks and bounce it."

As I say, they bounced not just the check but me as well.

Not too long afterward, Bankers Trust exited the consumer side of the banking business altogether. I like to think it was because of my check.

So I switched to Citibank. And when I moved uptown to share a wall with Elaine May, I switched my account to Branch double-o-seven at Broadway and Seventy-second Street.

Citibank, long an aggressive, leading-edge player, had run into one of its periodic problems. Growth in earnings had dipped—well, earnings themselves had actually dipped—and while most were looking to Third World loans for the explanation, I realized, as I stood endlessly in line to cash a check, that most of Citibank's growth all these years must have come from Branch 007, the single busiest bank branch in the world, and that by 1977 it had become physically impossible for this branch to take on even a single new account. I think mine was the last one. With the refusal of the adjacent Yum-Yum Ice Cream store to vacate so Citibank could expand, all prospect of profit growth just melted.

Eventually, ATM's and other innovations would break the logjam (and Yum-Yum would go bye-bye); Third World loan problems and even the S&L crisis would fade from memory; Citicorp stock, bottoming at $8.50 a share in late 1991 amid fears of bankruptcy would climb well past 100 by 1997. Indeed, coming soon to Branch 007, I'm told, in an even larger location across the street, will be such customer-convenient astonishments as machines to dispense quarters (for parking meters and the laundromat). "*Quarters*, Jerry—*quarters*!" you can just hear Kramer cry in some upcoming *Seinfeld*.

But in 1977, when I opened my account at Branch 007, it was a madhouse.

Fighting my way to the only working ballpoint in the branch one day, I found myself at the protective barrier from behind which bank officers denied requests. Being in one of those moods, I asked one of the assistant vice presidents, "Is it always like this?" And as she was beginning to reply ("No, sir, this is an exceptionally busy day"), customers to either side of me began answering for her: "Worse! it's usually worse!" "Worst damn bank in the world!" "A zoo! It's always like this!"

Shortly thereafter, I received my bank statement. There were my forty entries for the month, in check-number order. But included with the statement were not *my* forty canceled checks (light blue ones) but forty belonging to a Chinese laundry in Queens (big yellow ones), drawn on an entirely different branch of the bank.

Down to the bank I went with these checks, where I was told that the laundryman was probably doing the same thing himself with mine, so why not relax and wait to get something in the mail? Sure enough, in less than a month I received a fat envelope from Citibank devoid of any covering communication but filled with my forty canceled checks, *plus seven others* belonging to a Mr. Sid Silvers.

What Citibank seemed to be moving toward was a system of sending out canceled checks *at random*, relying on its customers to sort them out among themselves.

"My checks?" asked a surprised Sid Silvers when I called to let him know I had dropped them in the mail.

"Yes."

"You got a bunch of my checks?"

"Yes."

"Holy Christ, are they idiots."

Sid Silvers proceeded to recount a tale of woe about his branch that would have horrified anyone but a client of my branch. "I'm just so disgusted that I'm ready to pull out of the bank altogether," he concluded.

In the nick of time, heralded with blue bunting and a sweepstakes, Branch 007's first-generation out-in-the-freezing-cold cash machine—which was always either out of cash or out of order—was replaced by a pair of second-generation indoor video-screen machines. I stuck in my card and from that day forth have not spoken to a human teller. Citibank service has become remarkably good

## 10—The Only Investment Guide *I'll* Ever Need

It was around this time I decided to write a little investment guide. Not because I expected it to do particularly well, but because I was really sick to death—flattered, but sick to death—of having everyone I worked with and everyone else I knew ask me what to do with their money. (As if I knew.)

My concept was that there were a few simple, basic things to know about money that would really stand a person in good stead, and that beyond that, knowing more not only wouldn't necessarily help—it could get you in trouble. I envisioned a little book about the size of *The One-Minute Manager*, or whatever was the fad back then, which I tentatively titled *A Simple-Minded Investment Guide for People Who've Gotten Burned Getting Rich Quick Before.*

The great luxury of having had a *New York Times* best-seller, of course—even a fairly modest one—is that when you go to your publisher with the next one, you don't have to worry too much about getting a fast answer.

The fast answer I got was . . . "Nah." They'd love to do another book with me, they said, but this wasn't it.

I begged and whined a little, and ran my proposal through the typewriter again. I even offered to do it without an advance, so the publisher would have next to no risk.

"Nah."

Which is how I came to bring the project to Harcourt Brace, who offered a decent little advance, retitled it *The Only Investment Guide You'll Ever Need*, and, through enthusiastic promotion, propelled it onto the list for the better part of a year. By now, one way or another, it has sold something over a million copies.* Of course, it originally sold for $5.95 (at which time I liked to tell friends, whom I found remarkably gullible on this point, that I got a $7 royalty on each one), and then for barely $2.50 in paperback, so even this book didn't exactly propel me into the Stephen King league. (Typically, the author and hardcover publisher split the paperback royalty fifty-fifty.) But I count as a defining moment the day I was out in San Francisco, on "tour" to promote the hardcover, shivering at a friend's kitchen table (it is always cold in San Francisco), when I got a call from my editor. How she tracked me down there I never did establish.

"Are you sitting down," she asked.

"Yes," I replied, tentatively (and immediately rising to my feet).

"We just sold the paperback rights for $250,000."

Suddenly, it wasn't cold at all. Do you hear what I'm saying? *A quarter of a million dollars.* OK, $125,000 for my share less 10

---

* The obvious moral: don't be discouraged if a publisher turns you down. There was, too, the classic case where some wise-ass retyped Jerzy Kosinski's National Book Award–winning *The Painted Bird*, after it had won that award, and sent it around as a fresh manuscript to twenty-seven publishers. As I recall the story, all twenty-seven turned it down (and only one or two said that it seemed familiar). But the best example is my friend John Berendt's *Midnight in the Garden of Good and Evil*. Year after year I would hear about that book, and about how his very well known New York agent had read the latest chapter and loved it, and so forth—and then, when it was done, listened as John told me this famous agent had, essentially, fired him. She liked the book, she wrote him, but just didn't see it as the sort of commercial success she knew he hoped it would be—he should find another agent. He did; it's sold 1.4 million copies in the United States and topped several foreign best-seller lists as well. Big names are attached to the movie. So if you think you're right, keep pluggin'.

percent to my agent less 50 percent or so for taxes—so $56,000. But still. To be able, at last, to be able to talk in fractions. A quarter of a million dollars. I just loved saying it. I *still* love saying it.

Fifty-six thousand dollars bought a lot more then than it does now, though in trying to shield the larger amount from tax, I probably wound up with even less than $56,000.

## 11—Running for Shelter

Painful as it was back then to pay half of every dollar in income tax, there was a consolation: at least you got to keep the other half. In trying to hang on to the first fifty cents as well—a natural instinct, like ducking to avoid a punch or yawning at the sight of a textbook—it was not hard, in the dismal Seventies, to lose the whole dollar.

Not that I didn't enjoy the Seventies. I had a great time. But it was the decade of Watergate and stagflation, a decade in which you could actually be clipped for *79 percent* of your income in taxes, never mind 50 percent, if you were a *really* rich New Yorker. Interest rates had climbed above 15 percent by the end of the decade and the Dow was actually lower in 1978 than it had been fourteen years earlier. And that was before inflation. Adjusted for inflation, it was back to the Pleistocene.

So when you did make a little money, as I so giddily did with the paperback rights to *The Only Investment Guide You'll Ever Need*, your first thought wasn't to buy stocks—stocks had been rotten forever. Your first thought was to keep it out of the jaws of the tax monster. (We were all liberals, but ideology breaks down above the 50 percent marginal tax bracket.)

The first tax shelter I ever participated in involved $1,500 and a play called *P.S. Your Cat Is Dead*, based on the very funny book by James Kirkwood. Kirkwood was opening another play the same month—*A Chorus Line*—but that one wasn't open to public investors.

It was through this investment I learned that Broadway angels—at least angels with wings as modest as mine—had to *pay* for their opening-night seats. Never mind. I bought them anyway. And who should I find myself sitting behind—rather, behind whom should I find myself sitting—but the venerable John Simon, *New York* magazine's fearsome theater critic.

"John," I said, drawing shamelessly on our passing acquaintance, "I have a stake in this show—and I will thank you not to drive it through my heart." John is Transylvanian, or nearly so, so I thought the imagery might in some vague way appeal. Simon headlined his review: "P.S. So Is Your Play." Total return on my $1,500 investment: $168.

The idea of a theatrical tax shelter—if you can even call it that ("contribution to the arts" might be a better term)—is to deduct your investment this year and then recoup it, and more, in future years. If it works, all you really accomplish is to transfer income from this year's tax bill to future years' bills. As with most tax shelters, you are merely delaying, not eliminating, your liability.

I more or less knew this, and also knew that an awful lot of the deals out there were designed to separate tax-panicky city slickers from their money.

For example, there were the cattle-breeding shelters prevalent at the time, wherein you'd buy a bull and three cows, which, upon consumption of much feed and by means of much copulation, would someday multiply your tax-deductible investment into boxcars of hamburger at $2.19 a pound. That sort of thing. I ran into one such deal at *The Money Show* at the New York Coliseum in late 1978. From the brochure:

> Registered Black Angus Cattle can be an investor's dream. They offer you, the investor, an opportunity to breed for top purebred animals like the "Seattle Slew" of thoroughbred horse racing. It also offers the romance of owning your own cattle and visiting the ranches where they are maintained and bred.

> It's getting back to one's roots, the Old West, simply the good old days. [You know—the days before they invented the "investment tax credit" and "the 20 percent additional first year depreciation," which in 1978 applied to cattle, and the $17,000 in management fees, all described elsewhere in the brochure.] Although registered cattle are *Expensive and Risky* they offer *Prestige*, the *Speculative Chance for a Big Profit*, and *Significant Tax Benefits*.

Not only that, but each potential investor was given a card to which was affixed his or her own personal vial—and I do mean vile—of genuine 100 percent pure Black Angus bull semen.

Financially alluring as the Old West surely is (this company was located in Miami), no one I know invested in this particular deal, so I cannot report results.

I did have a friend, however, into beefalo. Beefalo are—well, I guess it's fairly obvious what beefalo are. My friend bought fifteen of them in the mid-Seventies, had them shipped to a farm he bought for the purpose in upstate New York (near Buffalo, I wondered?) and hired a couple of hands to look after them. From the back of the beefalo, this man was persuaded, will come the tenderloins of tomorrow, and he was out to breed all the pure thoroughbred bulls he could.

Yes, he was losing money, raising beefalo without looking to sell any at first—but that was just the point. It lowered his taxable income. When the world turned to beefalo, it would turn to those few farsighted individuals like him whose bulls would stand ready—nay, eager—to impregnate the thundering herd. That's when he'd begin reaping his reward, and by then tax rates might even have come down.

Well, tax rates did come down—from 70 percent to 50 percent in 1980, and then to as low as 28 percent for a while after passage of the 1986 tax act.

But imagine my friend's dismay when he learned that his beefalo were about to give birth (the good news) but that they were, without any question, a full two months early (the bad news). Either the beefalo gestation period had miraculously been shortened, or else one of the common longhorns from the neighboring pasture had jumped the fence, ——ed my friend's beefalo and, with them, his tax shelter.

Of course the real tax-shelter action in the Seventies wasn't Broadway shows or cattle, it was, as it had always been, real estate and oil-and-gas.

The first oil deal I went into was with some classmates from business school, one of whom has since fled the country. I am not implying it was a bad deal, but after more than 20 years I have yet to see a dime.

The second deal I did not go into. It, too, was the creation of a classmate. (You are thinking, Ha! The one he skipped was the Big Winner. Not quite.) The deal offered a *guaranteed* oil well, all my very own—or your very own—for just $28,500. Admittedly, the well was not guaranteed to produce at any specific rate of flow. But even a few barrels a day, at the then prevailing $14 a barrel, added up in the course of a year. These wells were to be drilled in places where you could hardly avoid hydrocarbons, just as digging into the sand at the seashore will almost certainly draw seawater after a few feet. On the off chance the driller did miss—well, then he would drill you a second hole at his own expense.

My own well. A dribbler, perhaps, but one that would allow me to deduct most of that $28,500 from my 1978 taxable income and that would provide a pleasing stream of (mostly taxable) royalty checks for years and years to come. Not unappealing.

I toyed with splitting the investment with friends; I read the lengthy prospectus two or three times—all right, I skimmed it—and tried to puzzle out the pitfalls; I checked out my classmate's qualifications. Impeccable.

My classmate, for his part, had checked out the driller's qualifications—also impeccable, he said. And although I finally decided the stakes were too high for me, "guarantee" or no, he actually managed to attract about a million dollars to the deal, in $28,500 chunks.

As it turned out, the driller, whose reputation is now peccable indeed, took the million dollars and relocated. Somewhere. My classmate—at least as devastated as the investors who had sought a million dollars' worth of tax shelter in this deal—made a show of trying to make good the money out of his own pocket one day, but I don't think that day ever came.

Happily, I had hung back. But by 1980—had they shown *Giant* on TV the night before?—I don't know what pushed me over the edge, but I could resist no longer.

Sure, the maximum tax rate on New Yorkers was coming down to "just" 60 percent or so, but it still precluded rational thought. With royalties flowing in from *Fire and Ice* and *The Only Investment Guide You'll Ever Need*, I became a limited partner in a deal that succeeded in drilling no fewer than seventeen commercially producing oil wells—contracted for when oil was just $12 a barrel, but pumping as the price climbed, briefly, to $40—the income from which, despite this price-rise bonanza, never quite covered the interest on the bank loans incurred to drill them.

These wells, I'm a little embarrassed to admit, were in Ohio. You know the expression "a drop in the bucket?" Every week or so, when the fields weren't too muddy, a truck would pull up to each of our wells and empty the bucket.

I am not trying to give the impression that all tax-shelter deals of the Seventies and early Eighties were lousy. At least 5 percent were not. I know of one investment banker, for example, who managed to parlay a zero-cash outlay (he borrowed the front money) into enough of a write-off to wipe out his entire 1977 tax bill while actually producing enough oil revenue to put him in even greater need of tax shelter for 1978 and, it would appear, years after that. After all, there *is* oil in the ground, it is in much demand, and people do find it. It just never seems to be us. That particular deal was not open to the general public—not a doctor or a dentist in the crowd.

Unfortunately, I eventually realized, just because 5 percent of the tax-shelter deals were good (if that was the number), you were not assured a one-in-twenty chance of finding one. Unless you were favorably situated—as a partner in a large investment or accounting or law firm, for example—you may *never* have gotten to see a good deal. Why? Simply because the lawyers and investment guys who designed the deals were in serious need of tax shelter themselves, as were the tax accountants and others who peddled them. So if the deal was really good, it was likely to sell out to the pros long before there might be a half unit left for you or me.

I tell you all this, of course, not because you're on the lookout for tax shelters. Tax shelters are largely a thing of the past.* I tell you because of the general principle that applies. When there's a really hot new issue of common stock, for example, guess who will not be offered a chance to buy five hundred shares?

Faced with this stacked deck, a business writer I knew at the time and some of his friends decided to create their own shelter. That way, there would be no fees to pay, no promoters to skip town—just a solid, tax-advantaged business opportunity. And perhaps a little fun. They decided to shelter their income by setting up a minor-league hockey team in—well, there already were teams in New York and Chicago—Macon, Georgia. (Surely a better choice than, say, Key West

---

* Once the top bracket dropped to 28 percent, in the late Eighties, the tax shelter business largely dried up. Partly it was that loopholes had been closed, partly that, at 28 percent, few saw the need to jump through hoops seeking shelter. If they had, they would soon have found themselves having deferred income that could have been taxed at 28 percent into future years when it would be taxed at today's higher rate.

or Port-au-Prince.) My friend contributed, along with his dollars, the idea for the name of the team: the Macon Whoopees.

As he subsequently explained it, "The tax shelter in the Whoopees was the accelerated depreciation of the players' contracts. If a player had a $500,000 multiyear contract, you might be paying him $80,000 the first year but taking an *additional* $80,000 in depreciation on his contract."

Whoopee.

"As it turned out," he continued, "you couldn't take the depreciation this way for minor-league teams. Only in the majors." (A pothole in the loophole.) The Whoopees skated off the ice and into obscurity in about the time it takes to pry off a goalie's headgear and pound his face into crushed ice.

I did have a few that went well—a "research and development" partnership that invented something and got swallowed by Johnson & Johnson, tripling our money in only a year; a cable TV outfit that took quite a bit longer but doubled or tripled our money, too. It was not an unmitigated disaster. But by and large I learned that the worst thing you can do is invest with the rationalization that "it's good for taxes."

### 12—IBM Names a Computer After Me

While all this was going on, a fellow named Steve Jobs—who would subsequently buy the top three floors of my building all for himself and spend something on the order of $20 million remodeling them, only to get married and *never move in* because he had designed the space as a bachelor pad—was inventing the personal computer.

Its impact on me came first with the Apple III, which, for all the scorn heaped on it, was a wonderful machine. How amazing to be able to word-process instead of type and retype, and retype yet again.

The personal computer had its second impact on me in 1982, when I was invited to be the so-called celebrity behind a piece of software that came to be called *Managing Your Money*, with my face on the box.

PCs were in their infancy—Atari had pretty well secured the lead spot, it seemed—and it was the idea of a company that came to be called MECA (rhymes with Decca) to break through the forbidding techie clutter with a line of "celebrity software." They already had Jim

Fixx for *running*; they were thinking about Julia Child for *cooking*; and—Louis Rukeyser being unavailable—they wanted me for *money*.

Research quickly determined that homemakers might not clamor for computers in the kitchen to manage their recipes. Jim Fixx suffered a fatal heart attack while jogging alongside a country road, which made his fitness program a tough sell. So that left me. And though there were those who assumed that I merely showed up for a photo shoot and licensed my name—could a fragrance be next?—I actually put the better part of twelve years into *Managing Your Money*. (It was on our companion program, *Taxcut*, that I was quick to disclose I was little more than a figurehead.)

These were the bonanza years, and they were fun.

The money—huge quarterly royalty checks, once the $199 program, launched in 1984, came to dominate the field—was, I will admit it, giddifying. A few times, *a single quarter's* check might equal the $400,000 in NSMC stock options I had once dreamed of cashing in. Shoeless children throughout Ecuador and Southeast Asia were soon cheering in the streets. And I did eventually get to endow a scholarship or two. I did a few less conventional things with the money, as well, the three looniest of which are described in the chapters that follow.

But it wasn't just the money. What was really fun about these years was working with Jerry Rubin (not the yippie Jerry Rubin, the genius Jerry Rubin) and the cadre of seventeen-year-olds he recruited to develop *Managing Your Money* from scratch.* I did most of the English, and got to make a lot of the decisions regarding function. The geniuses did the coding that actually made the thing *work*. Realistically, I'd say they deserved 90 percent of the credit for the program, though life being unfair, most of it went to me.

*They* made breakthroughs like developing their own private coding language—C-Saw it was called—to do things on an IBM PC that could otherwise never have been done. (Atari was the leader, but Jerry had the foresight, early on, to bet on IBM.)

---

* One of the earliest of these was so geeky and weird it was clear he would simply never make it in civilized society, so we let him go. I would have taken him for a squeegee person, or possibly a future unabomber, had I to guess whatever became of him. Then I noticed in *Fortune* the other day that he is no longer seventeen, he's in his mid-thirties, and worth a hundred million dollars.

*I* made breakthroughs like developing the forget-proof password. That may actually have been my only breakthrough, so let me describe it. The problem was simple: we thought people would want at least some rudimentary, if not hacker-proof, way to keep their records private. Hence a password. But we could only begin to imagine the tech support hassles of trying to deal with people who'd forgotten their passwords.

So I decided to have people, when they chose their password, also specify a "hint" we could use as a reminder. "The name of my first puppy," they could write, or "the girl I sat next to in the sixth grade"—something no casual snoop would be likely to know. Then, if they misentered their password three times upon trying to start the program, we'd present them with that "hint"—"It's the name of your first puppy, you senile old fool!"

Perfect.

Other innovations I came up with were not so felicitous. For one, I assigned ESCape as the key to press whenever you needed HELP. (We had HELP behind every screen. I wrote endless HELP. The main reason computers had to become more capacious each year was to accommodate all my HELP. I provided HELP by the heap.) F1 I reserved for the main "action key"—the key you'd press to *do* whatever the screen you were on was about, whether printing checks, adding a stock to your portfolio, calculating your life expectancy, or estimating your taxes. Of course, there was HELP to guide those who, in the early days of computers, did not notice that row of "function keys" on their keyboard and pressed F and then 1 instead of F1. ("No, you idiot," I would helpfully guide them. "Don't you see that for $2,000 you get an extra row of 'Function Keys'?" Sometimes we were the first program they had ever used. Sometimes we were the *reason* they bought a computer.)

Needless to say, at least to those of you who've entered the computer world, ESCape for HELP and F1 for "action" did not come to be adopted as industry standards. As the years went on, MYM was getting more and more of a devoted following, but becoming a bit like Esperanto in that regard. *No one* else did it our way.

Needless to say, also, I didn't actually address our hundreds of thousands of users as "idiots" (although there was one woman who took her 5¼-inch floppies, if anyone is old enough to remember those, and trimmed them down with a pair of scissors thinking this would make them work in a 3½-inch disk drive). Indeed, one of the joys of all this—and one that remains so on the Internet—is that it turns out there are just *scads* of really nice, smart people out there, most of whom provide feedback in a highly constructive, entertaining way.

But while I called no one an idiot, and rarely even muttered it (and then mostly at myself), I did try to inject a note of humor here and there, which as a little start-up we had the luxury of doing. An example of this—and, simultaneously, how I could goof up even the simplest thing—was in our on-screen tutorial, sappily titled "Hello, New User." Because as I say, in Version 1, back in 1984, we really could assume nothing. We had to start from hello-hello, teaching people how to move their cursor around the screen, how the TAB key could move you from field to field—and so on.

Anyway, on the Hello, New User screen where we were teaching people to enter numbers I asked them to enter their age. And, for fun, I had the program give hem an "error message" if they entered 39. Normally, they'd enter their age and proceed with the tutorial. But if they entered 39, it would say: "Sure, sure. You, me and Jack Benny."

My thought was that every once in a while this would produce a laugh.

What I did not anticipate was that people would simply get stuck. (Or that a lot of our users would turn out to be thirty-nine.) Rather than just enter 38 or 40 and move on, they kept entering 39, kept getting that message—and calling our jammed phone lines to try to find out how to get the program unstuck. What they didn't realize, I guess, was that what they entered here made no difference at all. It was just *a joke*. But a costly one, as it turned out, because every phone call cost MECA money. And having to make it (let alone be put on hold), annoyed our customers. Oops.

Other little quirks worked fine. In the life expectancy module, if you said you were a smoker, and reported your age as under thirteen, we flashed: YOU'RE 12 [OR WHATEVER] AND YOU SMOKE? ARE YOU CRAZY?

In the section where we added everything up and displayed—ta-da!—your Net Worth, I added annoying comments and a randomization mechanism to keep them from being the same all the time. The beginning of the display was always straightforward: "Taking contingent tax liabilities on your unrealized capital gains into account would make your net worth: $362,415.67." But then we'd append something like this: *Enough to buy about 37 shares of Berkshire Hathaway stock, at mid-1995 prices. Don't look now, but Warren Buffett and his wife own 515,000 shares.*

It was the Don Rickles approach to insulting the consumer. (Because some of our users were not amused by stuff like this, we soon added an option to the preference menu that allowed people to hide all this stuff if they didn't want to see it.) And it also helped enliven the demos I had to do over and over again, to retailers, user groups and occasionally even on TV.

That was part of the fun, too. Personal computers were so new then that even I, who knew almost nothing about them, had something to teach. For example, in a moment I couldn't possibly have scripted, Merv Griffin held up a copy of the software and said to me and his millions of viewers, "I see you have a videotape now, too."

Gee, I thought, a little panicked—do you correct your host on national TV? But it seemed unavoidable, so I said, sheepishly, "Well, actually, Merv, it's not a videotape; it's a computer program."

"*Really*," he said with unfeigned surprise and curiosity. "What does it do?"

And off I went.

I had a blast.

The other thing that was fun about being in this nascent business is that the capacity of the hardware and software was expanding so fast. Imagine it this year, and there it would be the next. The 160K (160 thousand byte) state-of-the-art floppy disk that constrained the original IBM PC was quickly replaced by an IBM XT with a 10 *million* byte "fixed disk." And soon IBM came out with an even more powerful offering it called the IBM AT—the first personal computer IBM had ever named after *me*, I would tell the demo groups—and then . . . well, you have to have been living deep in the bush not to know the rest.

In short, as you can tell, I still enjoy thinking about all this. And I still use MYM version 12 to do everything from maintaining my Rolodex—2,187 "cards" as I write this, some with thousand-word memos attached—to my datebook ("Never forget a birthday or anniversary again," I used to say as part of my demo); from paying my bills to estimating my taxes and keeping track of my portfolio; and more. It is a nifty, nifty piece of software, which in my own mind was meant to be *The Only Personal Software You'll Ever Need*. But you'd be nuts to buy it, because the one I'm describing is the old DOS version, long since made obsolete by Windows and removed from sale.

Just how we got caught flat-footed without a Windows version until far too late, and just how we came to be acquired by H&R Block (which then sold MYM to a consortium of large banks) is a long story. The relevant portion here is that as part of the deal, H&R Block insisted on buying out my contract and putting a stop to those lovely royalty checks. It was, on the one hand, the largest check I ever saw in my life. (OK, it was a wire transfer; but that didn't stop my visualizing it every which way.) On the other hand, it was a tiny fraction of what my contract would have been worth if the royalties had kept on coming. But sizing up the then management of MECA (things have changed), the competition it was up against (a program called Quicken we should easily have been able to outfox early on, but didn't) and the handwriting on the wall, it seemed to me as if I might otherwise get nothing at all.*

So in 1993, my vast fortune swelled by one last mighty gulp.

It would be tasteless to blurt out a specific number—my IQ and my net worth are the two numbers I try to keep to myself, being substantially lower than I'd like—but I think you get a sense of the ballparks involved. Bigger than a breadbox; smaller than those guys who fly first-class without an upgrade sticker. "With this much money," the net worth section of *Managing Your Money* scoffs at me, "you could pay the entire interest on the national debt—yourself!—for [several] minutes. And we'd be very grateful if you did."

Along the way there were some amusing investments that worked out surprisingly well and a few crazy splurges. About these, a few words later. But my main endeavors, once I had accumulated a spare dollar or two, were three. One in Miami, a second in Russia, the third in California.

* "Did I make the right decision?" I would later ask one of the surviving MECAteers I had been negotiating with. "Were you guys bluffing, or would the company really have gone under if I hadn't taken my half-a-loaf and gone along with the deal?" "We weren't bluffing," he said. MYM is no longer sold at retail.

# 2

## Miami

# NEVER BUY REAL ESTATE OVER THE PHONE

### 1—The Bait Is Laid

It all started with a 1981 cover story in *Time*, "Trouble in Paradise."
"So many bodies now fill the Miami morgue," the story ran, "that
Dade County Medical Examiner Joe Davis has rented a refrigerated
hamburger van to house the overflow." Of course, when *Time* puts
something on its cover, it says a lot. What it said to me was that it was
probably time to buy.

"Peter," I said to an attorney friend in Miami, "I need a condo or
something."

"What for?" he asked. (I practically owned his guest room.)

I explained my contrarian *Time* theory.

He said he would call his friend the Big Real Estate Agent and have
her call me in New York.

I had all but forgotten about this when, months later, the Big
Real Estate Agent did call. She had found me the perfect place, she
said. Had I ever heard of the Palm Bay Club? It was home to folks
who raced their horses at Hialeah, docked their yachts in the Palm
Bay Marina and parked their Rollses under forest-green-striped
canopies. It did not sound like my buying-tuna-by-the-case kind of

place. What caught my ear was that the young fellow selling this unique duplex was really anxious to sell. So anxious, in fact, that he had dropped the price from $195,000 to $135,000—did I want to come down and see it?

See it? Truthfully, that was something that just hadn't occurred to me when I called Peter. It did make sense—you don't buy real estate sight unseen. But what was I supposed to do? Fly down to Miami every time there was a condo to look at? Airfares weren't cheap in those days, though I was, and it wasn't even winter anymore. Who flies to Florida in the summer?

"Gosh," I said, "I don't think I can. But"—a moment of naive inspiration—"why don't you offer a hundred and ten and see if they'll negotiate. Then maybe I'd come down." I didn't want to visit; here was a face-saving way not to have to. The old leave-it-up-to-them decision method.

"A hundred and *ten*?" she asked sharply. "That's awfully low. I don't want to insult them. But . . . well . . . OK, I'll see what they say."

Eight minutes later it was mine for a hundred and ten.

Oh, *no*! I immediately thought to myself. What have I *done*? (My next thoughts: A hundred and *five*! A hundred and *four*!) True, I hadn't signed anything. But my word is my bond, so unless there was something drastically wrong with this place, I was committed. And now, it seemed to me, I should fly down to Miami.

## 2—My New Condo

But I didn't. I sent Peter. Not that $110,000 wasn't a lot of money to me. It still is. But I was really busy, and . . . well, having said that I would buy it, I felt I had to. *Seeing it* wouldn't make the transaction any better. In fact, it would make it worse, because the airfare would just add to the cost. And what did I know about Miami real estate? Peter's eye would be cannier than mine anyway.

The next day Peter called to confirm that, although somewhat unusual, the condo certainly seemed to be a good deal.

Unusual?

Well, to begin with, it was in an unusual part of town. You've heard of Coconut Grove? Coral Gables? Key Biscayne? The Palm Bay Club was in none of these. It was in a rather dicey area, but well protected. Not to worry. It was a fashionable oasis developed by a Miami socialite, recently deceased, who had attracted all her rich and horsey friends. And, yes, Peter confirmed, there were a lot of Rollses.

The condo itself—two separate studio apartments that the seller had joined with a circular staircase—was mirrored everywhere. Even the built-in desk had a mirrored surface. (Writing on it can chill your elbows to the bone and make you dizzy, I would later learn, but it must have been great for cutting lines of cocaine.) It was plushly carpeted, Peter reported, with a fancy bathroom on each small floor and beautiful views of the bay from its two double-length balconies.

I was beginning not to worry too much about overpaying.

There was even an illuminated custom-made king-size bed, a custom twelve-foot modern curvy couch, track lighting—and a submachine gun in one of the closets. It seems the apartment belonged to a bright young attorney, but that, like so many bright young people who surely could handle a little cocaine from time to time, cocaine had come to consume and wreck his life. He was moving because Uncle Sam had agreed to provide him—well, had insisted on providing him—with sparer quarters. He would not be at the closing.

### 3—The Interview

Not just anyone could qualify for membership in the (now defunct) Palm Bay Club. I could *buy* the condo without difficulty, and did. But actually being permitted to use it was another thing. For that I had to fly down and be interviewed. And of course by this time I had become more than a little curious to see it.

Basically, I was quite pleased. The surrounding area was indeed a bit scary, but talk about your marble lobbies and fresh-squeezed lemonade! Talk about championship tennis being played right there on your own courts! And a beautiful pool (since filled in with dirt, but wait). And crisp air-conditioning! (Which was important, because it was August. You might rethink your complacency over global warming if you ever visit Miami in August.)

The condo itself was pretty neat, too. What I most loved about it were the balconies: low enough to hear the lapping of Biscayne Bay against the boats, high enough for a view out over the islets the artist

Christo had not long before made pink, and of the Miami skyline beyond.

The interview was just a formality. But like my condo, it, too, was a little unusual. It took place at 11:30 A.M. with a gentleman in dark glasses at the dimly lit bar. I didn't get to say much but learned he had just returned from Europe in someone's private jet, leaving behind more jowl than his surgeon—the world's finest—had ever removed before. And now there was some problem with the floating helipad he had wanted for the marina, and something about a $1 million IRS payment that had his accountants in a tizzy, and he hoped I'd be very happy at the Palm Bay Club. Sign here.

## 4—I Launch My Real Estate Empire

To this point, the only real estate I owned was my apartment in New York, which, as you know, I had purchased for $41,000 back when New York—FORD TO CITY: "DROP DEAD"—was in crisis. By now, just a few years later, its value had begun to rise, along with my Keogh Plan (I'm telling you: slow but steady does indeed win the race) and my account at Smith Barney (to be joined not long after by a discount brokerage account).

My great mistake, of course, was in not finding the extra $10,000 it would have taken to secure a New York apartment *with a view*. That extra $10,000 would now be worth more than half a million.

Live and learn. At least I had a view from my condo at the Palm Bay Club.

Across the bay, that view could hardly have been more magical. Landward, it was more problematic. "Keep your windows up and your doors locked," one friend advised earnestly. My mother started sending clippings about car-jackings. Yet I was not shot at even once. Soon I began to think the horror stories were overdone.

One day a FOR SALE sign caught my eye. It was on the lawn of a three-bedroom house almost directly across the street from the Palm Bay guardhouse. There was an avocado tree in front, a concrete pool and citrus trees in back, a working fireplace, a big kitchen, three bathrooms and a wrought-iron fence. A bank foreclosure.

Now, what would you expect a house like that to have cost in 1985? Ask someone from Duluth, Minnesota, or Stanley, Kansas, and you would get a sensible answer. But I wasn't from Duluth or Stanley. I was from New York. I was from *Manhattan*. A studio apartment back then could easily command six figures. So a good-size house with chirping birds and clean air, in a no-income-tax state just yards from a fleet of Rolls-Royces and fifteen minutes from everything else—including a major international airport—well, let's just say that most New Yorkers I have asked guess $225,000. They guess that to be nice but really are thinking they wouldn't pay a dime over $189,500. I paid $71,000, which included closing costs and a new roof.

I was hooked. The fact is, for the price of a fancy two-bedroom apartment in Manhattan you could buy virtually an entire neighborhood in Miami.

### 5—Official Residence

It was about this time the New York City Department of Finance decided that income I earned giving a speech in Houston was not only subject to New York State and New York City income tax—no argument there—but also to New York City Unincorporated Business Tax ("for the privilege of doing business in the City of New York"). I had never thought of myself as a business, incorporated or otherwise, and I didn't see how giving a speech in Texas or Utah involved doing business in New York. But the tax guys did and decided to go back ten years, hitting me up for $44,695.29. It wasn't so much the money that got me as the injustice. And it wasn't even the injustice so much as the heavy-handedness. I could go on about this—and did, for four thousand words in *The New York Times Magazine* (which made them *really* mad)—but the long and the short of it is that I moved to Miami, into the three-bedroom house with the birds, the avocado tree and the pool.

Soon I bought an even bigger house up the street—this one with a *designer* pool. In Greenwich, Connecticut, a steal at $575,000. In my neck of Miami: $120,000.

The smaller house and the Palm Bay condo I rented out. Other rental houses and condos followed. And buildings! Well, little buildings. But imagine: a fourteen-unit building on now fashionable South Beach for $140,000. (South Beach at the time was still scary and dilapidated. There was only one pioneering restaurant on Ocean Drive.)

My thinking was that I could get into a lot less trouble in real estate than in stocks, where with just a few reckless moves I could ruin myself. In real estate, it takes longer. My feeling was also that things go in cycles. Miami—perhaps even Miami Beach—could one day come back.

(Needless to say, even *I* probably would not have gotten into too much trouble with stocks during these years had I just bought them and held on. But I didn't know it at the time.)

### 6—The Monk Arrives

For a couple of years I was doing this largely myself. I'd buy a house, rent it to friends of friends for $100 a month less than it was worth, and expect them not to call me with problems. It worked reasonably well. The building on South Beach already had a manager living in it, so I stuck with that.

Then I got a chance to buy a second little building on South Beach in partnership with a Young Attorney I'll call Bob. In return for my putting up his half of the down payment, he supplied the management. A nice arrangement, and a way, ultimately, to profit if South Beach—which had by this time come alive—continued its resurgence. Only a couple of years had passed, but now Ocean Drive was lousy with restaurants. My second little building was just a block from the beach and a block from the convention center.

At this point in the story I have to ask you to leave Bob, my Young Attorney partner, in charge of Little Building No. 2, as I did, and flash all the way back to 1972 for a minute. That's when, living in New York, I became good friends with the Vice President of Compliance for a small old-line brokerage firm. At twenty-eight, his job was basically to make sure all the brokers toed the line and that the firm was in full compliance with regulations. He wore understated fur-collar overcoats that cost more than my entire wardrobe, belonged to the New York Athletic Club and had occasional dealings with the president of the New York Stock Exchange—the works. A fine, fine guy.

And then he disappeared. Something about California, people said.

"Whatever happened to Jimmy?" I would periodically ask the broker Jimmy had fixed me up with.

"I don't know!" my broker would reply.

"Whatever happened to Jimmy?" he would ask me a few months later.

"I don't know!" I would reply.

This went on for about eleven years.

And then one day, out of the blue, my broker said, "Do you know what happened to Jimmy? [Long pause.] He's in a monastery!"

Apparently, Jimmy had moved to California and gotten heavily addicted to alcohol and cocaine, to the point where he might have died. (One way he knew he had a problem, he told me, is when he began drinking bourbon out of a mayonnaise jar.) All day long he would drink and drug and sit and watch television. Public television. And that's what saved his life. Because one afternoon he was watching a documentary on a monastery in upstate New York and saw his salvation. Not that he was particularly religious. He just saw this peaceful place on PBS and knew. Sort of like Richard Dreyfuss in *Close Encounters of the Third Kind.*

So the next day he flew to New York, showed up at the monastery door, unannounced—and stayed for seven years. Given his administrative skills, it was not long before he was more or less running the place. (Years later I was with him when he met an ex-monk from a neighboring monastery. The conversation was animated. "You made bread?" the other ex-monk asked Jimmy, incredulous. "I thought you guys made cheese! We made jelly.")

By the time I called (and wasn't *that* a scary call to make—what do you say to whoever answers the phone, "Brother?" "Father?"—what if this is one of those monasteries where they've taken vows of silence?), Jimmy had just left.

When I caught up with him, Jimmy was, very tentatively, rejoining the secular world. (Well, Los Angeles.) His routine consisted mainly of multiple twelve-step meetings each day, interspersed with trips to the gym. It was like the comeback sequence in *Rocky.* When he first came to Miami to live with me until he got fully back on his feet, Jimmy would stay in his room all day and watch public TV. Bill Moyers never had a more committed fan. His only forays were to the local twelve-step meetings. When I suggested things like finding a job back on Wall Street—or even just opening a checking account—he shuddered. Too much responsibility.

But gradually things changed.

## 7—The Monk Becomes a Saint

Jimmy never moved out from downstairs. And I don't think he ever once used any of the fifty-two channels on his cable box besides PBS. But as time passed he took on more and more responsibility. Soon he was running my little properties, including the first building on Miami Beach (but not Little Building No. 2, owned jointly with Bob, the Young Attorney); leading twelve-step programs himself; guiding runaways on Biscayne Boulevard to drug treatment; and managing not just his own checkbook but the checkbook for the real estate.

Biscayne Boulevard, a.k.a. U.S. 1, is a sort of Forty-second Street with palm trees. To the east lies Biscayne Bay (so the neighborhoods to the east range from middle-class to posh). To the west lies mostly crack-wrecked squalor. The Boulevard itself down by me has more than its share of hookers, vacant commercial space and welfare motels. There have been improvements in the last few years—Jimmy helped make some of them—but with crack on the west side of the Boulevard, it's very tough. Drugs ruin everything.

Anyway, I was off doing whatever it is I do—helping develop *Managing Your Money* and so forth—happily leaving my little real estate empire, in the main, to the former Vice President of Compliance (and, as regards Little Building No. 2, to my partner Bob, the Young Attorney).

## 8—A Bench Warrant for My Arrest

The good news was that, while the real estate wasn't making any money, I was making some on *Managing Your Money*, so it didn't matter. We were buying places, fixing them up, mowing a couple of the worst vacant lots and just trying to improve the area generally. I felt confident that with time the value of some of these places would rise.

The bad news was that the Palm Bay Club itself, which started me on this whole thing, was becoming less fashionable by the month. There were still Rolls-Royces, but with the socialite developer gone, the place was suffering from a serious cachet short-fall. The look of the surrounding neighborhood kept new people away (except me, apparently), which cut demand and, thus, prices.

The club/pool/marina/tennis portion of the property—a separate legal entity—went broke, as did one of the adjacent luxury high-rises. Without going into the excruciating details, suffice it to say that at its nadir, a new owner actually *filled in* the beautiful swimming pool and *bulldozed* the marble-lobbied clubhouse. The condo I had snagged nearly fifteen years ago for $110,000 is now worth $85,000—maybe.

Of course, I'm the kind of guy who tends to buy *more* when prices fall (some call this averaging down, though in my case it's usually just simple folly), so I now own several Palm Bay condos. Each time I buy one, the local real estate agent sees me as a better prospect for the next.

"Julie," I moan, "you have to be kidding. You know better than anyone that the last thing I need is another condo."

"Aw, don't you want to at least come see it?" she coos. "It's beauti-ful!"

So I go, anything being preferable to sitting at my keyboard, and meet Julie around the corner at the condo. Well, at 4F, for example—a terrific white-tiled one-bedroom with a $130,000 asking price. Julie thought the owners were really sick of holding it (they had long since moved) and might take $90,000.

"Julie, it's very nice, but what on earth do I need it for?"

"You could rent it out."

"Sure I could. But it would only bring $750. When you take out $500 for the common charges, taxes and insurance, that leaves $250 a month—$3,000 a year—before repairs, vacancies, hassles. What sort of return on $90,000 is that?"

"Not good enough, huh?"

"No. It might be fine for someone who wanted to live in it. *I'd* like to live in it. But as an investment?"

"Don't you want to make an offer?"

"No."

"Aw, c'mon." Julie is all smile. You cannot fail to like her.

"All right," I say, in mock exasperation: "$40,000."

And so it was that, a few weeks later, this terrific apartment became mine for $40,000. I use it for guests. (The pool is filled in, but we have perpetual rights to use the adjacent pool, tennis courts, sauna and gym—you really wouldn't hate it. Come visit!) These days, 4F would probably sell for about 50 percent more.

And then there was the three-bedroom, four-bath unit on which an out-of-town bank held a $250,000 mortgage. The bank had turned down a $105,000 lowball offer from someone else a few months earlier, but then just threw up its institutional hands—banks do this sometimes—and accepted $78,000 from me. Don't ask me why.

I like to think that was the low point of the Palm Bay bear market: March 10, 1993. At least so far, nothing else there has sold so cheap. Then again, the rent it brings in just covers its costs. Current annual yield: zero. But how could I resist?

Anyway, the bad news, as I say, was that my original brilliant $110,000 investment had turned out not so brilliantly after all.

The other bit of bad news was handed to me by a process server: a bench warrant for my arrest. Obviously, this was a mistake. I'm just not the bench-warrant type. Yet there it was, referring to some sort of infractions on Little Building No. 2. My Young Attorney partner, Bob, when I reached him, quickly assured me that the whole thing was ridiculous and had already been taken care of—I would shortly be receiving confirmation that the bench warrant had been canceled.

After a couple of weeks, I figured I ought at least to find out what a bench warrant was. Apparently, it meant that if I were ever stopped for speeding, say, or a broken taillight, and the officer ran my name through his computer, I would be hauled off to jail. Yes, I'd be out the next day. "But trust me," another attorney told me, "this is not something you ever want to experience."

As the weeks stretched into months, I was becoming increasingly alarmed—and driving very carefully. Jimmy, who had a lot of experience with these things, told me that Bob obviously had a coke problem. Then again, Jimmy said that about almost everybody (to a hammer, every problem looks like a nail); and when I broached the possibility, Bob was so hurt, and so genuine and forthcoming about it all, that he made me feel really terrible for not trusting him.

Long story short—because you've either gone through this with someone yourself or you haven't, and if you have, you know exactly how awful and endless it is, and if you haven't, I hope you never do—Bob was finally whisked off to a drug-rehab program, too late to prevent the loss of his legal practice. And it was then that Jimmy and I actually went to see the building. The first thing I noticed, because the sun was setting and it was getting dark, was that the hall light was out. The second thing I noticed was that all the other lights were out, too.

"Can you believe that?" I said, really steamed. "He let all the bulbs burn out!" And here he was supposed to be managing the place.

Of course, as you have already surmised, the bulbs were fine. It was the electric bill my Young Partner Bob hadn't paid. And the garbage bill. And the water bill. And any of the other bills. There was just enough waning light to read a gallery of citations on the hallway wall announcing $250-a-day fines for all manner of infractions. Nothing had been paid, or done, in months.

We promptly set things straight, and not long after sold the building for a small profit. But the fire marshal told us that if there had been a fire during the period Bob was in charge, he would have sought criminal indictments—our building was one of the worst fire-safety violators he'd ever seen.

So Jimmy was right about Bob's drug problem. Indeed, Jimmy's street savvy was one of the things that served us best. He could generally spot the addicted souls, and though he often tried to help them, he encouraged them to rent from someone else.

## 9—The Other Side of the Boulevard

I forget now which was the first place I bought west of the Boulevard. I remember driving past it with Jimmy and being scared to get out of the car. The abandoned crack motel had made me nervous enough, but at least that was on the Boulevard itself, and on the east side, to boot. That one, with seventeen rooms and not a single working appliance, had been shut down by the city. In the six months it had been closed, the police told us, they had removed three dead bodies. It didn't smell very good, either. But $125,000 of renovations later (on top of the $125,000 purchase price), it had become quite decent. We replaced the MOTEL—WATER BEDS neon with an understated "Belle Meade Studios." Of course, it's not nearly as profitable at $275 a month as it was at $20 an hour. And that's part of the problem. How do you get motel owners to convert to far less profitable apartment houses? Or, if not, to screen out the hookers and drug dealers? It takes a lot of guts to turn someone away just because you suspect seedy or illegal activity. Yet that's what the city requires and the neighborhood needs. But what if the person you reject was OK after all? Or wasn't, but takes offense and shoots you?

And ultimately, where are these people supposed to go, anyway? I'd love to get the drug dealers to move west of the railroad tracks that abut our neighborhood, deeper into the slum. But because a lot of their clientele are middle-class folks (who lament urban blight but want their drugs anyway), they thrive on the edge of decent neighborhoods, where a car won't have to venture too deep into alien territory. If there aren't enough prison cells to keep the bad seeds off the streets—with drug rehab, job training and a specific job to report to when they're off the drugs—the problem will never go away. It may shift from my neighborhood to yours, if I'm successful, but that's hardly a solution.*

I know what you're thinking. You're thinking: run! The only sensible way to invest in an area like this is *not* to invest in an area like this. And that may be true. But then what happens to the area? I'll say this: few things help you get inside the headlines about drugs and crime and racism and jobs and welfare and jails and corruption and teenage pregnancies—and all the rest—better than owning property in an area like mine. It doesn't give you many answers, sadly, but it sure makes the questions real.

(One answer for certain: drug treatment on request. At the very least, anyone who *wants* to get off drugs shouldn't have to wait twenty seconds for treatment. It's a lot cheaper than paying to catch, try and incarcerate the same people, whom drugs drive to crime.)

But I'm getting ahead of myself. So far, we're still on the east side of the Boulevard. Then one day Jimmy showed me a place on the west side—the one where I was scared to get out of the car. "Are you sure you'll be safe?" I asked him. "Do you really want to do this?" He did, and with a vengeance.

In the course of just a couple of years, he had gone from being a guy afraid to go out of the house or open a checking account to being Mr. Everything. He had seven guys helping to renovate, mow, paint, landscape, repair and collect the rent; a car phone, beepers—the works.

---

* Right now, the police tell me, most Miami crack offenders don't get five years. There's not enough prison space, and many judges recognize how unfair five years is, so they're back on the street in ten days. Yet as expensive as prisons and rehabilitation are, crack addicts on the street cost more.

The places we bought on the west side didn't cost much, but fixing them up did. In theory, the numbers should have all worked out—and still may. That aforementioned motel, for example, has a rent roll of about $60,000 a year. Subtract half for expenses, and you still have a pretty good return on $250,000, especially given that it's partially sheltered from tax by depreciation, and that the building's value could rise with inflation—or even faster if the neighborhood gradually improves. (The landmark Pussycat theater has merely been transformed into a *two*-screen playhouse, renamed Madonna. But the long-abandoned Playboy Club has finally been torn down and replaced with a large, modern auto-parts retailer.)

So the numbers may work out. But numbers are numbers. Real life is less neat.

What do you do when a tenant loses his job and falls two months behind with the rent? Or when a Haitian woman moves in with her child, and then within weeks there are eight or nine refugees living there, mostly under the age of ten, using four times as much water as you expected (not cheap in Miami) and destroying the electric stove every couple of months because of the enthusiastic way they cook? Evict them, of course! But really? Where are they supposed to go?

What do you do about tenants who think it's racism when you fix, rather than replace, a refrigerator? Where are the African Americans and Haitians willing to be landlords here? Most who can afford it would rather live someplace else.

What do you do about drug dealers who stand on the corner in full view of the police? Who shoot out your security lights at night? What do you do about an undercover police raid the drug dealers somehow know about two days in advance?

In the movies, it's simple. But in real life, whom do you complain to? How deeply involved do you really want to get?

But I digress. I was talking about Jimmy.

Most people on both sides of the Boulevard really liked Jimmy. White, black or Latino, old or young, police or civilian. Whatever they wanted, he tried to provide, including a smile and respect. And for a little added influence on the west side, Jimmy hired a three-hundred-pound Rastafarian I'll call the Prince. Jimmy told me we would need the Prince for only a while; he told the Prince he had a job for life (or so the Prince alleges) and that we would put his three beautiful baby girls through college. After Jimmy died, this led to a clash of expectations.

## 10—Big Trouble

I guess it was the Häagen-Dazs when I really knew for sure, but by then it was too late.

Up until the fall of 1993, I'd say, things were going pretty well, more or less as I've described. We were spending a ton renovating slum properties, but I got frequent-flier miles for a lot of it (a dozen stoves here, $2,500 of tile there—Visa kept calling to ask whether my card had been stolen) and no small satisfaction from seeing the improvements.

The problem was that even once the renovating pretty much wound down and we should have entered our "reap the rewards" stage, with rents coming in but no new tile or stoves to buy, it didn't happen. When I got back to Miami in the fall of 1993 (having spent the summer up north), everything looked great, physically—you could tell at a glance which places on the west side of the Boulevard were ours. But the numbers weren't working out.

Something to focus on, Jimmy and I agreed.

But the fact is, I'm a lousy manager, especially when it comes to friends of twenty-five years who are not just ex-monks but virtual saints. And who are clearly working very hard and with a lot more courage than I'd ever muster. On top of that, Jimmy was not in great health that winter. Fat and happy up until that time, he had contracted some sort of walking pneumonia in December and then a nasty cold or sinus infection he just couldn't shake. So I was doubly reluctant to press him for better results. But I was getting worried.

I got more worried when Bob, the former Young Attorney—now back from rehab and in a new line of work (which has worked out very nicely, I'm happy to report)—told me he feared Jimmy was on drugs. Jimmy? C'mon. No one was more antidrug than Jimmy. He'd *been* there, man. It was not possible Jimmy had got back onto drugs.

I went up north the next summer worried, but with Jimmy's solemn promise that he'd get the expenses down and the rents collected. I was pretty sure I was going to have to "do something" when I got back, but the prospect was so awful I could hardly bear to think about it. "Doing something" would presumably mean relieving Jimmy of some or all of his responsibility. But this stuff had become his whole life! As he told me often, he loved it. And he worked so hard at it! What's more, "doing something" would mean having to find some way to replace Jimmy. But how? Who could possibly have the gumption, intelligence and grace to deal with all these different kinds of people, cajole the drug dealers into moving a few doors down? I mean, where do you find a former Wall Street wunderkind ex-monk who wants to spend his life struggling to turn around a slum for a property manager's wage?

So I went up north. But the reports were not encouraging, to say the least, and soon I asked Jimmy to go for a drug test. He made me feel terrible for not trusting him, but went . . . and passed. I was relieved, but deep down I knew I was kidding myself. I called Jimmy's doctor and asked as delicately as I could whether he felt there was any way we should be helping Jimmy. Nope. Jimmy was fine, as far as this doctor knew, or let on.

And then other things happened that led me and my assistant Mary to be almost sure Jimmy was where Bob had been when he was whisked away to treatment in Atlanta. So I called the same treatment center, booked flights and planned to fly down to Miami—no one flies to Miami in the summer—and "confront" Jimmy at six one morning (that's when you're supposed to confront someone) and go straight to the airport and to Atlanta, where the clinic would be waiting for us. I wouldn't be doing this alone. Mary would be with me. Friends of Jimmy would be with me. The young man Jimmy was adopting would be with me. (His mother had raised him to be "retarded" in order to collect an extra $400 a month in Social Security. But he wasn't retarded, and Jimmy had been teaching him to read and tell time; had been working to get him into the right kind of school; had sent him to the orthodontist—the works.)

But what if we were wrong? What if he hadn't just beaten the drug test, and his long-running congestion really *was* accounted for by the punch in the nose he had not wanted to tell me about (but now said I could check the police records if I doubted it)? Here he was risking his life on the west side, getting punched, and I'm accusing him of snorting coke? Or crack? The very things he was dedicating his life to fight?

I was not looking forward to this. So when Mary, who knew and loved Jimmy, too, and who was my eyes and ears in Miami while I was north for the summer, told me she was having second thoughts—that she wasn't sure we should do something so drastic—I was relieved. I'd be back down in a few weeks. Maybe we were just being paranoid. But in my gut I knew.

I got back and was shocked to see Jimmy, leaner than he'd been in twenty-five years, eating a pint of Häagen-Dazs rum raisin—ice cream, not yogurt—out of the container. This was a man who wouldn't eat a pretzel for fear of gaining weight, who had somehow shed fifty pounds eating Häagen-Dazs? And whose nose was *still* stuffed up? And who had, for the first time ever, somehow missed picking me up at the airport? It was clear that after a good night's sleep I would have to deal with this.

The next morning, long before I had planned to get up, there was a pounding on my door. "Come quick. I think Jimmy's dead." And he was.

## 11—Sunshine and Storm Clouds

According to the coroner's report, Jimmy had suffered a massive heart attack brought on by a massive asthma attack. I heard secondhand that the autopsy turned up no drugs, though I'm not sure they even looked for drugs. I didn't have the heart to pursue it.

Things were happening very fast. That morning, I discovered that Jimmy had had a floor safe installed in his room. Only the Prince, whom I finally met that morning (and who really did weigh three hundred pounds), had the combination. When he opened it—shades of Geraldo Rivera—there was nothing inside. "He's been robbed" was the Prince's conclusion. A secret safe? For what?

I had understood Brando, the German shepherd Jimmy acquired, even though I didn't like him ("Christian Brando," I nicknamed him, after he had cornered me once in a particularly terrifying way); Jimmy felt he needed the protection. But a secret safe? I had trusted Jimmy completely. Why didn't I know about this?

Later that morning, the man came to turn off the water in a couple of our houses. It seems the water bills hadn't been paid in months. In fact, as it turned out, a great many bills hadn't been paid, including little things like the payroll taxes that the IRS is pretty keen on collecting in a timely manner.

It was the Young Attorney and Little Building No. 2 all over again, except on a far larger scale—and with a far sadder ending.

Jimmy's brother and sister came down on Friday, their only visit in the half-dozen years Jimmy had been here. His brother had requested we do the memorial service that same weekend, to spare the expense of two trips, so the service was held that Sunday. It was really nice, although, as it turned out, neither sibling was able to stay for it. We held it outdoors in our local park, in the late afternoon, with a mix of sunshine and storm clouds overhead and a diverse collection of people Jimmy had touched looking out over the bay.

A lot of people were tearful, including Jimmy's "son," whose adoption was just three weeks shy of becoming final. All the papers had been signed and filed long ago, but the lawyer hadn't placed one of the legal advertisements the judge unexpectedly required—a technicality—so that was that. By law, none of the retirement money I had set aside for Jimmy would be going to him. (Had the adoption gone through, by law it all would have gone to him.)

Others rose at the service to tell stories of Jimmy's incredible generosity. Since Jimmy had arrived in Miami with only what he had saved up in the monastery, and since monks don't get paid, I began to get at least a little better picture of where some of my money had gone. And stories people told me afterward, if true, would account for a good chunk of the rest. All told, I'd guess we were talking in the quarter-million-dollar range.

But anything he did wrong I blame on the drugs. Drugs ruin everything.*

## 12—Ending to Be Announced

When the dust settled, Sal, one of Jimmy's former lieutenants, stepped in and an amazing thing happened. The hemorrhaging stopped. The bills got paid, the rents got collected and things are back to being

---

* I speak here of addictive drugs, because there really is a distinction. "Did you ever really look at ketchup?" is the sort of thing people stoned on grass or acid say. A problem, perhaps, but not the stuff of hopeless lives or devastated neighborhoods.

more or less what they should be. He's even worked out a way to turn some of the vacant lots on the west side into vegetable plots for our tenants, hoping that this will help build a sense of community.

Not to say we will succeed. It would be far safer to buy shares in a real estate investment trust, not to mention easier. If the Big Real Estate Agent had called and asked if I had ever heard of South Beach and started me buying properties there instead of in the shadow of the Palm Bay Club, I'd be *rolling* in it. Talk about serendipity! Location, location, location. (At least I still have that one little building on the beach. It's about tripled in value.) But having gone this far with it—and there being no obvious buyers to sell many of these properties to, anyway—I'm going to stick it out a while longer and see what happens.

# 3

## Russia

# MY PARTNERS' WIVES
# ARE ALL NAMED TANYA

It all started, if you don't count the time I was arrested by the KGB for selling my blue jeans, in the summer of 1992. That was when I read in *The Wall Street Journal* that you could buy thirty seconds of commercial time on the Russian nightly news for $3,000.

Three thousand dollars? To reach the entire former Soviet Union?

Remember, this was a country that then had just two or three channels; where viewers couldn't zap you with the mute button (because they had no mute button—about the only remote function Soviet-made TVs were known for was spontaneous combustion); and where they couldn't go into another room for a beer during the commercial because they had no other room. So for $3,000 you captured a hundred million eyes.

*I have $3,000,* I thought. *With a little scraping, I even have $30,000.* Wouldn't it be neat to run ads ten nights in a row to tell Russians the story of tobacco? The true story?

Wouldn't that just annoy the heck out of the fine tobacco lobbyists from RJR and Philip Morris?

A little background.

## 1—I Am Twelve

All the smart kids were opting for French, Spanish or German. As you already know, I signed up for Russian. I liked the alphabet. It was like a secret code. I have been fascinated with things Russian and Soviet ever since. Not least because . . .

## 2—I Am Arrested

Junior year, at the ripe old age of sixteen, in 1963, I coaxed my parents into sending me on that trip behind the Iron Curtain, with twenty other kids, that resulted in my acquisition of the Lenin Library card and that had so disconcerted them. My two most vivid memories of the trip were, first, arriving in Czechoslovakia and finding that it was in color. I had somehow not expected this. And second, being framed by a very junior division of the KGB—specifically, the division charged with scaring the wits out of inquisitive sixteen-year-old Americans who strayed from the group.

While the other kids were dutifully following our Intourist guides around monuments and museums, a friend and I would regularly strike out on our own and just see what we could see. We made a good team: he spoke no Russian but possessed a magnetic sense of direction; I get lost at every opportunity but knew a little Russian. We would board the Moscow subway, headed no place in particular, and ask perfect strangers to "guess where we're from." ("Germany?" was the closest anyone got. "The moon" is probably what they were thinking.)

This was fun for us but angst-making for our Intourist guides, so a small team was dispatched to strike the fear of . . . not God, presumably, this being an atheist state, but . . . *something* in me, and they sure as heck did. I handed over a pair of blue jeans, expecting to get enough rubles to buy a ten-volume Soviet children's encyclopedia (which I did wind up buying anyway), and instead found myself being interrogated for four hours with the prospect of many years in jail.

They let me go because I was so young but claimed the "purchaser" (who was almost surely in on the sting, I realized later) would be executed. I can't remember if I ever got the jeans back. But the main thing is that we stopped misbehaving for at least a week, until we got to Poland. There, Soviet books were subsidized even more heavily than in Russia, so great was the supply and so slight the demand. I got a second set of the same encyclopedia at half the already ridiculously low price—something like $20 worth of black-market zlotys—as a gift for my high school.

I came back to the U.S. something of a socialist for reasons only a sixteen-year-old would understand. I wasn't sure what I wanted to do with my life, but business—capitalism—was clearly out of boundski. My dad, the advertising executive, had already placed the ad game off limits. Anything but that, he said. He didn't want me to suffer the frustration. (He was a man who could have written great novels but, to support his family, wound up writing great jingles. Remember "Man, oh, Manischewitz"? His. "Ronzoni, sono buoni"? His. "Calling all boys to Barneys"? I used to get all my clothes from Barney's son at 20 percent off.)

### 3—I Am Converted

I remained steadfast in my socialist principles until, as described, I wound up running the student business conglomerate at Harvard. Funny what a profit share will do to your political philosophy.

I still wanted to end the Cold War—I knew the Soviet *people* were peace-loving, with nice if impractical ideals. So I majored in what I thought of as "Soviet stuff" but Harvard insisted on calling Slavic Languages and Literatures. This meant reading *War and Peace* in English and taking Czech long enough to discover that all Czech words are accented on the first syllable, except those also accented on the second syllable. Hello? Does this just mean you are supposed to say the whole word louder? I dropped the course the next day.

It is a matter of no small personal shame that after four years of high school Russian, a major in Slavic Languages and Literatures, and decades of talking to Russian-born cabdrivers in New York, I still haven't mastered it. The cabdrivers compliment me on my Russian accent, but that is about the only thing they say that I can understand. "Slower, please. Slower!" I beg in Russian, hoping they will enunciate each syllable. But they just hit the brakes.

## 4—The Tobacco Thing

Well, the Cold War ended, and I had absolutely nothing to do with it. But now—1992, a full twenty-nine years after my trip to Russia—I am reading this thing in *The Wall Street Journal* about being able to advertise for $3,000.

Separately, I have become one of those really boring, obnoxious people on the subject of tobacco. I think people should certainly be allowed to smoke if they want to, but not where I have to breathe it. And I think it's nuts that we spend $5 billion a year in this country *promoting* the leading cause of preventable death.

So I've done some things here and there to try to help the pro-health activists in this ongoing dialogue. But in the U.S.—or practically anyplace else in the world—what kind of impact can you really have?

That's why this $3,000 notion was so startling. I knew that U.S. tobacco companies were rushing into the former Soviet Union. Wouldn't it be neat to issue a warning? "The Hessians are coming! The Hessians are coming!"—under the appealing cloak of the Marlboro man, Joe Camel and all those healthy, athletic, glamorous smokers who've been banned from U.S. television since 1965. *Listen up,* I would say, *because I can only afford to tell you once.* And then I'd tell them all the things we now know about tobacco and the cynicism of the tobacco companies.

I checked. Three thousand dollars was not a misprint. You really could buy airtime that cheap. (In fact, cheaper, as I would ultimately discover.) But producing Russian TV spots? Where would you even start? I just sort of filed this idea away. Like most of us, I have a large file of such ideas.

## 5—Opportunity Knocks

A few months later, serendipitously, I got invited to join a delegation to Moscow. Well, delegation sounds awfully grand—it was actually about fifteen of us, led by Congressman Barney Frank, hoping to persuade the Russian authorities to repeal "Article 121," Stalin's 1937 decree making intimacy between two adults of the same sex punishable by up to five years in prison. (And in fact, not long after our visit, very possibly thanks in some measure to Barney's efforts, the rule was quietly repealed and some prisoners released.)

Had the invitation been to Indonesia or Peru, I might not have gone. But Russia! I had been waiting twenty-nine years for a reason to go back to Russia!

And I remembered *The Wall Street Journal.*

One thing led to another, and pretty soon I was faxing furiously to Moscow, to an American friend-of-a-friend named Mark Slater who was over there producing documentaries with directors Lina Wertmuller and Werner Herzog.

"Sure," Mark faxed. "Why don't you write up some scripts and we'll try it."

## 6—Excuse My Pronunciation

Our little delegation reached Moscow on December 1, 1992, and got to do some neat things. One was to tour Butyrka prison, built by Catherine the Great and cleaned only twice since then. Well, that's not fair. But it is the single most depressing place I have ever been. It's here Russians are sent while awaiting determination of their guilt or innocence. This frequently takes three years. If guilty, they are sent elsewhere for the remainder of their term. If innocent, they are released. They cannot make outgoing calls.

It was very good to get back out into the cold Moscow air.

Actually, fresh air of any type is welcome in Moscow, because this is a country where everyone smokes. We visited Moscow's huge cancer institute and were told that 70 percent of the *doctors* there smoke.

This in a country where the average life expectancy was not so great to begin with, but is now slumping precipitously—down to fifty-nine or so for a male versus seventy-two in the U.S.

Yes, yes, if you had their problems, you'd smoke, too. But really: Should Russian kids give up on life just because communism has collapsed? Should they become lifelong slaves to the tobacco companies?

So there I was in Moscow with my scripts, which we had translated into Russian and which a crew had stayed up all night typing into a sort of makeshift TelePrompTer.

"Hello," I said at the outset of the first. "I'm a writer from Miami. Excuse my pronunciation, but I have something important to tell you."

I was reading from the monitor, following the stress marks that had been penned in for me. (Unlike Czech, Russian words are all stressed on just one syllable—and only a Russian knows which.)

"Not long ago, with the aid of some wonderful New York City schoolchildren, I wrote this little book [HOLD UP THE BOOK], *Kids Say Don't Smoke*. Now we are translating this book into Russian and hoping to distribute it to schools and hospitals. Over the next several evenings, I want to share with you some of the things I learned in writing this book.

"In America, every pack of cigarettes [HOLD UP CAMELS, LEFT HAND] carries a strong warning. For example: 'Smoking in pregnant women can cause fetal damage.' Yet in Russia, the exact same cigarettes [HOLD UP RUSSIAN CAMELS, RIGHT HAND] from the same manufacturer have no warning label. How come? Are *Russian* fetuses not important?

"Well, until tomorrow."

That was my sign-off line: "Well, until tomorrow."

The idea was to come back night after night with some factoid about smoking or the tobacco companies. We had been promised airtime for even less than $3,000—and for a full minute, not thirty seconds!—so we decided to tape fifteen spots. Of course, it was anybody's guess whether we could pull this off technically, and, if so, whether we could actually get them on the air. From the difficulty I was having pronouncing some of this stuff—"toy boat" is nothing compared with *"byeryemyenikh zhenshchin"* —I had grave doubts.

We had one guy standing by with a stopwatch—the ads had to be approximately a minute each, give or take a few seconds (is that how NBC does it?)—and another whose sole job was to listen with his eyes closed to see whether he could understand what I was saying. Plus the cameraman, a makeup woman, Mark (our director) and people from the studio running the monitor.

The ads in fact made it on the air in early 1993, broadcast on both main networks at the time, Ostankino and RTR, and on the regional (seventy million viewers) Petersburg TV. I was back in sunny Miami when they aired in dark and freezing Moscow but got copies taped off the air.

A not terribly scientific poll of 125 youngsters (OK, a terribly unscientific poll) determined that about half the kids in the country remembered seeing the ads. Comments ranged from "Keep doing this!" and "Please convince people not to smoke!" to "Make video with interesting plot. It's so boring just to see you lecturing." (The kid had a point.)

Better still, the ads were parodied. On what seemed to be a sort of Ed Sullivan hour, a team of powder-blue-tuxedoed stand-up comics did a bit where one of them stepped up to his mike and said, in what even I could tell was a bad American accent: "My brother-in-law quit smoking and three weeks later he was dead. My sister quit smoking, and three weeks later she was dead. And their dog died. They were hit by a car. Well, until tomorrow."

Finally, we heard a number of stories of adults being really annoyed with the ads, because their kids were bugging the hell out of them to stop filling the apartment with tobacco smoke. This made me very happy.

### 7—World Smoke-Out Day

Mark and I had *Kids Say Don't Smoke* translated and arranged to print fifty thousand copies. The first price we were quoted—by the publishing arm of Tass, struggling as it was to adjust to the new market economy—was about 10¢ a book, payable (in advance) in U.S. dollars. This was a sensational price, and we shook on it all around the table. The next day, when I returned to sign the final papers, the price had doubled. "Ah," they explained. "In our calculations, we forgot to include paper."

The books—which even at 20¢ cost barely a third what they'd have cost in the West—were delivered only a few weeks behind schedule and looked pretty good. With the help of the Russian journalist Vladimir Gubarev (first on the scene at Chernobyl and highly respected throughout the country), all fifty thousand were distributed across eleven time zones. For some reason he adopted our little project, even going so far as to hand one of the books to the president of Kazakhstan.

I was invited back to Moscow by some arm of the Health Ministry to hand out the first copies of *Kids Say Don't Smoke* and to participate in World Smoke-Out Day, May 31. Moscow is a lot nicer in May than December.

A few weeks before the trip I got word that Russian TV wanted me to come on as a guest. "I can't," I said. "I don't speak Russian." The word came back: "Oh, you speak Russian very well." They thought I was being modest. They actually believed this, because they had seen me speaking on TV. What they hadn't seen was the monitor with the stress marks. "No, I mean I really don't speak Russian!"

A simultaneous translator was engaged, and there I was on Russian TV, and later on a popular national radio-show broadcast from Ostankino. (Five months later, gunfire would crackle in the same lobby I passed through to go to my interviews, as the hard-liners attempted to overthrow Yeltsin.)

At a press conference Vladimir Gubarev arose from the back of the room unexpectedly, came forward and announced that—with our permission—he would be sending a copy of *Kids Say Don't Smoke* up into space with a Russian cosmonaut pal. The first such book in space.

It was so loony, and yet somehow he pulled off the moment with aplomb. I don't know whether the book ever orbited, but for a few seconds it all seemed to make sense. *Of course* he'd be launching our book. *Of course* this was newsworthy. *Of course* the proper etiquette in making the announcement was to ask our permission. ("No! You may absolutely not send a copy of *Kids Say Don't Smoke* into space. We have only *fifty thousand* copies, and we need them all down here.")

We got a bunch of press, and then the following winter we aired some more spots. This time we got two little Russian girls, six and ten, to look into the camera and read a letter to President Yeltsin.

"Dear President Yeltsin," they read. "The Supreme Soviet has passed a law banning tobacco advertising on TV, but everyone ignores it. Yet the companies that advertise tobacco on TV here can't show those same ads at home. Isn't the health of Russian children important to you? Please, President Yeltsin, enforce the law."

Night after night for two weeks, if memory serves. First the six-year-old, then the ten-year-old, on alternate nights.

I don't know whether Yeltsin ever saw these annoying ads, but I did hear that his number two, Viktor Chernomyrdin, stormed into a cabinet meeting one day and asked what *is* it with these kids.

Many months after those ads appeared—and most likely not in any way as a result—Yeltsin did decree the end of tobacco (and alcohol) advertising. A few days later, the highly popular head of Russian TV announced he was dropping *all* TV advertising while his team reassessed its impact (and wrested control of ad sales from the hands of the Russian mafia, but he didn't say that) . . . and a few days after that, at the age of thirty-eight, in front of six witnesses, he was shot to death in the lobby of his apartment building.

But hold that very sad thought. I have to back up.

## 8—We Start a Business

The thing is, I was dazzled by what Mark was able to accomplish. In a country where back then nothing worked, no one answered the phone, Kinko's was decidedly not on every corner and you had to carry around your own toilet paper, Mark managed miracles. Here was a thirty-five-ish Minnesotan who had just started learning Russian when he got to Moscow, whose accent was worse than *yours*, but who remembered everything, coordinated everything, managed to get everything done and never dropped a ball.

I quickly developed two basic refrains in my communications with Mark:

(1) "Thank you." I said that a lot. (He did all this smoking stuff for free. Also some stark ads we did with famous Russian actors to warn about AIDS.)

(2) "Find some business and let me back you." I said that a lot, too, because Russia was—is—a country where you could easily lose your shirt, and we still may, but where the potential is enormous.

So Mark began looking for businesses to invest in, and after several months' search settled on a small ad agency/computer graphics business run by three Russian partners—Ilya, Dmitri and Alexei—all twenty-six or so at the time (now pushing thirty), and all married to women named Tanya. They had brains, energy, integrity, some rudimentary computer equipment and a few local clients. What they lacked was $150,000 in Silicon Graphics workstations, Wavefront computer-graphics software, international connections and a nice office. We supplied all that in return for a controlling interest in the business, which was renamed Media Arts.

When friends ask me what "computer graphics" really are, I explain it this way. You know that winged horse at the start of all Tri-Star motion pictures? *It's not a real horse.* Not that we did that particular horse, or have done anything at all just yet for Tri-Star. But our equipment is in use virtually twenty-four hours a day. Indeed, by now we've moved into bigger, better offices, bought additional equipment and started a "media-monitoring" business. We have a bank of TVs and VCRs and a crew employed to tape everything that plays on Russian TV, keeping a log of what commercials are played when. That way, advertisers can verify they got the ad time they paid for—and get a clear idea of what their competitors are doing. We have about eighty employees in all.

My principal role in this is as wire clerk. And although the novelty is beginning to wear off, it's heady stuff. Picture it. To get the Wavefront software to our new office in Moscow, I wired dollars from our account in Miami to the Taipei account of the Dutch company that represents Wavefront in Russia. It then delivered the software in Moscow and (presumably) forwarded payment to Wavefront in California. Ah, brave new world.

Meanwhile, some of our business comes direct to the States, so again I get to play wire clerk. In February the bank called to tell me that a $450,000 wire had just come in from France. This was to pay for commercial time on Russian TV, so a few days later my partners E-mailed me instructions on wiring most of it back out: $235,000 to an account in Moscow and $201,000 to an account in Latvia. (Latvia!)

I dutifully fired off the wire instructions, and the bank dutifully fired off the wires.

Normally, that would have been the end of it, but later that day I got a call from Ilya in Moscow. "Have the wires gone out?" he asked.

"I think so—why?"

"Can you stop them?" he asked.

"I don't know—I doubt it," I said, growing ever so slightly nervous. "Why?"

Ilya reported that the aforementioned highly popular thirty-eight-year-old TV czar, Vladimir Listyev, had just been assassinated. Chaos reigned. Ilya thought it would be a good idea to stop the wires.

It was seven minutes to five in Miami (nearly 1:00 A.M. in Moscow), so I hung up and called the bank. "Well, it's not 100 percent guaranteed," I was told, "but we can recall the wires in the morning and chances are the money will come back."

So I asked them to do that—all of this confirmed in writing, of course—apologizing for the inconvenience. "The irony," I said, "is that things are likely to settle back down in a day or two and we'll have to send the darn wires out all over again. But better safe than sorry."

Sure enough, a day or two later, that's just what happened. I received word from my partners that it was OK to send the money.

The $235,000 from Moscow had already come back, so I instructed the bank to send it back out. "And if the $201,000 comes back from Latvia, send it back out, too."

Twelve days passed. I was out of town, thinking about other things, but then came an E-mail from Moscow. Where's the $235,000?

I called my counterpart at the bank. "Oh," she said. "I was going to call you this morning."

"Yeah?"

It seems that instead of re-sending the $235,000 that had come back from Moscow, she had accidentally re-sent a second $201,000 to Latvia.

I won't take you through every twist and turn. Suffice it to say that Latvia is not Cleveland. The Latvians apparently thought this second $201,000 was a miracle. An answered prayer. Can you imagine how much money $201,000 is in Latvia? When the Latvians were apprised of the error and asked to return the money, they said, "No." The Latvian bank was contacted directly by a vice president of the Miami bank. "Forget it," he was told. "You're not getting the money back."

This made the Miami bank, which acknowledged it was its problem not ours (but which showed a $170,000 overdraft in our account all the same), highly nervous. The FBI was contacted; Kroll Associates, a private investigative firm, was poised to strike. At the eleventh hour, our partners in Moscow prevailed on their partners' partners in Latvia to force the bank to return the money. Something like that. All I know is that the money came back.

And now a nice wire has come in from Hong Kong, from a client who wants to sell TVs in Russia. Indeed, we've gotten wires for as much as $3 million. Granted, as with the high school dues I used to collect, most of this isn't *my* money. Most of it goes out to pay for ad time or else for running the business. But a little of it is. And I like "being with it." (There's also a little more you can do with a few days' float than when I was in high school—not that we do anything remotely fancy—and with the occasional $3 million balance it's worth doing.)

### 9—He's Baaaaaa-ack

The second World Smoke-Out Day I attended, in May 1994, got us a plug on the front page of *Izvestiya* and was a chance to meet my Russian partners in the flesh and to see our offices. They are fine partners. And, by Moscow standards, snazzy offices. I also saw the computers our money had bought. Given what they cost, they sure seemed small. But with them, our skilled artists and technicians can make goobers dance and horses fly.

While there, I made another series of commercials that aired the following winter. (Winter is prime time in Russia. Who on earth would be out of the house at night in that weather? And night falls around three in the afternoon.) Taking pity on the Russians, who have a lot to bear as it is, I made just five spots instead of fifteen—and we jazzed them up with computer graphics. My favorite of the five talked about the economics of this whole deal. The Russians feel they must play ball with Philip Morris and the rest because of the jobs new cigarette factories create and because of the ad dollars that come pouring in. What I tried to point out is that Philip Morris et al. aren't doing this as a *favor*. They clearly expect to take far more out of Russia than they put in.

### 10—Heads You Lose, Tails You Win—Big

So far, we're making money. Most of it will probably go to the accountants for trying to figure out how to pay U.S. and Russian taxes. And there's the obvious and real possibility that something disastrous will happen. Russia is a volatile place.

Then again, by now I've gotten 100 percent of my investment back, and there's the possibility we will one day sell out for a big profit. As Michael Katz, who runs Glenrock Global Partners in New York, told

*The Wall Street Journal* a couple of years ago, Russia's a coin toss: heads you lose everything, tails you make twenty times your money. It's irresistible.

One of these days it will be safe to invest in Russia. By then, of course, it will be time to invest someplace else. Uganda, anyone?

P.S. Tobacco ads no longer appear on Russian TV. I suppose that could change anytime, with the right combination of bribes and corrupt officials. But I'm keeping my fingers crossed.

# 4

<u>California</u>

# RALPH NADER IS A BIG FAT IDIOT

OK, he's neither fat nor an idiot. In fact, he's lean and smart and has done some extraordinary things over the years. But in 1996 Ralph Nader was the linchpin of a deceptive campaign that cost California consumers more than $3 billion a year. This is the story of how he shafted them—at no small expense to my own vast fortune—and how he stands in the way of needed reform nationwide.

The roots of this story go back a long way.

### 1—F. Lee Bailey

The year was 1971. I was at Harvard Business School, fresh from my National Student Marketing experiences with Cortes Wesley Randall, listening to a fellow named Glenn Wesley Turner address the topic "Con Man or Saint?" (Beware guys named Wesley?) It was Turner's contention that his company, Koscot Interplanetary, was a legitimate business selling mink-oil-based "Kosmetics." A great many state attorneys general disagreed. They contended Koscot was a pyramid scheme—like a chain letter at $5,000 a pop.

By the end of the hour we had concluded that Turner was immensely likable but, indeed, a con man. (He took a show of hands.)

"You know the problem with you people?" he told us. "You *think* too much! If you could just come down to Florida and see our operation, you'd believe, like everyone else. In fact, tell you what I'll do. I'll fly you all down there. Anybody want to come?"

Stunned silence. This was wintertime—in Boston.

A couple of weeks later we were deplaning from two of Turner's aircraft, greeted on the tarmac by Miss Orlando and Turner's 33-inch-tall twin lieutenants. By the time we left, all but one of us remained convinced he was a con man. (That classmate went on to found an astrological investment advisory firm.) But that's not why I'm telling you this. I'm telling you this because as part of the show, F. Lee Bailey flew down, piloting his own Learjet, to join us for dinner. In addition to representing Turner—one of the finest Americans he had ever met, Bailey told us—and in addition to serving on Turner's executive committee, Bailey in those years was helping to lead the battle against no-fault auto insurance.

(With true no-fault insurance, you buy coverage to protect *yourself*. There are no lawsuits. You can't be sued, and you don't have to sue someone else to get compensated for your injuries. A reckless driver can still go to jail, and will certainly see his insurance premiums skyrocket. But you'd no longer have to pray he was heavily insured if he hurt you. With true no-fault, billions that now go to lawyers and fraud would be saved for victims and consumers. Unfortunately, true no-fault doesn't exist. Most states that think they have no-fault don't—the lawyers sabotaged it. There are still scads of lawsuits and massive fraud.)

"I can understand why no-fault would be a very bad thing for *lawyers*," I said to Bailey at one point during cocktails. "But isn't it a good thing for drivers?"

Absolutely not, Bailey assured me. He wasn't fighting to protect lawyers' fees, he was fighting to protect the little guy. It wasn't the money, it was the principle.

## 2—Ralph Nader

Shortly after the Koscot Kaper, I was in Washington on my first "book tour." Whom should I see coming toward me down the street but a tall, serious man I instantly recognized as Ralph Nader. Unlike Bailey (who ultimately failed to save Turner), Nader was a hero to me in those days.

I somehow felt that my book, a Wall Street exposé of sorts (as much as a twenty-three-year-old who had never worked on Wall Street could expose it), was vaguely related to his own antiestablishmentarianism. So I screwed up my courage, introduced myself and told him I would be honored if he'd take a copy. And I *was* honored. After all, this was the guy who had almost single-handedly forced General Motors to admit its sins and take safety more seriously. He had founded the consumer movement. Nader's book *Unsafe at Any Speed* was to consumerism what Rachel Carson's *Silent Spring* was to environmentalism. And if both movements have occasionally gone to extremes, few would dispute that in the main they have been enormously positive. So I was excited to be able to hand Ralph Nader my book, and even more excited a few years later when my dad worked with him pro bono to produce full-page *New York Times* ads launching Ralph Nader's Public Citizen and The Ralph Nader Congress Project. I have framed copies in my office.

I didn't know at the time that he—virtually alone among consumer advocates—opposed no-fault auto insurance of any kind. When it came to the little guy's right to sue—even his right to sue *other* little guys—Nader felt there could be no compromise, ever, no matter how great the benefit. It was almost as if he believed the right to sue was more important than the right to *get* anything (since suing only *gets* you anything if you can prove the other guy was at fault—and he has something worth getting). This was distinctly *not* the view of Consumers Union or almost anyone else.

Thirty-five years ago, in 1962, Consumers Union declared that the traditional auto-insurance lawsuit system **"produces results which are so unjust, capricious, and so wasteful of both the policyholders' and the accident victim's money that most laymen find it hard to believe the facts when they are first presented."** All that's changed since then: it's gotten worse. And Ralph Nader has done more than any man in America to keep it this way.

### 3—Gay Talese

Cut to 1978. I am out of business school; I've been lucky with a couple of best-sellers, as you know—my vast fortune has mounted well into six figures. The phone rings. Nan Talese, then with Simon & Schuster, would like me to do a book. "Everybody knows the banks have so much money," she tells me. "And everybody knows Wall Street has so much money. But what a lot of people don't realize is that the insurance companies—*they* have so much money, too! Think of all those billions! The power it represents! What do they do with it? The reading public hasn't a clue. You should do a book called *The Invisible Bankers*." I am paraphrasing here, but that was the essence of it.

The day after we signed the contract, or so it seems to me now, Nan showed up with a huge stack of dog-eared insurance texts.

Hello? Nan is a marvelous literary soul. She is not someone you'd expect to own, or even to have seen, an insurance text.

Ah. Well. Her husband, Gay, it developed, had been researching this book, but had decided it wasn't for him. These were texts *he* had accumulated, and now they were mine.

Only with time did I realize what had happened. I had been tricked. While Gay Talese spent years and years of *his* life "researching" and writing a book about sex, called *Thy Neighbor's Wife*, I was left to spend years and years of mine on insurance. Not for nothing does Talese get the big bucks.

And so, I have long told the legions of insurance-industry professionals who hate me (the book was subtitled *Everything the Insurance Industry Never Wanted You to Know*), "Don't blame me. Blame Gay Talese."

### 4—Fantasy Sex Hangings

I quickly found I had a problem. This was supposed to be a serious yet absorbing peek at how insurance companies invest their money. Well, as it turned out, for the most part they buy bonds. Now, *there's* an exciting paragraph or two.

With Nan's permission, I broadened my focus. I discovered that the insurance business is actually quite fascinating. "They Just Want Us to

Think It's Boring" was one of my chapter subtitles—because the less we know about insurance, the more easily insurers can rip us off. I learned, and wrote, about everything from fantasy sex hangings (life insurance adjusters know they're accidents, not suicides, but use the family's shame to keep from having to pay) to accounting (and you think *your* tax returns are creative!) to fraud (a Chicago pastor claimed thirty auto-accident injuries in four years).

The insurance industry hated *The Invisible Bankers*.

Sure, there were a few open-minded souls—"[The author] has done his homework," opined *The Actuarial Review*; "The book is basically fair," said *The Actuary*. But most of the good blurbs came from outside the industry: *Fortune, Newsweek, The New York Times*. One I was particularly proud of came from Ralph Nader: "Fun to read, crackles with wit . . . shows how much consumers can save if they learn what to demand from insurance companies."

I tell you all this not to line my pockets—the book is resoundingly out of print—but rather to establish my credentials. I am no more "a tool of the insurance industry" than . . . well, Ralph Nader.

### 5—Zero Impact

In writing my book I naturally gave the most space to the stuff I thought was most interesting or important. One area I skirted almost entirely was health insurance. I knew it was important; I could just never get my head around it. (As the baby elephant said to the crocodile, "This is just too buch for be!" If you don't know what I'm talking about, sue your mother.) An area I *did* find easy to understand was automobile insurance.

I had never had more than routine contact with car insurance—like you, I had never thought much about it. But as I did my research I began to realize that we have in this country, to varying degrees (Michigan being the exception), about the worst, most inefficient, inhumane auto insurance system you could possibly devise. It costs a fortune, yet little of that money makes it through to the people most seriously hurt. In California today, nearly two thirds of the $7 billion paid annually for the "people" portions of auto insurance (damage to people, not theft or dented fenders)—two thirds!—goes to lawyers and fraud. The remainder is split between insurance companies and honest victims, with the great bulk of the "victim" money going to those least badly hurt. The really seriously injured recover, on average, just 9 percent of their actual losses from that $7 billion pie. Nine percent. And this is the system Ralph Nader fights to preserve.

But I'm getting ahead of myself. The point I want to make for now is: unlike health insurance (or Bosnia, or poverty), where there's no simple answer—*with auto insurance there is.*

Step one, I have always maintained, is to collect the bulk of the premium at the gas pump (with the rest, to be sure bad drivers pay extra, at registration and through surcharges on traffic violations). That would slash selling costs and end the uninsured-motorist problem. Step two is to adopt true no-fault auto insurance. More on that in a minute.

So two of the chapters of *The Invisible Bankers* laid out the auto-insurance solution. Not that I expected anything much to happen as a result.

And guess what? I was right! Nothing *at all* happened.

## 6—Prop 103

That was 1982.

It is now 1988, and out in California—crazy California—they are promoting a thing called Proposition 103 that would lower auto-insurance rates by 20 percent. How would they achieve that miracle? Well, just by passing a law.

Isn't that wonderful?

The insurance companies spent $63 million fighting Prop 103. Rates were sky-high, they said, not because they were gouging consumers—they actually earned *less* in California than elsewhere—but because *claims* were sky-high. ("Hit me, I need the money," was a popular California bumper sticker at the time.) This was true; but who wants to believe an insurance company?

It got very messy, with three "counter propositions" added to the ballot and lots of angry shouting. The one thing that pierced the confusion was Ralph Nader. He said Prop 103 was the one to vote for, and 52 percent of the voters that November did. In fact, it was an organization Nader had helped establish that wrote Prop 103 and

started the fight in the first place. That organization—Voter Revolt—
was headed by a Nader acolyte I would come to know well, attorney
Harvey Rosenfield (Georgetown Law '79). Ralph and Harvey. Harvey
and Ralph.

I was only vaguely aware of the Prop 103 battle at the time. I do
remember being asked about it on *Good Morning America* and
saying, Well, there's no question rates are too high in California, but
the way to solve the problem isn't to just decree lower prices;
you've got to get at the *causes* of the problem—huge legal expenses
and massive fraud. Otherwise, why not do this for hamburgers and
gasoline and anything else we'd like to see cheaper? I didn't say it
with any particular passion—it just seemed kind of obvious. But to
my surprise, by remote TV hookup from three thousand miles away,
someone (who I now realize must have been Harvey) was replying
with considerable heat. Prop 103 was terrific, he said—I clearly
didn't understand.

I was a little struck by that encounter. But more than that, I was
struck by the fact that this boring old topic, *auto insurance,* was actually making the front page in states like California, Massachusetts and
New Jersey. Who'da thunk it?

So after Prop 103 passed (and auto insurance rates did *not* decline
20 percent, but I'll get to that), I wrote a story in *Time* describing the
problem and explaining how to solve it for real—basically just reprising the two chapters from *The Invisible Bankers.*

*Time* reaches four million households.

I got two calls.

## 7—NICO

One was from my mother, who always calls. The other was from Bob
Hunter, the nation's leading consumer advocate on insurance. He ran
a Nader offshoot called the National Insurance Consumer Organization (NICO). Formerly Gerald Ford and Jimmy Carter's federal insurance administrator, Bob is a man of great physical and intellectual
stature, and the actuary perhaps least loved by the insurance industry.
He had been gracious with his time when I was researching *The Invisible Bankers,* and had long been privy to my thoughts about fixing the
auto-insurance mess.

Anyway, Bob called. "I think maybe it's time," he said, suggesting that I fund a NICO study on the topic.

You have never seen someone more eager to be tapped for $10,000. I figured, wow: It's one thing for me to *write* this stuff. But imagine if NICO and the nation's leading insurance critic, Bob Hunter, actually decided to advocate it. I happily wrote the check.

## 8—Bingo!

It had taken more than two years, but there we were in Washington at the National Press Club, Bob Hunter and I, May 18, 1992, unveiling our proposal for Pay-at-the-Pump, Private, No-Fault auto insurance. The insurance press (and pretty much only the insurance press) noticed, ridiculed us a bit and went back to sleep.

I realized that if this thing was ever going to happen, I'd really have to spell it out. Not just *say* there'd be a way to make pay-at-the-pump fair—explain exactly how. Not just *say* no-fault would lower premiums and increase benefits—prove it point by point.

So I fleshed it all out into a little $5 paperback, *Auto Insurance Alert!* (which I am not flogging, either, because it too is out of print, and all the royalties, such as they were, went to NICO and an environmental group). Basically, it was still the same two chapters from *The Invisible Bankers*, the same article from *Time.*

But because this time I hoped something might actually happen— what with great quotes from people like NICO's Hunter ("Join the crusade!") and *Newsweek*'s personal finance columnist Jane Bryant Quinn ("I love this idea")—I was more aggressive. I sent pre-publication copies of the manuscript to all fifty governors and insurance commissioners asking for comments.

My purpose was partly to get feedback and partly to make state officials feel they were part of the process, not under attack.

And the most remarkable thing happened.

Months before the book even came out, I got a call from the office of the chairman of the California Senate insurance committee. "We want to turn your manuscript into a constitutional amendment," his chief aide said.

"Who is this really?" I said.

"No, really!" he said. "But don't get *too* excited. It will never pass."

The lawyers and insurance companies would never allow it. But we should try anyway, he said—raise the public's consciousness on this issue and, well . . . you never know.

## 9—Stumping for Reform

It was fun. Three of us went on radio and TV plugging Pay-at-the-Pump No-Fault—Art Torres, Senate insurance committee chair; John Garamendi, California's elected insurance commissioner; and me.

We got endorsements of one sort or another from *USA Today, The Wall Street Journal,* the *San Francisco Chronicle, The Sacramento Bee* and *Consumers Digest,* among others.

The highlight of our campaign may have been a three-hour live televised hearing with "viewer call-ins"—a first in California legislative history. One woman called in and said, in effect, "I don't understand what the hell you're talking about, but if the lawyers are against it, I'm for it."

And of course the lawyers *were* against it. Like anyone else, the lawyers didn't want to see their livelihood threatened.

The difference is that when ATMs came along and threatened bank tellers, or fax machines came along and threatened bicycle messengers, there wasn't much they could do. What class of employees in this country *hasn't* faced the trauma of "downsizing" or "reengineering"? Not many come to mind. Even doctors have seen their old ways of doing business crimped. The difference is, doctors and bank tellers and bike messengers don't write the laws. Lawyers do. The second difference is that doctors and bike messengers don't make massive contributions to the Democratic party. Trial lawyers do.

And for the most part, I'm glad they do. I give the Democratic party a lot of money, too. But when it comes to prying loose their stranglehold on the auto-insurance system—a system that provides trial lawyers and insurance-defense lawyers $2.5 billion a year in California alone—their political clout is a virtual veto. We learned that the lawyers will say and do almost anything to keep from letting go of that money.

As predicted, Senate Bill 684, my-book-as-constitutional-amendment, failed to make it out of committee.

## 10—Cue the Trumpets

And that might have been the end of it, had it not been for an April 6, 1993, *Los Angeles Times* column lamenting the demise of the bill and urging me to "go the initiative route."

(California is one of those states that allow voters to end-run the legislature. For better or worse—often worse—all you need to put a proposed constitutional amendment on the ballot is seven hundred thousand valid signatures, at a cost of about $700,000.)

I read that column and heard the music swell. Each of us has a calling and—appalled though I was by its total lack of pizzazz—auto-insurance reform seemed more and more to be mine.

Not that I was about to spend $700,000 to do this all by myself. I'm not even *from* California. And to me, $700,000 is megabucks. But because so much was at stake—*nationwide, a sensible auto-insurance system could wring some $30 billion of waste from the economy*—it seemed to me I should try. I have a few California friends to whom $700,000 is a rounding error. I figured: maybe we can split it three ways.

Sure, it was a long shot. But think for a minute what $30 billion a year means (for if California fixes its auto-insurance mess, would not other states follow?). For just *nine* billion—once—Craig McCaw and Bill Gates intend to girdle the Earth with 840 satellites to provide a whole new global communications network. For five more, as reported on the cover of *The New York Times Magazine*, some serious visionaries believe we could mount a privately financed manned mission to Mars. Or look at it this way: $30 billion is more than twice our entire foreign aid budget for *the whole world*.

It was irresistible.

I hired a young guy, Mike Johnson, from Garamendi's insurance-industry-bashing staff—and off we went.

Johnson, I should explain, is one of those junkyard-car-driving liberals who make Republicans so nervous. After Harvard ('86) he went to work for Ralph Nader's Public Citizen at $10,500 a year; then on to Voter Revolt at $22,000 a year, fighting for Nader's Prop 103. The night before the election, he and some other zealous Voter Revolters even scaled the H-O-L-L-Y-W-O-O-D sign, in dense fog, adjusting it to read 1-0-3—Y-E-S. (Well, actually dawn started to break before they could finish, so it read 1-0-3—Y-E-S-O-D.)

I paid him $3,000 a month, no benefits.

Mike recognized that Prop 103—though he'd helped pass it—hadn't worked. The courts had ruled you couldn't just slash rates 20 percent. ("You know it will never work," an old chum had told Nader at the time. "I know," Ralph supposedly replied, "but they"—meaning the evil insurance companies—"*deserve it.*")

In the eight years since Prop 103's passage, $1.2 billion in auto-insurance premiums had been rebated to California motorists. But that amounted to only about $75 per car. The irony is that in the four years *preceding* passage of Prop 103, auto insurers' profit margins were about 2 percent *lower* in California than nationwide, while in the years since passage, they've been more than 3.5 percent *above* the national average. (The reason? Just around the time of Prop 103, California entered its steep recession. Recessions mean less driving, less partying, fewer accidents, fewer claims. In some states auto-insurance rates actually dropped. Not California. There, because of Prop 103, auto insurers were afraid to drop their rates, fearing they'd never get approval from an elected insurance commissioner to restore them when the recession ended. Thus rates stayed steady, claims dropped and profits rose.) Thanks to Prop 103, auto-insurance profits in California went from subpar to fat—the very thing Ralph Nader and Harvey Rosenfield were railing against. Brian Sullivan, publisher of *Auto Insurance Report,* estimates that Prop 103 has actually *cost* the people of California $4 billion.

Not being widely known or understood, this unintended consequence was not bad for Harvey or Ralph. Their crusading image was intact. And Harvey now earned a good living running a thing he set up called the Prop 103 Enforcement Project, trying to force the insurance companies to disgorge the excess profits he believed Prop 103 required them to. His services in this regard were billed to the California Insurance Department at the rate of $295 an hour (although it's not known how much of that, if any, he personally got to keep ).

## 11—Mike and I Get to Work

Mike and I set about to fix California's auto-insurance mess for real. All we had to do was write the initiative, raise $700,000 to get it on the ballot, and win 50.00001 percent of the vote. Fortunately, there were two of us.

• We leased a "suite" of offices at Hollywood and Vine—$346 a month.

• We hired an actress-to-be gal Friday.

• We wrote a terrific initiative. Mike did most of the drafting, but we both slaved over it, with lots of expert help, because that's the trouble with initiatives: if they do pass, you're stuck with them. They're not easily amended. It's really, really important, if you get into this game, to write an initiative that will *work*.* Normally, initiatives are an all-too-rabble-rousing way to make laws. But when it comes to legal reform, how else are you going to succeed? The lawyer-dominated legislature won't do it.

• I gave NICO $57,000 to hire Tillinghast & Co.—the world's leading actuarial firm—to analyze our initiative. A bunch of money, to be sure, but a bargain I figured, naively, if it proved, once and for all, our numbers were right. And it did. Tillinghast estimated that with our 25¢-a-gallon premium, the extra required at registration each year to provide the plan's generous benefits would be a modest $91 to $141 per vehicle.† This was very good news for us. It meant our plan was eminently affordable, saving all but the worst gas guzzlers a lot of money. (Harvey dealt with the Tillinghast findings simply by ignoring them. He just proclaimed that our 25¢ surcharge would hike the price of gas by $1 or more. Hunh? He exploded when, privately, I suggested he was just doing the bidding of the trial bar by opposing us. Less than 10 percent of his support came from trial lawyers, he told me. Mostly it came in small contributions from consumers.)

---

* I was more than a little mindful of the terrific piece Richard Reeves had written for *Money*, showing how Prop 13—which all but froze property taxes in 1978—had come ultimately to hurt the state.

† We were pretty sure Tillinghast wasn't skewing its findings in our favor. A huge chunk of its revenue each year comes from the insurance industry. Why would they go out of their way to jeopardize that for $57,000?

• We started looking for money. "Would you match me on this?" I asked one Croesan friend, thinking the idea might amuse him. (He could match me with *one day's interest.*) After all, how often do you have a shot at making the world $30 billion a year more productive and prosperous? Didn't grab him.

A less wealthy friend (just a few hundred million) was more sympathetic. In the sketchiest way, he had heard of my project. "I will give you any amount of money you want," he said, when I reached him, "*on one condition.*"

Long pause.

"You have to promise that you will never, *ever*, tell me anything about it."

"But—"

"No—you have to promise."

"What do you mean, 'any amount of money'?" I asked, deciding I could live with this one condition.

"Any reasonable number with five zeroes. But you have to promise . . ."

Only later did it occur to me that $900,000 is a number with five zeroes. But I knew he didn't mean that—$25,000 or $50,000 was the kind of number he meant. And so, while I was touched and even somewhat elated, I had hit upon a big problem: I was raising money for *auto-insurance reform.* Do you see what I'm saying? *Who cares!* Certainly not rich people, to whom auto insurance is a trivial expense. It was not going to be as easy as I had thought to find a couple of guys to split that $700,000 with me.

• We forged ahead and retained a political consulting firm.

• We hired a signature-gathering firm, and I fronted the money— from my vast fortune—to buy some new computer equipment for the all-important signature-verification process. (You've got to be sure the opposition isn't feeding you bogus signatures; you've got to track your validity rate so you get enough extras to make up for all the illegible, invalid and duplicated ones; yet you want to avoid paying to get a hundred thousand more signatures than you need.) Ballot initiatives, it turns out, are not about neighbors visiting one another with petitions. No one does it that way. You pay by the signature. (Gee, I quickly came to wonder, why doesn't the state just charge a $700,000 fee—or at least allow that alternative—and save everybody a lot of trouble?)

• We enlisted Voter Revolt, Ralph and Harvey's old organization, in our crusade. (This did not sit well with Ralph and Harvey.)

• We met with some important people we hoped to get on our side. Lunch with some big-shot editors. Lunch with John Gamboa of the Latino Issues Forum and with other members of the Greenlining Coalition (which did wind up giving us its support). Conversations with the Union of Concerned Scientists (which also signed on). Coffee with the head of the Chamber of Commerce (who did not). Meetings with representatives of Consumers Union.

CU had advocated strong no-fault insurance for decades and was receptive until its West Coast director, Harry Snyder, returned from sabbatical. He said CU would not help us in any way, or review our initiative, because people would never vote for higher-priced gas.*

## 12—The Limits of Stupidity

Even at our first press conference—before anyone had actually *seen* our initiative—we had opposition. The big oil and insurance companies had formed a group called "Californians to Save Our Economy."

What a joke. As if California's auto-insurance system were something worth saving. Here are the facts (and they apply in large measure to every state in the nation, save Michigan):

• **It's a system that pays out more money to lawyers, when someone's hurt, than to doctors, nurses, hospitals, rehabilitation specialists and chiropractors—*combined*.** California lawyers reap nearly $2.5 billion a year from auto insurance, according to the state insurance department. That's a pretty big chunk of the $7 billion or so Californians pay for auto insurance to cover injuries.†

---

* "I do not believe that an initiative that calls for an increase in the cost of gas can be passed by the California voters," Harry wrote to me in October 1993. "I don't care how good it is or what a good deal it is or how you pitch it or what the polling says or how much money can be raised or who will support it. We have not recently examined your proposal because we are engaged in other issues. We have, in the past, supported the concepts contained in your proposed initiative. We are sure that your efforts will be intended to improve the system and protect consumers, but we do not intend to review or support an initiative for auto insurance reform, particularly one based on [blending the premium into the price of gas], at this time. . . ."

† They pay another $6 billion or so to cover bashed fenders and theft, which no-fault does not affect.

- **It's a system that encourages massive fraud.** Californians—who've learned there's good money in saying your neck hurts after a fender bender—are three and a half times as likely to claim injury after an accident as Michigan drivers, who have no such financial incentive. *Three and a half times!* Clearly, most or all the extra claims are bogus. But, not being able to tell which, insurers grudgingly pay. Another huge cost.

- **It's a system that overcompensates minor injuries but grossly *under*compenates serious ones.** With minor injuries, there's often a $10,000 or $15,000 settlement. But if someone's badly hurt, forget it. The RAND Corporation's Institute for Civil Justice estimates that for injuries involving $100,000 or more in actual economic losses—medical expenses and lost wages—California victims receive from today's auto-insurance system, on average, as mentioned earlier, an amount equal to just 9 percent of those losses. For the other 91 percent, especially if the victim is among the millions with inadequate health and disability insurance, *tough luck*. It's like homeowner's insurance that pays triple if your stereo's stolen (or you say it was) but only 9 percent if the house burns down.

- **It's a system so costly, more than five million vehicles are driven uninsured.*** It costs a typical San Francisco motorist with an unblemished driving record $624 for the minimum $15,000 in liability insurance. For a Los Angeles family with two cars and one occasional teenage driver: $3,314—not to mention theft, collision, medical payments or uninsured motorist coverage (and not to mention that $15,000 is not remotely enough coverage to protect your own assets or to adequately provide for someone you seriously injure). Now, you may say—"Five million uninsured? Well, that's not so bad. It's only 25 or 30 percent of all California drivers." But it's actually worse, because *the riskiest and least responsible drivers, for whom the rates are highest, are even less likely than average to have coverage.* So the proportion of *accident-causers* driving uninsured may well be closer to 50 percent. If you're injured, half the time there won't be anything to sue for (uninsured motorists rarely have

---

* Given the choice between eating and buying liability insurance—which doesn't even protect *them*, just the car they might hit—most lower-income California families choose to eat.

big bank accounts). The rest of the time, whatever you do get will ordinarily pale in the face of a serious injury. Even if the accident-causer had $100,000 coverage—and fewer than 10 percent of insured California motorists have more—that's still barely $65,000 after legal fees. (And what if it was a hit-and-run? The *Los Angeles Times* reported 18,317 hit-and-run injuries in 1992 in Los Angeles County alone. Or a "one-car" crash, as at least 15 percent are—you skidded or rolled over or swerved to avoid a dog and hit a tree? Whom do you sue? What if, finally, it *wasn't* the other guy's fault? *You* goofed. All you collect from today's system, despite your own severe injuries, is a lawsuit.)

*Why, you might ask, would Ralph Nader help protect a system like this? Why would he stand in the way of efforts that could help solve this problem nationwide?*

"The authors of this book are not in favor of no-fault in its present forms," wrote Nader with coauthor Wesley Smith in 1990—and did not suggest any form in which they *would* be in favor. "We believe that the compensation is often inadequate" (true everywhere but Michigan) "and that the victims of accidents are asked to pay for the wrongdoing of those who cause the accidents. In other words, safe drivers are penalized while unsafe drivers benefit through no-fault." (Actually, safe drivers are penalized far *worse* by today's system.) "And why should people give up compensation for pain and suffering in order to expand insurance company profits, anyway?"

Phrased that way, clearly they should not. But expanding insurance-company profits isn't why we made pain-and-suffering coverage optional in our initiative. Nor why Consumers Union steadfastly backed no-fault for thirty years.

The case for our initiative was overwhelming. But how can you make the case without money? How can you fight the most powerful interests in the state?

The opposition of the trial lawyers I had naturally expected. And of the insurers. But when the oil companies piled on (heaven forfend we should burn a little less gas into the California air), bringing with them the Chamber of Commerce . . . and with Ralph's boy Harvey telling people it would add $1 to the price of a gallon of gas . . . and with Consumers Union refusing even the mildest endorsement . . . well, it was daunting. But here it was the first week of January 1994, and I had to put up or shut up. If we were going to proceed, the $700,000 signature-gathering effort couldn't be put off any longer. It would cost something like $35,000 a week. Was I in or out?

Hey: even I'm not that stupid.

## Intermission

It was a longer story than that, of course. Like the time I was waiting to testify in Sacramento and saw one of those "Have you been injured?" ads on TV. I called and said my friend had been horribly mangled by an uninsured motorist. The attorney was sympathetic and articulate; but once he had ascertained there was no one to sue—the county hadn't been negligent with branches overhanging the STOP sign, it wasn't the automaker's fault—well, gosh: he wasn't running a charity. You can't get blood from a stone.

"But my *friend*!" I cried as convincingly as one can for an imaginary friend.

"Sorry," said the lawyer. Given the circumstances, there was nothing he could do. That's just the way the system works. Accident victims hear this every day of the year.

But enough of that. On to the second half of the story.

## 13—We Regroup

After allowing me to grieve for a few days—pay-at-the-pump no-fault having become like a child to me—Mike Johnson suggested I face reality. "I know you're in love with the 'pay-at-the-pump' part of this," he said. (And I was! It had been so much fun devising a system to make it fair and to keep it in private, market-driven, capitalist hands.) "But you also know that 80 percent of the benefit comes from the no-fault side—eliminating most of the legal fees and fraud."

I said nothing. I knew he was right, but hated to admit it.

"So look. What if we just did a really good no-fault initiative? That would be 80 percent of what we're trying to accomplish, and we'd only have the lawyers and Nader against us."

Hmph, I said. I'd think about it.

We kept our office; I kept paying Mike; I kept thinking about it—and looking for money.

After a few weeks, swallowing my pride, I agreed that 80 percent is a whole lot better than nothing. "Pay-at-the-pump no-fault," clever as I thought it was, became just "no-fault." But *true no-fault* that would really eliminate most of the lawsuits and fraud, that would really lower costs and raise benefits—not *fake no-fault* of the type they had in Massachusetts and so many other supposed no-fault states, where all you have to do to be able to sue is build up a few thousand dollars in medical expenses to exceed a magic "threshold." *Those* systems give you all the problems of today, plus they have people purposely going for unneeded care in order to meet the threshold.

### 14—A Pilgrimage to Menlo Park

The reason I wasn't rich enough to finance all this by myself was a company called Intuit. As you know, *my* vast fortune had been hatched from a software program called *Managing Your Money*, published by a company called MECA. Intuit—started over a kitchen table a few years later by Scott Cook and his then twenty-two-year-old partner, Tom Proulx—had a program called *Quicken*. You've heard of it? By 1994 *Quicken's* success had pretty well ended what for me had been a wonderful run.

It occurred to me it might be worth trying to meet these guys. Not only were their fortunes *genuinely* vast (at my expense, as I perceived it)—*they were from California*. Maybe they'd feel guilty about wrecking my life and chip in for California auto-insurance reform.

I made the pilgrimage from MECA to Menlo Park and spent an hour with Scott Cook. As we were leaving he introduced me to his cofounder, Tom Proulx (pronounced "Pru"), who was by then thirty-three, and who, as it happened, was on his way to Los Angeles, too. Same flight.

So there we are, flying down to Los Angeles, and I'm trying to think how to get him to laugh—yet maybe turn the conversation to my main interest at the same time.

"You know, Tom," I said, "you're getting to be a pretty old guy. You've been with Intuit what—eleven years now? It's got to have become kind of a rut." (In fact, of course, Intuit was on the cutting edge.) "You know what you ought to do?"

"What?" he asked.

"You ought to take a year off from Intuit and do something really exciting—like auto-insurance reform." It was *so* preposterous, I knew he would crack a smile.

He turned to me, deadpan: "You know, I've been thinking about that," he said.

We had known each other for all of ninety minutes, so I realized he was pulling my leg.

But (long story short) he wasn't. Within about six months he had left Intuit, kicked in $100,000 of his own, and was soon working sixty- and seventy-hour weeks at no pay.

## 15—Tom's Strategy

After thinking about it for a little while, Tom concluded it would be very hard to raise money for auto-insurance reform. What we ought to do, he said, was develop a package of *three* initiatives, all lawyer-related, to achieve a sort of critical mass.

"Now, Tom," I said, slowly. "If it costs $700,000 to get one initiative on the ballot, it will cost $2.1 million for three." *Am I going too fast for you?* Of course, I didn't say it this way, I just thought it. *This* was the genius whose software program had outflanked mine?

But of course he was right. With a little help from me and others but very largely on his own, Tom wound up raising $12 million (not a penny of it from the auto-insurance industry) to promote three initiatives for the March 26, 1996, California primary ballot:

- **Prop 200, the no-fault auto-insurance initiative.** No longer could you be sued in connection with an accident (unless convicted of driving drunk), but—more to the point—no longer would you have to sue someone else to get compensated. You'd be buying auto insurance to protect *yourself*—and you wouldn't have to split the proceeds with a lawyer.

  RAND was asked by the California Insurance Department to evaluate Prop 200. It concluded that drivers who today purchase only the statutory minimum $15,000 liability coverage—coverage that doesn't protect *them* if hurt, just whomever they hit—would actually *save* 17 percent buying Prop 200's standard $1 million-per-person policy. Thus, for less money than they pay now, the typical family of four would be covered for up to $4 million in medical care, rehabilitation and lost wages. (You could purchase more coverage if you wanted; or as little as $50,000 per person—not nearly enough, but more protection than most have today.)

Under Prop 200, every pedestrian, skateboarder and bicyclist hit by a car would automatically have been covered for up to $1 million in medical, rehab and lost wages, even if he or she had no insurance—plus up to another $250,000 in scheduled "pain-and-suffering" compensation. And every child in California under the age of eighteen would have been covered for at least $50,000 while riding in a car, even if her parents hadn't bought insurance at all.* All this without the need to catch the other driver and prove he or she was at fault and then split the cash with a lawyer.

Premiums down, benefits up. Magic? No. Just redirecting nearly $2.5 billion a year from lawyers to consumers and crash victims . . . along with billions more now lost to fraud.

- **Prop 201, the "strike suit" initiative.** This was our version, for California, of what Congress had overwhelmingly passed in 1995 at the federal level to discourage ill-founded securities suits (while allowing the real ones to proceed). Among those voting to restrict the abuse: Ted Kennedy, Barbara Mikulski (who won a Consumer Federation of America award the same evening I did) and Diane Feinstein. So even many good liberals agreed there was a problem. Congress was addressing it at the federal level; Prop 201 was meant to address it the state level.

- **Prop 202, the "contingent fee" initiative.** This would have kept a lawyer from taking more than 15 percent in cases where the initial "demand letter" resulted in an acceptable offer within 60 days. The

---

* In the meantime, in addition to suing convicted drunk drivers, you could still sue GM for bad brakes or the county for bad roads or your insurer for bad faith. (Today in California you typically *can't* sue an insurer for bad faith, because it's typically *the other guy's* insurance company stiffing you, and you have no contract with *it*.) If an insurer dragged its feet providing the benefits you had contracted for, Prop 200 imposed a 24 percent annual interest penalty for the delay.

goal: to leave more money in the victim's pocket—and encourage early settlements. (For details of Propositions 201 and 202, see Appendix A.)

To me, all three of these seemed really important. I knew winning would be a long shot; also that there was something faintly comical (ridiculous?) about a a complete novice—from Miami, no less—helping to lead the charge. But remember: I had heard the trumpets. How often does a guy get a chance to make the economy billions of dollars a year more efficient? And thus, more prosperous?

Armed with these three initiatives, the scruffy, low-paid, idealistic young troops of VOTER REVOLT—from which Harvey Rosenfield had by now been forced by his fellow board members to resign*— knocked on doors signing up more than a hundred thousand supporters, including fifteen thousand small contributors. But the overwhelming majority of our money came from high-tech executives and venture capitalists incensed over the "strike suit" issue. Our Silicon Valley backers—people like Gordon Moore, chairman of Intel, and the late David Packard, cofounder of Hewlett Packard—liked Prop 200 and Prop 202 well enough. But what they really cared about was Prop 201.

## 16—The Lawyers' Strategy - I

The trial lawyers' strategy was to say whatever they had to in order to confuse the jury and win. But to get others to say it for them, since they knew that their own credibility was at a fairly low ebb.

Naturally, the fight would not be portrayed as an effort to protect lawyers from a huge pay cut. No, it was a matter of protecting the little guy's right to sue. Self-interest? Never!

Indeed, lest there be any misunderstanding whose side they were on, the California Trial Lawyers Association—five thousand members strong—changed its name to the Consumer Attorneys of California, or "CACA," as we happily noted.

Even so, they kept a low profile. When radio and TV shows called the trial lawyers for someone to debate us, they almost never got a

---

* Their characterization; Harvey remembers it differently.

lawyer. Heavens, no. Instead CACA gave them a "consumer advocate" like Harvey Rosenfield . . . or a particularly annoying woman named Kelly Hayes-Raitt whom Harvey had hired ("If you were my wife," one exasperated radio talk-show host told her, on air, "I'd hang myself") . . . or Nader coauthor Wesley Smith, whom Harvey had also hired. Nader himself refused to debate.

Virtually all the money to defeat us came from trial lawyers, but the front group Harvey set up was called Citizens Against Phony Initiatives. Our initiatives were phony, because—well, here's a taste of the rhetoric:

> An exhaustive investigation of documents from court proceedings, reports filed with the Fair Political Practices Commission and other confidential sources reveal an elaborate Ponzi scheme. Political mercenaries, whose histories are fraught with misdealings, fraud and hypocrisy in which the interests of consumers are ignored or abused for personal gain, have organized a highly-lucrative campaign guaranteeing themselves hundreds of thousands of dollars in consulting and signature-gathering contracts from big business and the insurance industry . . .

Mike and I, it seems, were in it for the money.*

It's true that once we got Tom on board, and once Tom was able to raise millions for the campaign, people would make money from it. Not Mike, to any appreciable degree. And certainly not Tom or I—we were *paying* hundreds of thousands of dollars for the privilege. But printers, TV stations—and, yes, the pollsters and campaign managers and signature gatherers who are in this business. Call them mercenaries if you want; but they didn't hatch this effort. I did.

## 17—Hawaii

Out of the blue, Hawaii's legislators passed a "true no-fault" bill of their own. (Perhaps they were in on the Ponzi scheme, too.) It wasn't perfect, but it would have cut auto-insurance premiums by an estimated 45 percent or more—in part merely by shifting costs to

---

* A Ponzi scheme, of course, has nothing to do with any of this. It's where someone promises high returns, using money from more and more new investors to pay old ones.

Hawaii's universal health-care system, but largely through savings on lawyers and fraud.

Here was a state with just about the lowest accident rate in the nation yet nearly the highest auto-insurance rates. This bill would have fixed that, while providing better protection to the worst hurt.

Ralph and Harvey flew to Hawaii to try to persuade Governor Ben Cayetano to veto it. Which wasn't hard—before entering politics, Cayetano was a trial lawyer. What they were really there to do was give him some political cover. After all, if Nader's agin' it (and the insurance industry's *fer* it), maybe it ain't so good after all.

In fact, the insurance industry was not of one mind on this bill. The *stock* companies, like Allstate and AIG, care first about profits. A 45 percent premium reduction would have made auto insurance a 45 percent smaller business. So they weren't *fer* it at all. ("Don't let it pass," AIG chairman Maurice Greenberg is said to have instructed the head of AIG's Hawaii operation.*)

The *mutual* companies—those owned by the policyholders themselves, like State Farm and USAA—were for it. After all, their customers *are* their shareholders. So where a stock company sometimes has to choose between the interests of its customers and the interests of its owners, a mutual faces no such conflict. In truth, the dilemma for the mutuals is to choose between its customer/owners and its employees, or, in this case, its agents. If slashing lawsuits and fraud cuts premiums 45 percent, it also cuts agent commissions 45 percent.

To my surprise—and to its considerable credit—State Farm and its agents actually chose to put its customer/owners' interests first. (State Farm's executives weren't affected either way. They are paid straight salary, no bonuses, profit shares or stock options. For years the CEO earned a flat $600,000. In 1995 it was bumped up to $1.25 million— but for the CEO of the twelfth-largest Fortune 500 company, this is modest pay. The guys at Allstate and GEICO, smaller companies, make considerably more.) State Farm ran a series of full-page ads advocating public support for the bill.

The trial lawyers retorted with an ad in which Nader was promi-

---

* If true, as I believe it is, Greenberg is a bum for having done this. But he was just serving the interests of his shareholders, of whom—because he's the smartest guy in the business—I am one.

nently featured: "Does it bother you that most information you're getting comes from an insurance company that stands to gain immense profits?" Not explained was how State Farm would gain "immense profits" by cutting its rates 45 percent, nor why other companies, if it were such a gold mine, wouldn't compete and drive prices down, nor how a change in its Hawaii auto-insurance profits could really impact the twelfth-largest company on the Fortune 500 in any noticeable way—nor what terrible thing State Farm would *do* with all those immense Hawaii profits. (When a mutual has profits in excess of what it needs to build reserves to cover catastrophes, it pays them back out to its policyholders as dividends. For example, in 1995 USAA paid a $480 million dividend to its 2.3 million auto-insurance policyholders. Between 1991 and 1995, in states where profits had been more than adequate to boost reserves, State Farm paid out $790 million.)

Nader must understand this stuff. He must know the difference between a stock company and a mutual. He must know, at least more or less, that the gargantuan State Farm reserves he rails against amount to barely $500 per policy, and that the executive compensation at State Farm is not unreasonable compared with the rest of American industry. (Heck: Rhoda Karpatkin, the lawyer who heads Consumers Union, pulls down $237,000 a year—why isn't he railing against *that*?) He must know all this, but it just doesn't seem to matter.

Cayetano vetoed the bill.

But wait! Would the legislature override? It had never happened since Hawaii achieved statehood, but it looked as if the votes might just be there.

Out I flew—sixty thousand frequent-flier miles—for a two-day trip to Hawaii. (I love Hawaii, but not in a suit and tie in June.) I addressed an informal session of the legislators, urging them to stick by their guns; I made the ritual three-minute TV news appearances; I flew home.

It was a cliff-hanger. To keep it from going over the edge, the governor's insurance commissioner, Wayne Metcalf, issued a complaint on June 28, 1995, the crucial moment, blasting the State Farm ads as deceptive and effectively banning any further ads in favor of the bill. Of course, the complaint was eventually dismissed, but only months later. In the meantime, it had its desired effect. The override effort narrowly failed.

Personal injury lawyers continue to do a nice business with auto-accident lawsuits in "no-fault" Hawaii. The insurance company lawyers continue to do a nice business *fighting* those suits. The governor and his friends are happy. Ralph and Harvey scored another victory.

## 18—Harvey's Lie

Meanwhile, Citizens Against Phony Initiatives was gearing up to achieve the same victory in California. Who exactly were these "citizens"?

They were, in a word, Harvey Rosenfield. Citizens Against Phony Initiatives shared the same office and phone number as his Network Project (also known as the Proposition 103 Enforcement Project), and its mouthpiece, Kelly Hayes-Raitt, had been working for Harvey before taking on her new role.*

It was our contention that Harvey's group was the phony one—that he and it were a front for the trial lawyers.

As I have mentioned, talk like this really got Harvey steamed. He told anyone who asked—including *The Sacramento Bee* on December 17, 1995—that no more than 10 percent of his support came from trial lawyers. His right-hand man, Jamie Court, told the Los Angeles *Daily News*, July 8, 1995, "Our returns show we are funded by foundations and consumers." "Rosenfield acknowledges getting some financial support from individual trial lawyers," reported the *Bee* a few months earlier, "although he says it's only about 10% of his organization's $350,000 budget."

Imagine our surprise, therefore, to find misfiled in the state attorney general's office a report—signed by Harvey himself and stamped

---

* "What did you say?" Kelly asked the talk-show host after a long silence. Perhaps she had misheard. "If you were married you'd hang yourself?" "No, if I were married to *you* I'd hang myself," he said. "You know, John, you have your right to your point of view," she said, "and you'll be able to express that point of view next Tuesday when you go to vote. I have my rights and my point of view. And you've invited me to be a guest on this show—" "And you've been— you've been the worst guest I think I've ever had. Ever," he interrupted. "And you've been incredibly insulting," she shot back. "Yeah, I know, because I can't stand people who don't— who aren't truthful," he explained. "Well, I am truthful," Kelly protested. And so it went.

NOT SUBJECT TO PUBLIC INSPECTION—showing that Rosenfield's Network Project had received more than $400,000 from trial lawyer sources from 1991 through 1994. Indeed, 100 percent of the listed contributions were from, or directed by, a trial lawyer—every one of them.*

Nor were these contributions from supportive consumers who just happened to be trial lawyers. Most of the money came from past presidents and other leaders of the trial lawyers' lobby. Rosenfield's little organization even received $9,000 a month for most of 1993 from the Los Angeles Trial Lawyers Association. Perhaps most remarkable of all, trial lawyers funneled to him just over $100,000 from two special funds established with money from class action settlements that are supposed to be used to benefit consumers—not to campaign against reforms that would help them.

After we released this information, Harvey took a less visible role in the campaign, leaving those he had hired—Wesley and Kelly—to do most of the talking.†

Feeling sure we had found the smoking gun that would wreck the Rosenfield/Nader credibility on this issue for the rest of the campaign, we put on press conferences in Sacramento and Los Angeles. Nobody came. Maybe everyone was glued to the TV watching F. Lee Bailey defend O. J. Simpson (not for the money, you understand; for the principle),

---

* Only contributions of $5,000 or more were reported. It's possible some smaller contributions were not from trial lawyers. But trial lawyers clearly provided the bulk of his support, and were the contributors to whom he was most indebted. (On a personal note, Harvey purchased a $357,000 home in 1990. A colleague at the time overheard his telling famed trial lawyer Bill Shernoff that without Shernoff's $10,000, he could never have swung the down payment.)

† Kelly will tell you that, gosh, the lawyers didn't fund her work—it was mostly unions and nurses that did. And technically, tailored to the public-reporting needs of the campaign, that was true. But it was our guess that the California Nurses Association's sudden interest in denying medical care to crash victims stemmed not from any deep-seated nursely conviction but rather from political favor swapping. Ralph and Harvey were key supporters of a ballot initiative that would have established mandated nurse staffing levels for HMOs. What's more, a week after the election, it was reported that the trial lawyers had donated $190,000 to the nurses' campaign from the checking account of "Consumers and Their Attorneys Against Prop 200, 201 & 202." California law (Section 89512.5) requires that any such disbursements be "reasonably related to a political, legislative, or governmental purpose of the committee." How would disbursing $190,000 to the nurses' campaign be related to defeating Props 200, 201 and 202? There may be another explanation, but the one that jumps to my mind is: the nurses were being paid for services rendered.

Still, at least some of the key newspaper reporters came to realize that Harvey was not entirely who he purported to be.

Of course, we had no problem with Harvey and his crew receiving so much of their support from the trial lawyers. What we found unbelievable was that they would repeatedly have denied it. This wasn't some embarrassing but relatively trivial fib. This cut to the core. It was as if a scientist funded by the tobacco industry identified himself as "an independent health advocate" and reported that—hey, he was as surprised by this as anybody—tobacco doesn't cause cancer . . . and then, when asked whether he was funded by the tobacco industry, called that outrageous: "No more than 10 percent of our support comes from the tobacco industry; most of it is small contributions from concerned citizens."

At what point would such a guy cease to be identified as a health researcher rather than a tobacco-industry flak? At what point, we wondered, would the TV stations stop putting "Consumer Advocate" below Harvey's face?

Did Ralph know that his close associate was lying all these years, and actively seeking to hide the source of his support?

## 19—Did Ralph Lie, Too?

Shortly after *The Sacramento Bee* reported Harvey's claim that "no more than 10 percent" of his support comes from lawyers, *The New York Times* did a lengthy Nader profile. One tidbit that caught my eye: "Public Citizen and other Nader groups take less than 1 percent in contributions from all lawyers, not just the trial bar, Mr. Nader said."

Could this be true? Perhaps. It's the same thing he faxed *Forbes* when it profiled him in 1989. But here's what four major trial lawyers from around the country told *Forbes*:

"We are what supports Ralph Nader."
—Fred Levin (*Forbes* says Levin earned $7.5 million in 1988)

"Nader supports all of our issues and we support all of his."
—Bob Gibbons ($3.7 million)

"We support him overtly, covertly, in every way possible. He is our hero. We have supported him for decades. . . . I would think we give him a

huge percentage of what he raises. What moneyed groups could he turn to other than trial lawyers?"
—Pat Maloney ($6 million)

"I can get on the phone and raise $100,000 for Nader in one day."
—Herb Hafif ($40 million)

In a subsequent article, Hafif was quoted saying that in 1988 Prop 106—a fee-limiting measure vaguely similar to our Prop 202—"was certain to pass. It had 70 to 80 percent approval ratings. . . . Finally I asked Ralph to help, and he did . . . and I helped his [Prop 103] initiative, and it passed by a few points, and we beat 106 by a few points."

It was "win-win" for everyone but the public.

You might think that as the world's squeakiest-clean consumer crusader, who doesn't even own a car (so what does he care about the cost of auto insurance, or being sued by a scam artist?) and who only owns a black-and-white TV, Nader wouldn't have the slightest hesitation at disclosing his tax returns and other financial records. But this is something he has always refused to do—even now, in 1996, as he was running for president. (Of what—*California*? I marveled when first told.)

If Ralph Nader says less than 1 percent of his support has come from lawyers, you just have to believe it. *He's Ralph Nader.* If Ralph Nader identifies me as "a business consultant" and characterizes Mike Johnson and me as "consumer protection impersonators"—well, then, that's what we must be.

In slamming Mike, Nader wrote the governor of Hawaii (in a letter released to the press) that "[Johnson] bills himself as a 'former policy analyst for Ralph Nader,' when in fact he was turned down for a position at this office some ten years ago and instead worked in the mid-1980s for an organization [Public Citizen] I have not run since 1981."

Makes it sound as if Ralph may never even have *met* Mike, no? But in the first place, Johnson does *not* "bill himself" as a "former policy analyst for Ralph Nader," but rather as a "former policy analyst for Ralph Nader's *Public Citizen*"—which he was. And while Nader did resign as president of Public Citizen in 1981, he remains intimately involved and regularly signs the organization's fund-raising letters, with his name emblazoned on the outside of the envelope. So it very much *is* Ralph Nader's Public Citizen. Nader's assertion that Mike was turned down for a job is just false. And would you be surprised to know, from Ralph's description, that Mike ghostwrote an op-ed for Ralph? Or that he accompanied Ralph—just the two of them—on trips to Florida, Kansas, California and New York?

Not to say Mike was a key Nader aide. Just that, like hundreds of other young people over the years, Mike had been inspired by Ralph's work and hoped to do some good as one of his troopers. "As you know," Mike wrote Ralph when he resigned from Public Citizen in October 1991 before going to work for the insurance commissioner, "I have devoted much of my time and energy over the last five years [to] working for insurance reform. I was attracted to this issue, despite the mundane subject matter, because I believed that it presented us with a golden opportunity to demonstrate to people that the kind of work we do can make a tangible difference in their lives. Recently, however, I have come to the conclusion that our rigid opposition to no-fault runs counter to honest insurance reform and citizen empowerment."

And don't blame *my* corrupting influence. This was two years before I had ever even heard of Mike Johnson.

## 20—The Bombshell

Traditionally, no-fault has been a good bipartisan issue. Only Nader, virtually alone among consumer advocates, has consistently opposed it—in every form in every place no matter what. This is particularly ironic, because true no-fault increases consumer choice and auto safety.

(Today, under the system Ralph protects, you don't get to choose the insurance company that settles your claim if you're hurt—the guy who hits you does. You have to settle with *his* company. And today insurers can't give people much incentive to purchase safe cars, because they're largely covering the injuries you might cause someone else—and they don't know what kind of unsafe car *he'll* be driving.)

First proposed in 1916 as an analogue to Workers' Compensation (another no-fault system—would Harvey and Ralph repeal *that*?),*

---

* Workers' Comp certainly has its problems. But replacing it with a system where every injury results in a contingent-fee lawsuit, and victims must prove fault to get compensated, like auto insurance, is not the solution.

no-fault has been advocated over and over, but almost always defeated by the lawyers.

In Massachusetts, when the trial lawyers realized they couldn't win outright, they just performed a clever maneuver they would repeat almost everywhere else, when needed: they got the legislators to throw in a "low threshold" above which you could sue. When the law was first passed in 1971, anyone with $500 or more in medical expenses could sue. That "threshold"—since raised to $2,000— quickly became a target, instead. How hard is it to rack up $2,000 in medical bills? When the threshold jumped from $500 to $2,000 in 1988, guess what? The number of doctor's and chiropractor's visits for the typical injury claim jumped from thirteen to thirty.

Of course, almost none of these cases actually goes to trial. Almost all are settled, typically for three or four times the "actual" expenses—which provides a further incentive to pad the claims. Every extra MRI scan means thousands of dollars in cash for you and your attorney.

The brilliance of the trial lawyers' maneuver, back in the early days of "no-fault," was not only that they more or less gutted it in almost every state where it was adopted (Michigan again being the prominent exception), dooming it to continued lawsuits, fraud and failure, *but that they would be able to point to this failure when the next generation of reformers came along.* Us. "See?" they could say. "No-fault hasn't worked. It's expensive. It's an old idea. Everyone hates it." And, of course—because they sabotaged it in the first place—they're right.

Most informed consumer advocates know all this. Consumers Union has been writing about it for decades. "The verdict is unanimous," CU wrote, via its *Consumer Reports* magazine, in 1971. "Something must be done to make insurance do a better job of paying the cost of highway injuries." Yet in California, and most other places, despite CU's long-standing good intentions, *nothing has been done.* "CU agrees that no-fault auto insurance"—real no-fault, not phony low-dollar-threshold no-fault—"is an idea whose time has come," it wrote in 1973. "Car owners get more value for their premium dollars under no-fault," it wrote in 1984.

That 1984 article ("Whatever Happened to No-Fault?") led off with two real-life horror stories. The first was of a terribly injured young man who got nothing from the traditional lawsuit auto-insurance system because there was no one to sue. (Under Prop 200, all his expenses and hundreds of thousands of dollars in lost wages would have been paid.) The second story was of a terribly injured little girl who—because she lived in Michigan—did much better. (With Prop 200, she would have done better still.) Both examples CU chose to highlight fairly shouted for support of Prop 200.

STILL NEEDED: GOOD NO-FAULT LAWS, ran a 1988 *Consumer Reports* headline.

STRONG NO-FAULT LAWS, STILL THE BEST ANSWER—1992.

Given that background, I had naturally been disappointed when Harry Snyder, CU's West Coast head, had declined to help with even the mildest endorsement of pay-at-the-pump no-fault, or of Prop 200's no-fault.*

But imagine my dismay to receive, upon returning from Hawaii, a copy of a three-page press release, sent, as best we could tell, to every news outlet in California, dated June 29, 1995, headlined: PUBLIC INTEREST GROUPS WARN PUBLIC ON "ALLIANCE" TORT INITIATIVES. (The official name of our three-initiative effort was The Alliance to Revitalize California.) Not only was Consumers Union among the signatories; at the top of page 1—"For Immediate Release"—the lead contact was "Harry Snyder—Consumers Union." Just below was the other contact: Harvey Rosenfield.

## 21—Counter-Attack

The press release was not about accuracy or thoughtful public policy, in my view. Rather, it seemed to me, it was about gulling well-intentioned liberals who hadn't heard our side of the story—or known where Harvey's support had been coming from all these years—into joining Ralph and Harvey in doing the trial lawyers' dirty work.

One of the reasons I find this whole enterprise so fascinating, in hindsight—while recognizing that I may be the only one who finds it so—is that it shows how things actually get done, and not done,

---

* On pay-at-the-pump the excuse was that it couldn't pass, so Harry was too busy to study it. On Prop 200, it was that this "strong" no-fault law was *too* strong, cutting lawsuits—and thus costs—even more than in Michigan. Harry preferred a plan that would have provided just $15,000 in benefits, but a lot more opportunity to sue.

in the real world. Just as it is wondrous to me that, in a democracy, a dramatic tax *cut* could have been engineered for the wealthiest 1 percent of Americans while at the same time shrinking most workers' pay checks via a heavier Social Security tax—Reagan-era magic!—so it is (morbidly) wondrous to me how a jury could be persuaded to set O.J. free, or good-hearted liberals could be persuaded to *fight* reform of a system that, going back to CU's 1962 characterization, "produces results which are so unjust, capricious, and so wasteful of both the policyholders' and the accident victim's money that most laymen find it hard to believe the facts when they are first presented."

I spent the Fourth of July weekend preparing an annotated version—forty-one footnotes pointing out what I considered to be forty-one inaccuracies, false impressions, ironies, and attempts to deceive. (Least important, but indicative, was my being presented as a "corporate consultant." There's nothing wrong with being a corporate consultant, of course; but that's simply not what I am.)

My thought was that when these seventy-five folks saw what they had put their name to, they'd want to disassociate themselves from it.

To their credit, a few, like the Reverend Cornelius Taylor of the NAACP, did. But very few.

Realistically, once Ralph and Harvey had recruited their most faithful—many of the seventy-five had direct ties to Nader organizations—and then used that impressive list to sign up others, it acquired a sort of snowball effect. What decent consumer advocate *wouldn't* want to be in company like that? *Wouldn't* trust Ralph and Harvey and Consumers Union to do the thinking for them?

The problem is, once you've signed on, it becomes very awkward to sign off. What are you going to do: issue a statement that you haven't done your homework? Risk disappointing or embarrassing friends you work with all the time?

I began calling names on the list. With some, who even knew how to reach them? Grandmothers for Peace? It sounded good, and doubtless existed in some form—but not in any California phone book I could find. So I just picked groups that made me particularly nuts.

For example, I called Valerie Papaya Mann, who runs the AIDS East Bay Project. At first, she had no idea what I was talking about. She vaguely remembered, sort of, agreeing to having her name used on some kind of statement, but she was very busy—caring for AIDS patients in the East Bay is more than a full-time calling—and, no, she didn't remember getting my forty-one point rebuttal.

"Ms. Mann," I said, in effect, "I am awfully sorry to take your time with this. But you have signed a statement that's really harmful. I have more than a hundred friends who have died of AIDS. I'm a sponsor of the GMHC AIDS Walk in New York every year, APLA's event in Los Angeles, HCN's event in Miami. I give to ARC in Boston . . . I mean, I just would never be party to something that would hurt people with AIDS. Are you sure you really considered the pros and cons of our three initiatives before lending your name to this?"

That was the essence of it, and after repeated calls and faxes, to *her* considerable credit Ms. Mann agreed she didn't know the first thing about what we were doing, or the statement she had signed, and agreed to disassociate herself from it.

But do you know how much work that took?

Was I really going to be able to persuade Mary Raftery, head of CALPIRG (one of the many state public-interest research groups Ralph Nader inspired) to disassociate herself from Ralph?

One of the others I did try was Bob Fellmeth, a law professor and "children's advocate." Heck, we had law professor Jeffrey O'Connell—basically the father of "no-fault" in America—endorsing Prop 200. We had Prop 202 based on a concept endorsed by two Harvard Law School deans. We had a provision that would provide a minimum of $50,000 in auto-accident coverage to every child in California. Why would a children's advocate be so opposed to *that*?

I had long since learned that many Nader allies wouldn't talk or meet with me. So to get Fellmeth to return my call, I did something I wouldn't normally do. I faxed him a note that I was writing an article in which he was identified as "corporate consultant Robert Fellmeth" and just wanted to be sure it was accurate.

He called, perplexed. He had no idea who I was and he was certainly not a corporate consultant—why would I identify him that way? Well, I said, because that's how you identified *me*.

I then explained what I meant, and we had what I took to be an excellent chat. It turned out he was a user of *Andrew Tobias' Manag-*

*ing Your Money* from way back and that he had read some of my stuff—we had a fine old time.

He promised to retrieve my forty-one-point rebuttal from his pile and send me some sort of fax disassociating himself from the statement that, in truth, he had not been very deeply involved in drafting.

Later that night I got a handwritten fax: "Dear Andrew,"—it read in full—"My apologies for any indication that you did not believe in good faith that your initiative was meritorious. I have no reason to believe that you do not believe fully in the merits of your proposal. I have some problems with it, but not with you."

Well, isn't that nice? What he apparently did *not* have problems with was keeping his name on an inaccurate, misleading statement.

It was the last I ever heard from Bob Fellmeth. I tried *so hard* all summer—and really nicely, deferentially at first—to get him back on the phone. I offered repeatedly, via fax and his secretary, to fly to San Diego and buy him dinner. Finally, I decided to try a harder edge. On November 2, 1995, I faxed and sent via certified mail an "open letter" I had drafted to run in his university newspaper. I asked him to please call if it was in any way inaccurate (a courtesy he had not extended me) and let him know that I'd love not to run the ad if he'd only be willing to talk.

I waited and waited. On February 8 I ran it. "Others, like Reverend Taylor of the NAACP," it concluded, "have disassociated themselves from the June 29 statement you signed, yet you won't even discuss it. Is this the standard of intellectual debate at your Law School?"

Apparently so. To this day I've not heard a word.

## 22—More Counter-Attack

How do you reach people if they won't even talk? It had begun with Nader himself, and in my more paranoid moments I fantasize that he simply spread the word: Don't talk to this guy.

As early as March 1989, I had written him an almost fawning (but sincere) letter reminding him of his work with my late father and thanking him for his help in suggesting me and *The Invisible Bankers* for the Donahue show, and so on, but also asking whether, given the current auto-insurance mess, a distinction could not be made between the right of little guys to sue corporate giants, on the one hand, versus the need for little guys to sue *each other*. Could he give me a little advice on how to proceed?

No answer.

Six months later, because Bob Hunter told me Ralph answers *all* his mail, I sent it again with a nice little cover note invoking Bob's name and suggesting that perhaps the original hadn't reached him.

No answer.

A year later I tried sending it via his closest associate in the world, Joan Claybrook, head of Public Citizen (or "Ralph Nader's Public Citizen," as it's often known).

No answer. From him. From Joan I got a letter written as if it had come from the American Trial Lawyers Association itself. (Only later did I learn that Joan was actually on the board of Trial Lawyers for Public Justice—and, while we're at it, that she was the most prominent and forceful member of the Consumers Union board. Are you seeing any connections here?)

I had this insane notion (at least Mike said it was insane) that if I could just spend some time with Ralph, I could persuade him that— far from launching consumers down the slippery slope to having no rights—true no-fault would actually relieve some of the pressure for more extreme tort reform.

In April 1993, noticing that Nader and I were scheduled to attend the same Social Venture Network conference (a sort of Ben & Jerry's confab), I called the organizer and asked whether somehow he could put in a word for me and get me twenty minutes.

"I can do better than that," he said. "It's about an hour's drive from the airport—why don't I ask Ralph if it's OK to have you pick him up? You'll have a nice quiet hour to yourselves."

Perfect.

Except that he then called back to say Ralph had said no.

It was like the movie *Roger and Me*, about one guy's struggle to get an appointment with Roger Smith, then chairman of General Motors, only it was "Nader and Me."*

---

* The director of *Roger and Me*, Michael Moore, actually worked briefly for Ralph's Center for Responsive Law. After the movie became a hit, Ralph reportedly demanded that Moore contribute $30,000 to the Center, claiming that Ralph had gotten him thinking about GM in the first place. Moore refused.

At the conference itself I left a message with his room asking for ten minutes; and when there was no response to that, I finally just went over to him at lunch—he's only a man, after all, not a god, and there were only about two hundred of us in the room—and asked whether he could find even just a few minutes for us to talk.

Visibly upset, he said it was incredibly rude for me to approach him this way—he had a speech to give in a few minutes—and that we had "irreconcilable differences." There was "nothing to discuss."

I guess that's when I gave up on Ralph Nader.

But as I say, it was almost as if Nader had told Fellmeth and every other consumer leader he'd ever mentored—which was pretty well all of them, it often seemed—not to talk. He'd do the big thinking for them.

The only other example of this I feel the need to share was a woman who joined the fight against us named Margery Tabankin. I've never actually met or spoken with Ms. T—though Lord knows I've tried—but I gather she is one of the key liberal "Hollywood women," her influence not lessened by her position as Barbra Streisand's policy person.

Not only had she joined the effort against us, she had also written a letter to a colleague expressing disappointment over the way our campaign manager, her old friend Bill Zimmerman, had (in her view) sold out.

Bill was amazed that she would not even call first to hear his point of view. After all, they had shuddered in a *bomb shelter* together in Hanoi when Bill was arranging for medical supplies for the North Vietnamese. (And later, as she doubtless knew, he had risked his life piloting an airlift of supplies over the heads of the FBI to the Indians at Wounded Knee. Whatever you may think of such exploits, they are not trivial liberal credentials.) So in addition to writing to Margery himself, Bill asked me to send her a point-by-point answer to the various misimpressions she seemed to have of Props 200, 201 and 202.

This took two days of my life—seventeen pages. "Because this letter is so long," I led off, "I'll make you a deal. Read it all the way to the end, and I'll give $1,000 to the candidate or charity of your choice, since I assume we support almost all the same ones anyway. Just don't be really cruel and make me support the opposition to our initiatives."

Right? A little bonding? A little incentive? A little humor?

The only response I ever got—and I also called hoping to take *her* to lunch, and so forth—was that she was too busy to respond right then, but would.*

Every time I see Margery's name listed alphabetically right above mine as a "patron" or "benefactor" for some liberal cause—because given the munificence made possible by my vast fortune I often find myself following Tabankin or Tisch and preceding Trump—I think to myself: How can she think of me as the enemy? We support all the same things! Can she really support a system where two thirds of consumers' money goes to lawyers and fraud, leaving the worst hurt victims practically nothing?

## 23—Denouement

I'm mindful that I haven't offered *you* $1,000 for reading all this, and that the time is long past to begin wrapping it up. It's not *your* fault this was such a foolhardy enterprise, spanning so many years, eating up so much money. What kind of idiot actually thinks he can beat the trial lawyers, anyway? When enough cash is at stake—and never was there more than in California on March 26, 1996—they will find a way to triumph.

I found it more than a little ironic that twenty-five years after meeting F. Lee Bailey at Glenn Turner's mansion, we would both be in California—he, fighting successfully for O. J. Simpson; I, unsuccessfully, for no-fault.

Nader, too, was in California, briefly. He was running for president, as I've mentioned. The 7 percent he was polling would come straight from Clinton, in a state crucial to Clinton's reelection. Didn't Ralph

---

* One woman I did manage to take to lunch was Candace Lightner, founder of Mothers Against Drunk Driving, a wonderful group. Because our initiative singled out convicted drunk drivers as people you could sue (but paid your benefits anyway, since few drunk drivers have much to sue for), I was hoping for her support. "Why are you so tough on trial lawyers?" was her opening statement after we sat down, lending weight to our suspicion that she was already working with them in some way—and it got little better from there. Needless to say, she did not support us. A month after the election, she was paid $2,512.34 by the Consumer Attorneys Issues Political Action Committee for "consulting." I do not know whether there were other payments as well, or any quid pro quo. I just know the trial lawyers have a lot of influence and a lot of friends.

care about issues like tobacco, equal rights for gays and a woman's right to choose—to take just three where the contrast with the Republicans was so stark? "He's stayed conspicuously silent on the tough social issues," says Congressman Barney Frank, who wishes Nader "wouldn't spend so much political energy attacking those who *are* fighting these battles." ("Gonadal politics" is how Nader sometimes dismisses the concerns of women and gays.)

Anyway, the battle lines were quickly drawn. And discouraging as it was to have so many of the "good guys" (as I thought of the seventy-five on Harvey's list) coming out against us, we enlisted a few good guys of our own—people like Medical Education for South African Blacks cofounders Herb and Joy Kaiser; SmokeFree Educational Services founder Joe Cherner; gay rights leader Tom Stoddard; and Democratic Leadership Council founder Al From. (My favorite good guy was former Democratic congressman Chet Atkins, who said we should hope people would mistake him for the country-and-western star.)

We also had a motherboard of Silicon Valley CEOs—people who have shown themselves more than a little adept at analyzing and solving problems rationally. And of course we had all the Republicans, which was a weird feeling for me, to say the least. Not that there aren't a lot of fine Republicans out there. There are. But this should have been a fully bipartisan effort. Yet given the trial lawyers' clout in the Democratic party, we Democrats weren't doing our part. The worst was when, in the last week, our liberal campaign guys (wincing) got Charlton Heston to do a TV ad for Prop 202. Charlton Heston was swell as Moses, not half bad as God, but we could hardly have more different political views. "You're kidding," I moaned. But it was our only chance, they felt.

A huge problem: it's so much easier to get people to vote NO than YES—for a NO, you just need to raise one nagging objection, even if you have to be untruthful or misleading to do it.

**On Prop 200**—which would have greatly *reduced* costs and *raised* benefits—the trial lawyers took every opportunity to say the reverse. RAND had estimated that, for many people, auto-insurance rates would fall by nearly 40 percent. So the lawyers ran commercials claiming Prop 200 would *raise* rates 40 percent. (Well, I thought to myself darkly, at least they got the number right.) I believe George Orwell called this technique The Big Lie.

"Join Ralph Nader in voting NO!" ran the refrain. Hike insurance rates 40 percent? Heck: if I hadn't known the truth, *I'd* have "joined Ralph Nader" and voted NO.

Now, you may be saying to yourself, C'mon. The lawyers can't just tell a big fat lie over and over on prime-time TV—can they? But the answer is: Sure they can. There is no law against lying in a political campaign.

Columnist Jane Bryant Quinn called the fellow on whose data the lawyers' "40 percent" claim rested, Robert Klein, research director for the National Association of Insurance Commissioners. Klein told her that his data absolutely could not be used to draw conclusions like that. (He subsequently told me that in his seventeen years of insurance research he had never seen his work misused in a more irresponsible, misleading way.) "Consumer advocate Ralph Nader, who opposes Prop 200, thinks the principle of open access to courts is too important to curtail," concluded Quinn. "[That] argument has merit, but Prop 200 seems to be the greater good."

The other part of the lawyers' strategy against Prop 200 was this simple notion: *When someone is hurt by a reckless driver, don't you think the victim should be compensated? Don't you think the wrongdoer should pay?*

Who could disagree?

But guess what?

Today in California, the seriously injured victim is *not* compensated. As noted, RAND estimates that the current system pays the most seriously injured victims just 9 percent of their actual losses on average. Prop 200 would have ratcheted that up to more like 70 or 80 percent—not ideal, but better.

And today in California the wrongdoer does *not* pay—his insurance company does. Or, if he's uninsured or flees the scene, no one pays.

Prop 200 would have done nothing to soften criminal penalties for reckless driving; would still have allowed suits against convicted drunk drivers. Accident-causers would still have seen their insurance rates hiked. (But Prop 200 specifically *forbade* an insurance company from raising rates after an accident that *wasn't* your fault—a common practice today.) So, despite the unfortunate term "no-fault," for all practical purposes reckless drivers would have been no more let off the hook than they are today.*

They beat us on this one 65 percent to 35 percent.

Not exactly a close shave.

Frankly, I'm a little surprised we got even 35 percent of the people to vote YES on a plan they'd been told, night after night, would raise their rates 40 percent. A claim that Ralph Nader had for all practical purposes confirmed—not technically, but by allowing himself to be the tag line of all the ads. A claim that Consumers Union had all but confirmed—not technically, but by allowing its name, and Harry Snyder's, to lead off each of the official opposition "ballot arguments" mailed to every voter in the state, and by never calling a press conference to disassociate itself from Harvey or to lay out the pros and cons of the initiative, in the objective, detailed way consumers have come to expect of CU.†

It was more than a little galling to me that in the thick of things CU was featured in elaborate four-minute segments on the news detailing the pros and cons of various low-fat peanut butter spreads—announcing to the world that (surprise!) low-fat peanut butter doesn't taste quite as good as the regular brands—and protecting consumers against the possibility that they might spend $2.39 on a less-than-the-tastiest brand. All this rigorously monitored by CU's incredibly impartial staff within the hallowed walls of its new $40 million building in Yonkers. But could CU release the same sort of careful pro and con on our initiative and let the consumers/voters decide? No. Could CU president Rhoda Karpatkin make time to meet with us? No—she's abroad a lot on business.

(Rhoda came to run CU direct from twenty years as a lawyer. Her husband was a lawyer. Her daughter is a lawyer. Lawyers and consumer advocacy are tightly bound. Ralph was himself a member of the American Trial Lawyers Association for a while and himself on the

---

* We had thought of using some different name, like "no-fraud" or "no-lawyer," but knew that whatever we called it, the press—and the lawyers—would brand it no-fault. We didn't want to seem to be trying to play it cute. Better, we thought, simply to explain the difference between fake no-fault and real no-fault—and to point out how little personal responsibility reckless drivers bear *today*.

† "Subscribe to *Consumer Reports* (800-234-1645), with its unbiased reports on virtually everything," I counseled eighty million readers of *Parade* in an unrelated article as our battle raged, not wanting to lose my own objectivity out of pique.

board of Consumers Union. Linda Lipsen, ATLA's senior director for public affairs, came to that spot after her stint as CU's legislative director. There is absolutely nothing wrong with any of this, but the ties are there. One item not likely to be high on most consumer advocates' agenda for reform is the legal system.)

As for Harry Snyder, back at CU's West Coast office after a sabbatical and then off to China for three weeks, and so forth—well, Harry had by now, I'm sure, come to *loathe* me, although to his credit he always kept his cool. He just wouldn't budge. He felt our initiative restricted too deeply the consumer's right to sue. Presumably, he realized that most of the time you get *nothing* from that right, or not much—what are you going to get from someone with no significant assets and minimal insurance? But he had decided that *compensation*— a guaranteed $1 million per person in protection for less than most people were paying today—was less important than *suing*. And maybe the people, had they been presented with that choice clearly, would have agreed.

From Harry's point of view, it was all a little academic. He told me he had $3 million in liability coverage (so anyone *he* hurt would certainly have made out fine). He'd been with CU for twenty-one years, and he told me I had to understand this was a long-term process. No, he'd never achieved anything for auto-insurance consumers in California, but he was busy with other important issues. CU didn't have the time to provide any "studies" or "analyses" of the pros and cons of Prop 200.

Harry is comfortable in his liberal credentials and wears them well. I have no doubt his heart is in the right place. But it's his turf, his comfortable home in exclusive Mill Valley, and if it takes another ten years, another twenty, to fix the auto-insurance mess out there, well— patience, dear boy, patience.

Harry objected to our plan because it cut back *too* far on lawsuits— it was *too* strong, leaving *too much* money for policyholders and victims, not enough for the lawsuit process which occasionally— lottery-like—wins the lucky accident victim even more money. No one would argue with him that justice is precious. But is justice really being served by the lawsuit auto-insurance system today?

The last thing I want to say about Harry is that it would have been hard for him, at least subconsciously, I think, not to have had a special place in his heart for the trial lawyers. His West Coast CU operation, he told *The Wall Street Journal*, gets about 20 percent of its budget from class action proceeds—not necessarily in cases CU has been party to, but simply "leftover" money where not every member of the class can be found. Rather than let the wrongdoer keep that money, judges frequently give a chunk of it to CU—hundreds of thousands of dollars that CU gets without having to write grant proposals, without having to organize benefit galas. It's about the sweetest money a nonprofit executive can imagine. And were it not for the fine work of the trial lawyers—much of which *is* fine—Harry wouldn't have had it to augment his budget.

(Perhaps to show his independence from the trial lawyers, Harry bravely blasted their tactics—after the election, once it was too late to do us any good. "Consumers Union is greatly disturbed by the deceptive tactics employed by 'Consumers and Their Attorneys Against Proposition 200, 201 and 202,'" his five-page April 8, 1996, letter to the state bar concluded. "We feel the actions of the group clearly warrant the imposition of disciplinary action and would appreciate some guidance from the State Bar in this regard.")

**On Prop 201**—the securities law initiative—the lawyers' TV ad morphed two faces back and forth: Charles Keating's and Al Shugart's. It ominously announced that Shugart (one of our key supporters) had been *sued for securities fraud* and reminded people of Keating's Lincoln Savings & Loan scandal. It suggested that if Prop 201 succeeded, stock swindlers like these would have a field day. This was, to say the least, a bit unfair—but typical of the lawyers' tactics.

Keating was a convicted felon. (And nothing about Prop 201 would have kept his victims from recouping just as much as they did without it.) Shugart, by contrast, had never been charged by the government with anything. He had founded Seagate Technology in 1979 from nothing. Today it is the world's largest independent maker of computer disk drives, employing eighty-five thousand people. Yes, he'd been sued repeatedly for securities fraud, *but only by the same private lawyers who were paying for this TV commercial.*

The first time, in 1984, Seagate was accused of intentionally misleading investors by being too optimistic in its projections. (And perhaps it did mislead them—I don't claim to know.) The lawyers

demanded $100 million. Seagate, though certain of its innocence, felt
it would be cheaper and far less time-consuming to settle than to fight.
"We paid $1 million, our insurer paid $8 million, and the lawyers got
nearly $3 million." The lawyers felt this grievous wrong had been
done—but a quick $3 million was enough to make them go away.
Maybe $100 million was due, but they'd settle for getting the share-
holders $6 million instead, net of their own fees.

Not a bad deal for the lawyers, even if it hurt Seagate shareholders.
(If you own stock in a fledgling high-tech, you're not eager to see it
sued, or to see it fork over $1 million.)

The same lawyers sued twice more. This time, furious, Seagate
decided to fight. A judge threw out one of the suits—but it still cost
$4 million in legal fees, hurting the company's shareholders some
more. (Seagate's Japanese competitors must have been amused its
rival had expenses like that.) The third suit is still being fought.

At the time the ad was running, morphing Shugart's face back and
forth with Keating's, Seagate stock was at an all-time high. *Anyone
who had bought it at the time of the alleged fraud would have had a fat
profit*—though it would have been fatter had it not been for these
lawsuits.

Really, when you come to think of it, it's a great tactic. First you sue
somebody; then (though no court finds in your favor), you slam them
for having been sued. (Sound familiar? First you sabotage no-fault;
then, years later, you take ads saying, "See? It hasn't worked.")

In most cases, T. Rowe Price vice president Liz Buyer told the *San
Jose Mercury News*, these suits "not only aren't helping the small
investor,"—and few people know more about small investors than the
folks at mutual-fund giant T. Rowe Price—"they're causing significant
harm. The one who gets hurt is the small shareholder. The one who
gets helped is the lawyer."

But though Congress voted overwhelmingly to do something
about this racket at the federal level, Ralph, Harvey and crew would
not even concede there was a problem. We got 41 percent on this one.

Gosh, I kept thinking as we debated. Just what California needs:
fewer Intels and more lawyers.

**On Prop 202**—the 15 percent contingent-fee cap on early offers—
the opposition argued that "you couldn't get a lawyer" if it passed.

Trial lawyers would be so appalled at being limited to 15 percent in quick settlements they wouldn't take the time to hear your story and write a demand letter.

But what were they going to do—quit and become high school teachers? Talk about pay cuts!

Yes, lawyers would earn much less on cases that settled fast, and somewhat less on those that involved a rejected low-ball offer—*money that consumers would save.*

But the notion that the good lawyers would all just quit was preposterous, as was the notion that they'd all go to work for corporations instead. (With more early settlements and fewer auto-accident cases, why would corporations need them?) The fact is, if Props 200 and 202 had passed, a tremendous amount of legal talent would have been freed up to serve consumers.

Props 200, 201 and 202—"the terrible twos," as Harvey and the lawyers called them—would have been tough on lawyers, just as peace is tough on military subcontractors. But lawyers are smart, talented people—and we do need more smart, talented high school teachers (and more smart, talented entrepreneurs). Over time, if Californians were spending less on auto insurance, less on lawsuits, they would have had a more profitable economy and could afford to *hire* more teachers (and patronize more start-up businesses).

This was our opponents' main argument: if your plane crashed or someone amputated the wrong leg, no good lawyer would be available to represent you. It did not stand up to rational scrutiny; but that's not how elections are determined. We got 48.8 percent of the vote. No cigar.

## 24—Election Night

In short, we lost them all. Even when we were ahead 53 to 47 on Prop 202 around midnight—and for a minute I began to think, My God, all this work may actually have accomplished something! (albeit not something quite as sexy and exciting as auto-insurance reform)—the pros were telling me it was hopeless. They could tell from the pattern of precincts reporting what would happen.

We were beaten with big lies (your rates would go *up* 40 percent) and little lies (we were financed by the insurance industry).

In point of fact, "less than 1 percent" of our money (not to sound too much like Ralph here, but our records are on file to prove it) came from the insurance industry—from a company that doesn't even write auto insurance. We got not one dime from the auto insurers. We suspect the stock companies wanted us to lose (because lower premiums mean lower profits). And although we knew the mutual companies were quietly on our side, because they certainly knew Prop 200 would have been terrific for their customer-owners, they were afraid to help. They wouldn't even send letters to their policyholders advising them what their coverage and premiums would have been if Prop 200 had passed. They just didn't want to tangle with the lawyers.

Yes, there were trade-offs; there always are.*

The problem—hardly unique to our campaign—was that the trade-offs were not honestly laid out to allow an informed choice.

Which is a great argument against plebiscites (i.e., ballot initiatives) and in favor of "representative democracy" (i.e., electing some smart people like Senators Moynihan, Lieberman, McConnell and Dole to consider the issues carefully and make sensible trade-offs). But sometimes the legislature gets blocked by powerful special interests, like the trial lawyers.

I chose the senators in my example above, incidentally, because on June 11, 1996, they introduced a no-fault auto-insurance bill in Congress—The Auto Choice Reform Bill. Its approach is a little different from ours, but there is more than one way to skin a cat. Who knows?

One thing for sure: the thousands of Californians who will be seriously injured this year and get nothing, or next to nothing, from today's expensive lawsuit auto-insurance system—about 85 percent of all the cases—have a colossal bone to pick with Ralph Nader.

The millions who *won't* be hurt have a bone to pick, too. They're paying too much and getting too little. Because of Ralph, more than half the $7 billion they pay for auto-injury insurance will be eaten up by legal costs and fraud.

Not because Ralph is being "paid off" by the trial lawyers in any

---

* A good liberal wants insurance that pays generous benefits. But generous benefits cost money—and a good liberal also wants insurance poor people can afford. It's a trade-off. By slashing legal costs and fraud, we came as close as we could to satisfying both concerns.

literal sense—no one thinks that; least of all, me. No one doubts his zeal or commitment to doing what he thinks is right. But sometimes it's harmful to be so sure you're right.

Three last things:

- First, just as you don't have to be Jewish to love Levy's rye, neither do you have to be a Republican to think there's room to make some modest improvements in our legal system. As George McGovern put it: "America is in the midst of a new civil war, a war that threatens to undercut the civil basis of our society. The weapons of choice are not bullets and bayonets, but abusive lawsuits brought by an army of trial lawyers subverting our system of civil justice while enriching themselves." George McGovern!

- Second, it goes without saying—but is important to say anyway: most lawyers, including many trial lawyers, are terrific people. Anyone who doubts the important work trial lawyers do, the enormous risks they sometimes take, need only read Jonathan Harr's page-turner, *A Civil Action*. Ralph is right: we *need* good trial lawyers. We just don't need them helping us sue one another over auto accidents.

- Third, Ralph Nader, who I say again is neither fat nor an idiot (unlike a certain radio talk-show host), really has done some great things. But that doesn't make him right about everything. One of the greatest things he's done—perhaps *the* greatest—is to inspire a legion of younger people (many of them now running advocacy organizations of their own) to work for peanuts to make the world a little better. Let me give the last word to him—or perhaps to my dad. It's the end of that full-page ad they wrote launching Public Citizen: "Let it not be said by a future, forlorn generation that we wasted and lost our great potential because our despair was so deep we didn't even try, or because each of us thought someone else was worrying about our problems."

# 5

## Updates

# BLEEDING HEARTS VERSUS JERKING KNEES

I will admit to being one of these people who think everything is his fault, or certainly his responsibility. What is it they say—a psychotic is someone who feels responsible for nothing, while a neurotic is someone who feels responsible for everything? I am, friends will affirm, deeply neurotic.

You may recall the front-page story a couple of years ago about the universe containing a billion more galaxies than previously thought. I don't remember the specifics, but I do remember my chest tightening. My immediate reflex (quickly overcome, but still): Oh, God. That much more to worry about.

This is sick. But before bringing you up-to-the-minute on Miami slum dwellers, Russian smokers or California crash victims, all of whose distress I feel at least vaguely responsible for, not to mention the Ecuadorians or South Africans (sure, things are much better there, but the squalor remains), I want to take a few pages to make two things clear: First, not all my vast fortune is committed to help these suckers, by any means. A lot of it has been lavished on *me*. Second, not all of it has been amassed solely from writing, royalties and failed investments. I've actually had a few good ones along the way, too.

## 1—My Winners

Well, there was my apartment on Central Park West, as you know, $11,000 down which has by now appreciated fiftyfold. And there was the IRA money I had the good sense to entrust to Michael Price's Mutual Shares, up thirty-sixfold. I liked Mutual Shares, because it was one of those no-load, relatively low-expense funds that invested in value. The junk nobody else wanted or understood, which meant it was selling for even less than it was worth. (Mutual Shares still follows this general approach, but in 1996 Price sold out to the Franklin group of funds, so that for newcomers his funds now do entail a load. And as Price's involvement gradually winds down, it may not do as well in the future as it has in the past.)

One theme here is to buy what nobody wants and wait for the cycle to turn. When I bought my apartment in New York, the city was a basket case. If only I had made the effort to buy a Dallas apartment building at the depths of the S&L crisis! I was certain it made sense. But actually scaring up enough dough, let alone adding yet another complication to my life—owning buildings isn't quite as easy as owning a thousand shares of a Real Estate Investment Trust, though the rewards can be greater—was just beyond me at the time.

### Buying the Farm

A farm, on the other hand (so long as you don't have to work it yourself), is easy. I bought mine, in northwest Iowa, in 1986, for two reasons. First, I wanted to be able to echo the haunting preamble to *Out of Africa.* "I . . . had a farm . . . in Iowa," I wanted to be able to say softly, and with great feeling. Second, things down on the farm in 1986 were terrible. Federal agencies alone had more than a hundred thousand acres of foreclosed Iowa farmland overhanging the market, and Uncle Sam seemed headed out of the "price support" business, which could drive crop prices even lower. The world was awash in food. (It was trucks and supermarkets—supply lines—the Third World lacked.) Farmers were awash in red ink, driving tractor caravans to Washington in protest. Nobody in his right mind would have bought a farm at a time like that, which was precisely what intrigued me.

Ukraine (it was still "the" Ukraine back then) had recently gone radioactive—Chernobyl—and my friend Laura Sloate, the sharpest-eyed blind woman on Wall Street, who runs her own firm and manages upwards of a billion dollars, pointed out to me that Ukraine was Europe's breadbasket. Whatever happened with Chernobyl specifically, it was her thought that food in general might one day come back into fashion; that commodity-price cycles might turn. They always had before. So she was buying a farm, and that gave me the idea to buy one, too—although in keeping with the third rule of personal finance, NEVER INVEST IN ANYTHING THAT EATS OR NEEDS REPAIRING,* I made certain to choose one without animals or equipment.

The thing is, the stock market had about tripled in the prior few years, while the price of farmland, some of which had got caught up in the tax-shelter frenzy of the Seventies, had come crashing back by as much as two thirds. Farmland that had not long before changed hands at $1,500 an acre could be had for $500-and-change. (This was the kind of farmland for me.) Combined, there had been about a ninefold shift in relative values. One share of Ford Motor Company stock would buy nine times as many square feet of Iowa farmland as it had just a few years earlier. I decided it was time to sell Ford and buy a farm.

Not that I was without misgivings. For one thing, I was not at all sure farm prices wouldn't plunge further. Had my $500-an-acre land dropped in value to, say, $275, I had already planned on buying more. (This was the quicksand theory of soil management.) For another, I was worried that I might be perceived as the big bad city slicker driving a family off its land. "No," said the bank that sold me my farm. They had already foreclosed on it three years earlier—*they* were the heavies, not me—and a little outside capital would be welcomed by Iowans eager for signs of a bottoming out in the price of land.

Fortunately, it didn't take much to send one of those signs. For $35,000 in cash plus a low-interest $130,000 mortgage, I got three hundred acres in Monona County. I began eating popcorn and corn

---

* This was the precept of vaudevillian Billy Rose. Most of the other basic rules were laid down by either Mark Twain (OCTOBER. THIS IS ONE OF THE PARTICULARLY DANGEROUS MONTHS TO SPECULATE IN STOCKS. OTHERS ARE NOVEMBER, DECEMBER, JANUARY, FEBRUARY, MARCH, APRIL, MAY, JUNE, JULY, AUGUST AND SEPTEMBER.) or Benjamin Franklin.

flakes like crazy, doing what I could to boost prices, while some excellent folks at Security National Bank in Sioux City, who acted as my farm managers, arranged to rent my land to a farmer who needed extra ground over which to spread the cost of his equipment. Having just seen *The Grapes of Wrath* again for the umpteenth time, I pledged to be as understanding and supportive a landlord as possible.

Here we are little more than a decade later, and guess what? The value of the land has more than doubled, meaning that my $35,000 cash investment has nearly tentupled.

But it's much better than that, because I've been getting better than $15,000 a year in rent each year, net of expenses, along the way.

(It was only after getting rent checks for a few years that I was really fairly certain I owned three hundred acres of land and not just a large, parched football field. Because the one time I went out to see it, before making the purchase, that's all it seemed to be. Flying in, I had been imagining what three hundred acres must be. "All the land as far as the eye can see" was roughly how I pictured it. After all, our place in Bedford Village, New York—23.9 acres, and we were quite protective of that ".9"—was so immense, especially to a little kid, I had never actually been to its hilly, swampy, overgrown far boundary. So *three hundred* acres—"DUM-da-da-dum-da-da-dum-da-da-dum-da-da-DUM-dum" was the tune that kept jumping into my head.* And yet when I arrived, and Dick Thoreson drove me out past Mapleton, population 1,500 or so, to see this place, all I saw was a very large parched-clay football field. I still cannot imagine something so small could be three hundred acres, although I did subsequently calculate—because I really worried I was being scammed—that "as far as the eye could see," if the eye could see five miles in every direction, would be more like fifty thousand acres. So getting those annual rent checks was very important to me. I just assumed no farmer would be paying me $23,000 a year to rent a football field.)

The rent started out at $80 an acre. It has since inched up, over the years, to over $100. Even after the 7 percent management fee and some taxes and insurance (what's to burn down? it's *dirt*), the yield

---

* What—are you tone deaf? It's the theme from *Bonanza*.

has been better than 10 percent on the cost of the farm, and more than enough to pay off the mortgage.

Of course, this is poor soil. If you were to buy a farm with great soil, and/or located twenty miles from downtown Chicago, say, or Indianapolis, you would pay far more for the land without a proportional increase in rent or yield. In farming, as best I've been able to dope it out, the worse the land, the better the return—at least in the short run.

To give you an idea how this all works, my poor soil yielded 150 bushels of corn per acre one recent fall, which was a lot better than the 85 bushels it's officially rated at and about the best it ever did. (Go, soil! Rah!) But this was not as great as it sounded, I learned, because the crop was damp. True, that wasn't my problem; I just rent out the land. But I do always hope my tenant does well, so it concerned me. Yes, he had gotten a great harvest, but he had to spend a lot drying the corn. (I kid you not: they dry the corn.) As my farm manager reported: "Most grain elevators charge two and a half to three cents per point of moisture dry down; plus the grain shrinks as the moisture is removed." Ah, no wonder we got such a fat yield! It was wet behind the ears! Corn must be dried to 15 percent moisture to sell and 14 percent moisture to store. The corn from my damp farm was bulging with 27 percent moisture, so to bring it down to 14 percent meant bringing it down thirteen points at the aforementioned two and a half to three cents a point. Plus, as it dried, it shrank. (Had they heated it aggressively enough in the drying, it might have popped, but that's a different story, and a different kind of corn. Mine gets fed to pigs.) Shrinkage left my tenant with approximately a hundred twenty-five bushels of corn per acre, and a drying bill of about 35¢ a bushel. With corn going for $1.85 a bushel at the time, paying 35¢ to dry it was like giving up nearly 20 percent of the yield—bringing my tenant's net yield (adjusted for drying costs) down to around the equivalent of a hundred bushels per acre. Selling those hundred bushels at $1.85 brought him $185 per acre. Paying me $85 per acre left him $100 for his expenses, labor and profit. Not a lot, though in recent years, I'm pleased to see, the price of corn has often been much higher.

In my case, I don't have to know any of this; I'm just interested. In your case, if you ever decided to diversify into farmland, you might prefer an arrangement where you hired someone to farm the ground *for* you, taking all the risk yourself; or where you provided the land and split the return with your tenant. In either case, you'd then want to know a lot about the management of your farm, and the moisture of your crop, because your return would be uncertain. You could earn nothing one year, reap a windfall if you ever produced a truly epic crop of not-too-damp kernels.

(And that's the other thing that amazed me. For the first two years, I assumed "bushels" included the corncobs and tassels and husks, the way it's sold at roadside stands out in the suburbs. But no, to get a lousy couple of bucks for a bushel of corn in Iowa, you've got to produce a bushel of *kernels*! Something like seventy-two thousand of them, I calculated one rainy afternoon.* If I did not already have tremendous respect for the American farmer—and I did—I bowed even more deeply when I learned *that*.)

Should you be interested in learning more, I am happy to provide the names of the two farm managers I have dealt with, being quick to acknowledge that hundreds and hundreds of others may serve you every bit as well. But I've greatly enjoyed my association with Dick Thoreson (Rural Route 1, Mapleton, IA 51034)—where the soil is not altogether choice and the movie screens are few and far between but the people themselves first-class. And with Westchester Farm Management, at 2407 S. Neil, Champaign, IL 61820, where the soil is better (though far more expensive) and the movies, first-run. Note, though, that while it may be true a billion Chinese eating just one more egg a week will do magnificent things to the price of grain, U.S. farm prices are no longer in the bargain basement as they once were, by any means. I'm afraid the lesson here may not be to buy farmland (I'm not buying more at today's prices), but to find whatever is today's equivalent of farmland in 1986.

### Selling the Farmhouse

That said, there is one more farming story I have to tell you. The farm in Iowa was not my only agricultural plunge. With my mother

---

* There are 56 pounds of corn in a bushel; 100 kernels weigh about 1.2 ounces. I extrapolated from there.

and my stockbroker* I bought a farm outside Indianapolis several years ago. "Sight unseen" would be too strong, because I saw Polaroids. A big field, lots of furrows, a big old farmhouse in one corner. The tenant pays something like $95 an acre in annual rent, plus $250 a month for the house. (The house is so poorly insulated that the heating bill alone, I'm told, dwarfs the rent.) Fine. All's gone swimmingly with this farm, and Indianapolis creeps ever closer, like a glacier bearing down on New Hampshire. One day, we figure, we'll be rich.

Comes this past summer, and it seems that our tenant would like a nicer house, and so we're faced with three choices. We can sell him our house for $25,000 and let him fix it up. We can let him move out and rent or sell it to someone else. Or we can tear it down and cart it away to free up more land for farming.

Personally, I lean to choice number four: if he's offering $25,000, he'll probably pay $45,000—it's a big old *house*, for heaven's sake! But I decide to leave this one to my broker. I'm swamped with other stuff, and he's nothing if not money-savvy, so the decision is his. *You* deal with it, I plead, and he agrees to do so.

My broker has a few conversations with the farm manager and comes to a decision. Bulldoze the sucker. Why? Because once you sell the house, you no longer control it. When they come to build the skyscrapers, they'll shun your land because of the ugly old farmhouse—or else the guy who owns the ugly old farmhouse will get to call the shots. Plus there's the liability of owning it (he slips, he falls, he scores!). So my broker votes to bulldoze the thing. My mother's view is that this is not her department; we boys should figure it out ourselves.

Well, I don't know anything about Indiana real estate, and I did say I would stay out of it. But as one who can't even discard empty boxes (what if we have to move?), I can't see bulldozing a perfectly good, if drafty, *house*. Why not get the $250 a month? Better still, why not get $750 a month? But our farm agent checked, and $250 a month really

---

* Yes, if you trade stocks yourself—and no-load, low-expense mutual funds are probably a better choice—you should strongly consider using a deep discount broker. I do that, too. But this guy has been a friend since before there was ever such a thing as discount brokers, let alone deep discounters. It doesn't bother me that I'm helping to put his kids through college—they're great kids.

is about right for that kind of property, he says. (He's not on-site, either. He's in Illinois.) There's just not a lot of demand for drafty farmhouses out in the middle of the cornfields. He agrees bulldozing is probably best.

This is a true story.

We have a three-way phone conference, and I say, Look, before you bulldoze the house, do me a favor and get it appraised. If it's worth $45,000, why would we bulldoze it? Even if it's worth only $25,000, and this guy's first offer was his best offer, I'm wondering why we'd bulldoze it.

Two weeks later the farm manager, a lovely young guy, calls. "I guess I know more about land values than home values," he says sheepishly. The house, it develops, is worth $117,000.

This is very good news. First, it means that in a modest way, at least—*WE'RE RICH!* Second, it means I can stick it to my broker for the rest of time. *Decades* from now, if he starts to make fun of my hair-gel disaster (I have lost more money on a hair-gel stock than most hairy guys dream of making in a lifetime) or any of my other disasters, just a slight tilt of my head—the flicker of a smile at the corner of my mouth—will stop him in his tracks. He'll know I'm getting ready to tell the bulldozer story.

### Dead Nuns

Have you ever read *Opportunities for Industry and the Safe Investment of Capital—or—1,000 Chances to Make Money?* Written in 1859 by a merchant named Freedley, and out of print for a century, it is one of my favorite books. It identifies a long list of ways to make money (*"by Mining Silver in Mexico and Peru," "by Raising Sheep where pasturage is cheap," "by Army and Navy contracts, especially in War Times"*), one of which I find particularly delightful—namely: *"by Accident."* (He then tells the presumably apocryphal story of the young "scullion-boy" who, having nothing else to contribute to his wealthy employer's trading venture, gave up his cat. The cat made it all the way to the Dey of Algiers, who found it so efficient at ridding the palace of rats, he offered any price for her, making the scullion-boy rich and, eventually, mayor of London.) Until we had our little farmhouse bonanza, I had no idea this sort of thing could actually happen. But now that I think about it, it wasn't the only time I've lucked out. (I've always felt very fortunate, but never terribly lucky.)

As I mentioned above, one theme of my investing philosophy is to look for things others don't. Another—born more of my need for cheap thrills perhaps than a true investment strategy—is to take risks. You can lose a lot of money taking risks. But the rich get richer, I'm persuaded, not just because their money sits there earning *more* money, but also because *they can afford to take more risk*. Risk, prudently evaluated, is an investor's friend. The market, in effect, pays you to take it—and stomps you mercilessly, more often than not, for taking it casually, without the proper resources or research. Sometimes it stomps you mercilessly anyway.

Sure, you can buy a lottery ticket. But that's dumb. The odds are against you. And sure, you may even be able to back your brother-in-law's software start-up, or the restaurant he plans to open. But unless you have ten brothers-in-law and enough capital to back them all, gambling, as venture capitalists do, that one or two will hit big, while the others all fail, this is probably not prudent. What's more, venture capitalists and other big risk takers have at least two additional advantages. First, they see more of the good deals. (When was the last time a brilliant MIT physicist came to *you* with her invention?) Second, they have more resources and experience to evaluate prospective investments.

I don't have those advantages. But as my vast fortune swelled, Gates-like (just divide by a few thousand), I did accumulate the wherewithal to spread my bets a bit. The eight of ten that would fail gave me something to write about (I rationalized), and if once in a while I cashed in . . . well, there's no feeling quite like it. If you don't believe me, ask the millions of poor souls who troop to Las Vegas and Atlantic City each year, spending billions in search of just that feeling.

The difference is that a good investment, especially if you're one of the initial investors who actually make the venture possible, is more productive than a good run at roulette.

Not to say that everything that makes money is a boon to mankind. Take *Nunsense*, perhaps my most successful investment ever. Could mankind have thrived without a musical comedy about forty-eight dead nuns? I'm thinking: yes. But I wasn't thinking about mankind, or much of anything, really, when a friend called early one evening, years ago, and said it was playing in a high school theater a few blocks from my apartment. Five bucks. Did I want to see it?

Oh, sure, why not.

An hour later I was laughing almost as hard as the Catholics in the audience, and when the show was over I kept saying to my friend, "Why is this five bucks in a high school? Why isn't this on Broadway?" (By which I meant off Broadway.) Funny you should mention that, my friend said. The writer/director/producer, Danny Goggin, had the same idea, and happened to be right here—would I like to speak with him? To this day, I don't know whether I was being set up. But it worked out pretty well, because unlike the other shows I had put $1,000 or $2,500 into, such as the aforementioned *P.S. Your Cat Is Dead*, this one had a few special things going for it.

In the first place, it was being capitalized at a mere $150,000— which was ridiculously cheap even then to put on an off-Broadway show, let alone today. (Today's full-fledged Broadway musical might require $8 million.) So for a relatively small amount of money you could own a meaningful piece of the production, in case it went well. Second, unlike most shows, where for every 1 percent of the capital that the investors put up they are entitled to one half of 1 percent of the profit—with the other half going to the producer—in this case, because Danny was the producer, director and writer rolled into one, and really wanted to get the final money he needed to seal the deal, he offered me 1 percent of the profit for each 1 percent of the capital I put up.

Suddenly, the odds were twice as good as usual, and maybe four times as good as *that* because the cost of the production was so low, and maybe four times *again* as good just based on the fact that I wasn't buying some pig in a poke, or some high-falutin' somber drama—I was buying into a show I had actually gotten to see, in its entirety, and to "test" on the audience I happened to see it with. "Nunsense . . . is habit-forming," ran the theme song, "that's what people say. We're here to show that nuns are fun—perhaps a bit risqué—" and by the end of the evening I was nun-punning nonstop. When I *think* how Sister Mary Amnesia (played by the magnificent Semena DeLaurentiis) lost her memory and, in one of the most stirring country-and-west-nun renditions of all time regained it in the final act . . . well, don't get me started.

I dug deep into my pool of speculative capital—because as relatively good as the odds were, this was still a complete speculation—and, for 25,000 very tax-deductible dollars (assuming we lost it all), bought 16.66666666667 percent of the show.

I wouldn't normally extend it to so many decimal places, but as it turned out, this was not an investment one would have wanted to round down. The show played for ten years in New York, and in dozens of countries on five or six continents. The checks have tapered off, but I've surely recouped my investment thirtyfold and *still* get royalties.

It was, in short, a miracle.*

## 2—Spending It

Much of this money, and money like it, went to pay for the *dumb* investments. And much of it went to my follies in Miami, Russia and California, or to shoeless Ecuadorians. But charity begins at home, and there was plenty left over for me.

Fortunately, I'm largely a mail-order kind of guy. Yes, I have been given a $125 tie or two in my day (to my horror), and yes, I once had an $85 haircut just to see what it would look like (it looked like I'm not the kind of guy who needs an $85 haircut—I pay $10, plus a $10 tip). And yes, after a lifetime of never having spent more than $6,000 for an automobile I finally broke down in 1992, when Detroit was hurting, and bought a brand-new Chrysler LeBaron convertible for $22,000 (I went nuts and got the leather seats). But just because it's been stolen and slashed a few times, I'm in no rush to get a new one. So long as it runs and has an airbag, who cares?

Boats? The dumbest thing you can possibly do is buy a boat. For one hundredth the money and one thousandth the hassle, you can lavish a boat-owning pal with so many gifts he wouldn't dream of leaving port without you.

Planes? OK, I'll admit it. The few times I've flown in a private jet have been so neat I can remember every one of them. But owning a

* If you would like to lose money in relatively small chunks being a Broadway angel ($10,000 and up), one outfit I've dealt with in recent years—producing no huge hits for me, but quite often breaking even or making a little money, and generally making it fun—is Scorpio Entertainment, 180 South Broadway, White Plains, NY 10605.

jet is so far out of my league as to be laughable, and chartering one from time to time, though I could afford it, reminds me of the line I think Malcolm Forbes recalled about the wealthy woman who shunned expensive restaurants "because, darling, I don't like to eat my money." Something like that. Not to mention that they don't give frequent-flier miles at Butler Aviation.

I do splurge on computers. And I love buying huge carts of stuff at Costco. Cases of ketchup, cartons of Tide, fish farms of frozen shrimp. But spending several hundred dollars at a warehouse store, while good therapy (and not bad exercise), is less spending than saving, because the prices are so good.

I have ostrich burgers flown in from New Orleans, which is extravagant (the flying more than the burgers, which run $3.50 a pound). But, as you know, there are only two grams of fat in an ostrich patty versus sixteen grams in a burger of beef. I find it a lot less taxing to eat ostrich than to spend half an hour on an Exercycle.

Another thing I suppose I have to own up to is a $1,500 cashmere Neiman-Marcus overcoat. It was presented to me by a PBS film crew to wear on a cold stroll through Chicago. They had put it on a credit card and planned to return it later that day, saying it didn't fit. (A little scuzzy, don't you think?) But, oh, did it fit! Something just came over me—I would never have gone to the store to buy it, but the thought of letting it go . . . "Don't bother to return it," I found myself saying, shocking myself and all those around me. "I'll reimburse you." That doubled my clothing budget for the year.

(It also proved a point made by an earlier interviewee for this same PBS series, Dick Thaler, a professor at the University of Chicago, who talks of "loss aversion." As investors, he says, we tend to cling to our mistakes because we hate to recognize a loss. His research shows that $100 lost seems to matter to us about twice as much as $100 gained—even though to most investors they should be about equivalent. He gave every second student in his class a $6 coffee mug. One got, one not. One got, one not. Then he asked those with and without mugs what they'd buy or sell them for. Those without mugs figured, quite reasonably, *What the heck do I want with one of those stupid coffee mugs?* and offered just a dollar or two. Those *with* the stupid mugs, by contrast—because they now owned them—valued them much higher. Most were unwilling to let them go for less than five or six dollars. Well, by the same token, I never would have gone to Neiman-Marcus* and paid $1,500 for that coat. Ever. But once it was on me, once it was mine, it was worth $1,500 to me not to lose it. Q.E.D.)

What else do I go crazy on? Not much, in part because I'm lucky enough to have so much already (albeit not always in the swankiest neighborhood or with the best view), and in part because I know $22 a month—$264 a year—is all it takes to change a family's life forever through Save the Children or the Foster Parents Plan (now called Childreach—800-556-7918). It's sappy and corny, I know, and there's always the chance *your* kid will grow up to be a terrorist, or, saved from starvation, bring fifteen additional offspring into a world of misery and starvation, only making the problem worse. I'm not suggesting that we send all our money to Ecuador or Peru. Even so, $264 can go a long way. Makes you think twice about $1,500 over-coats.

But of course I'm lying to you, because there is a glaring, gaping hole in my dike of frugality. "My name is Andy, and I'm a 'historic-document collector,'" I blurt out at meetings. *"Hi, Andy!"* responds the chorus of fellow addicts.

I tell myself I'm "investing," not spending. I tell myself I'm not taxing the world's resources as I would if I were burning five gallons a mile to power my yacht. But whatever the rationalizations, I've spent a fortune on these things. There aren't enough walls in the world for it all. So rather than leave them all starved for attention in the dark confines of my file drawer (that's apparently what serious collectors do: they just file these things!), I thought I'd share a few with you. Here are a few of my favorite things:

- A note from Humphrey Bogart, then thirty-four, to the more established actor Clifton Webb, asking to borrow $200 to pay the rent. ("It's terribly embarrassing, but Mary and I can't think of anything else.")
- A 1933 letter from Clarence Darrow to a fellow in Little Rock vigorously reprising his argument in the Scopes "monkey" trial.

---

* Needless-Markup, as it is affectionately known.

- A souvenir prayer from Mother Teresa.

- A three-by-five manila note card on which John F. Kennedy jotted in October 1963: "10-12 Senators—High Places—Implication White House—1 Cabinet member—Q Club—Babes—require informant of F.B.I."

- A complete collection of signatures from all the munchkins in *The Wizard of Oz.*

- A letter from Einstein responding to a colleague distraught that her husband is cheating on her. "Men are pigs," he basically advises, compassionately. "If in most respects he's a good husband, you may just have to look the other way." I'm not saying he was right (or that I'm translating the German verbatim)—but here it is: the smartest man in the world on the subject of infidelity.

- A collection of newspaper columns financed by Henry Ford that appeared in *The Dearborn Independent* in 1920 and 1921. Reprinted in book form, it is entitled, THE INTERNATIONAL JEW: *The World's Foremost Problem,* and inscribed, "From your friend, Henry Ford." (Ford's anti-Semitism was huge and very public. Hitler had Ford's picture hanging on his wall.*)

- A 1950 letter from ambassador Clare Boothe Luce to actress Claire Luce thanking the latter for forwarding misdirected mail.

- A letter from Harry Truman, eight years out of the White House— and a bit rusty on his geography, from the sound of things—to Dean Acheson, that begins, "I have been reading the results of our situation in Asia east of the Caribbean Sea and I am very much worried." To which Acheson replies: "I have been worrying for

---

* Nor was it exactly an eight-by-ten glossy. According to *Henry Ford and the Jews,* by Albert Lee: "Next to Hitler's desk at Nazi Party Headquarters in Munich hung a life-sized likeness of Henry Ford. On the table in the antechamber, visitors were often shocked to find anti-Semitic booklets and books with Henry Ford's name and portrait on the covers. . . . Hitler often spoke of Ford to his followers, frequently bragging about financial support he had received from the American industrialist. . . . In 1931 Hitler summarized his feelings when a *Detroit News* reporter asked what the portrait of Ford on Hitler's wall meant to him. 'I regard Henry Ford as my inspiration,' Hitler said. [Gee. Without Henry Ford, we might not have had the Mustang—*or* World War II.] On the occasion of Ford's seventy-fifth birthday, Hitler sent personal congratulations, along with the highest honor which could be awarded by the Nazi government: the Grand Cross of the German Eagle. Ford shared this honor with only four other men, one of them Mussolini." Good for the modern-day Ford Motor Company for sponsoring the uninterrupted broadcast of *Schindler's List.*

some time that the Asia problem was creeping up on us, but I had not realized how close it had approached, and here it is now just a bit south of Bermuda. So I am worried too."

- The April 24, 1740, issue of *The Pennsylvania Gazette*, a four-page weekly newspaper "Printed by B. Franklin, Postmaster," which includes "A Short Description of CUBA." Just imagine: "The Soil is very fruitful; and the Abundance of Pasture has occasion'd all Sorts of Cattle, as Horses, Kine, and Swine, to encrease so prodigiously, that they run wild, belonging to no Man, but are free to any that will take them. . . . The Country in general is very delightful, being full of little Houses, with Gardens and Farms, where there is no Want of any Thing." Isn't two hundred fifty years of progress wonderful?

- A document signed in 1794 by Samuel Adams, governor of Massachusetts, with respect to a burglar's death sentence. The governor was not commuting the sentence—the man was a burglar, after all, compassion has its limits—but, rather, graciously postponing it six weeks, to Thursday, September 25, so the burglar could more properly settle his affairs before being hanged. (Apparently, he used those six weeks to escape. He became a traveling preacher.)

The seeds of my addiction were planted years ago at an investment conference. Awaiting my turn to speak, I sauntered over to the Historic Documents booth, wedged between the Oil-Drilling-Deal booth and the You-Can-Make-a-Fortune-with-Our-Franchise-Opportunity booth. I was struck by a remarkable letter from Darryl Zanuck to Marilyn Monroe. It was on Twentieth Century–Fox letterhead, scolding Marilyn for her "completely impractical request" to have a special dialogue director work with her on the set of *Don't Bother to Knock* (a movie rated "Don't Bother to See"). "You have built up a Svengali," the letter read in part, "and if you are going to progress with your career and become as important talent-wise as you have publicity-wise then you must destroy this Svengali before it destroys you."

The booth person and I had a brief conversation. "How much?" I asked, pointing to the letter. "You're kidding!" I said, when she pointed to the price. But I left my name and address anyway, in case they ever got serious about selling it. (They were asking $8,000. I was thinking more like $300.)

From then on I would periodically receive, unbidden, catalogs of historic documents. A group shot of Nixon, Ford, Carter and Reagan, signed by each: $4,000. A nice George Washington letter: $35,000. A thank-you note signed by Bobby Kennedy: $650. An autographed photo of Sitting Bull (signed, "Sitting Bull"): $17,500.

So it wasn't exactly a cold call when the phone finally rang, in that I had given this outfit my name years before. And the caller wasn't exactly a college kid reading a script—he was a former curator of the Smithsonian. Still, I was getting all set to find some delicate way off the phone ("Oh, wait—the ambulance is here") when I remembered the Marilyn letter. Forget Abe Lincoln ("Dear Sir: Herewith I send you my autograph, which you request. Yours Truly, A. Lincoln"— $5,000. *Boring*.). What about Marilyn?

It seems this particular letter was indeed still available, some four years later, and that now its price was $9,500. Bear in mind that this was not a letter *from* Marilyn Monroe, it was merely addressed *to* her (Miss Marilyn Monroe, 611 N. Crescent Drive in Beverly Hills); and that if it was still available, that meant nobody, apparently, had wanted it at $8,000.

This gave me several ideas. The first was that if letters *to* famous people could acquire such value, I should myself write a ream of them to Madonna, which, when they came back stamped "insufficient address" (we've lost touch), I would save for my old age and then sell.

My second idea was to buy stock in Rupert Murdoch's News Corp., which owns Fox, because so far Wall Street has only focused on the value of its film library. What about the value of all its business correspondence? All those canceled checks endorsed by famous actors and actresses? All those deal memos and contracts? A gold mine!

My third idea was to haggle.

I won't tell you how much I wound up paying for my Marilyn letter because you'll think I'm an idiot. (OK. I paid $7,500—far too much, I would say, now that I know a little more.) And I won't tell you how I managed to get the price down even that little bit. (OK. As part of the deal, I agreed to buy a second letter, for even more—a letter from Einstein describing Hitler as a lunatic—and so got a little bit of a break on both.) But I will tell you that once you finally do swallow hard and buy one of these things, ranging in price anywhere from $50 to $748,000 (the highest price ever paid for a letter, so far as I know—an amazing Lincoln letter defending the Emancipation Proclamation, not boring at all, purchased at Christie's in December 1991), you will be hooked.

And I think that Albert Einstein, if not Marilyn Monroe, is likely to loom as large in the human consciousness a thousand years from now as Renoir. So given the choice between a little slice of Einstein for $15,000 or a work by Renoir for $15 million (and given $15 million), I would opt for the Einstein.

An inexpensive way to learn more: join The Manuscript Society (350 N. Niagara St., Burbank, CA 91505—$25 for a "personal" membership). For example, from its review of *From the President's Pen: An Illustrated Guide to Presidential Autographs* (State House Press, Austin, TX), I learned that:

- Zachary Taylor "once refused to pay ten cents postage due on a letter, hence failing to learn about his nomination for president for several days."
- President Garfield "had the interesting and well-documented ability to write in Greek with one hand and in Latin with the other at the same time." I'd like to see Dan Quayle do that.
- Chester A. Arthur "was probably born in Canada in 1829, not Vermont in 1830," making him ineligible to have become president.

You might also write Christie's (502 Park Avenue, NYC 10022) and Sotheby's (1334 York Avenue, NYC 10028), among others, to request the catalogs from their latest or forthcoming "Printed Books and Manuscripts" sales. They typically have two a year and charge $25 per catalog.

And if you ever find yourself with a spare hour in Manhattan, go down to the Forbes Building, at 60 Fifth Avenue, and walk through the small but wonderful free museum in the lobby.

One last word: especially with the glitzier dealers you'll find listed in Appendix E, you should only pay the full asking price if that's also the way you buy Buicks. Sometimes, their prices are firm and fair. Other times they've bought something for $4,500 at auction—which means, by definition, no one else at the auction was willing to pay even *that* much—that they are turning around to offer you the next day for $12,500. They have every right to do it. You have every right to negotiate.

### 3—Russia—1997

As I write this, things in Russia are going well. Mark Slater and I (you will remember it was Mark who coached me through my antismoking commercials) have recouped our investment with a little to spare, and the eighty or so Russians that Media Arts employs now earn about double what they were earning just a couple of years ago, though still a pittance by U.S. standards. Our three young Russian partners and their three Tanyas seem to be thriving as well. They have Visa cards, travel abroad on business and vacation, even buy American marketing and management books via the Internet bookstore, Amazon.com. Brave new world.

We've moved to larger offices.

It's still a pipsqueak operation, and something awful could presumably happen at any time, but so far, so good.

Cigarette advertising is still banned from TV, but I hear that the Russian courts recently upheld cigarette makers' right to market their brand names on TV—buy a Marlboro Man T-shirt, I guess—so long as they don't mention or show cigarettes. This is discouraging, since it more or less guts the ban altogether (what kid fails to associate the Marlboro brand with cigarettes?). But I suppose it's the least of Russia's problems. Over time, things may improve.

Make no mistake: for all the proliferating McDonaldses, Moscow construction sites, and other signs of progress, this is still Russia. Witness, for example, my experience buying a couple of Russian stocks.

It was October 1995, and I was over visiting my partners. Although the safest, simplest way to buy Russian stocks is through an American-based mutual fund, I thought it would be interesting to visit a Russian brokerage firm and perhaps buy Russian stocks directly. Here in America, there would have been a big sign out front, an electronic ticker in the window, maybe a digital clock. But

Moscow's capital markets are still young. Merrill Lynchski this was not. We entered an unmarked door and were greeted by three big guys with holstered guns. They came at us with big plastic metal detectors and frisked us. Carefully. (In America, this is called the "Know your customer" rule.)

Then they led us down a quarter-flight of stairs, along a narrow corridor, around to the left, up a half-flight of stairs, around to the right, down some stairs, through a door, up some stairs—this was not a place you could escape from easily—and finally to the conference room, which may once have served as a tiny interrogation room, on the second floor overlooking the street. (Not that you could see the street—the curtains were closed.)

We talked turkey. Specifically, Rostelekom, Russia's main phone company, then selling for 91¢ a share.

Their notions of valuation were quaint—earnings? dividends? what this mean?—and had mostly to do with "market down, down—will up soon." But their English was better than my Russian, so I shouldn't scoff; and, in any event, I had read that Russian companies were wildly undervalued, even considering the risks, and I wanted to help these guys out. They were friends of one of my partners, trying to make it as beez-ness-men in the new Russia.

I had visions of being able to tell friends, "Can I call you back? It's my broker in Moscow." That should be worth *something*.

I bought 25,000 shares of Rostelekom. (That's also kind of fun to say; 25,000 AT&T would have been about 24,000 beyond my reach.) Then, a couple of weeks later, from back in the U.S., I bought shares in a giant Russian nickel complex, too.

It's easy. You just send an E-mail placing the order; receive your confirm by E-mail; wire the money to an account in Cyprus (I don't know and I don't want to know); and for the next eleven months you get weekly E-updates.

Paper? Who needs paper?

When Rostelekom had climbed from 91¢ to $2.56, and when my partner told me he was beginning to have his doubts about these fellows, I decided to sell. A small earlier sale had gone smoothly— $1,450 had actually cyberblipped from Cyprus to my bank account in the States. But this one, in late July 1996, was the real test. Would I get my money back and a rather huge profit?

I got my E-confirmations that the trades were done. Hello, $67,000!

I got E-confirmations that the paperwork would be completed in early August and the cash wired immediately thereafter.

I got an "unforeseen technical difficulties" E-message announcing a minor delay, and then another explaining that there would be two wires—one right away, returning my investment, the other a few weeks later, conveying my profit.

Eight weeks after the sale, that's *all* I'd got.

I got nervous.

And do you want to know something really silly? I actually thought I was going to get some of, and very possibly all of, my money. Shows you how naive *I* am.

Sillier still, and with $700 of help from a Russian law firm, I did—I got every dime. My Russian stockbroker coughed up every kopeck I was owed. What I don't know, and may never, is whether he was (a) actually trying to steal my money, (b) borrowing it interest-free for a little while to make investments of his own, or whether he had (c) genuinely encountered bureaucratic weirdnesses in getting it back to me. (If your hunch is (a) or (b), your cynicism is crushing—and probably dead on target.)

Isn't it nice to live in a country where, by and large, routine commerce can be conducted without much worry? In Russia, they still have no checking accounts or, for the most part, credit cards. Here we are going "check-free," and they haven't even gone "check."

The sensible way to speculate on Russia is through the Templeton Russia Fund (TRF on the New York Stock Exchange) or something similar, especially if/when it is selling at a discount to net asset value. (Avoid closed-end mutual funds selling at a premium.) But even then, it's really, really risky. And as I write this, with Russian stocks having soared from their lows, a good chunk of the upside has already been realized. But if Russia does stumble and stagger into the modern, free-market age—no sure thing by any means—Russian stocks have a long way to go.

## 4—Miami—1997

Here, too, things are going reasonably well. The Palm Bay, where I accidentally bought my first condo ("a hundred and five! a hundred and four!"), and subsequently a few more, may really have kissed the bottom good-bye. A dynamic new board of directors did some sensible things and managed to buy the bankrupt "common areas"—the marina, the filled-in swimming pool, the torn-down clubhouse, the neglected tennis courts—for a song. The huge French conglomerate that owned it all (*mon dieu*, what a bad investment!) had been asking $2.5 million for all this. But it was—what's French for stalemate? They couldn't really do anything with this property without our approval; we couldn't ever get back on our feet without it . . . but we had no money.

Fortunately, they blinked first. From what I understand, they told one of their people just to get the damn thing off their books before the end of 1996. With that in mind, they offered it to us for $850,000. We said yes. We'd try to raise that from the condo owners. It seemed to be a pretty great deal, not least because the French had just spent nearly that much—$650,000—totally refurbishing the marina. Yet with a few days to go before the end of the year, we had managed to raise only $300,000. *They took it.*

Of course, one targeted hurricane could be the end of the neighborhood. And there's the little matter of corroding pipes and other such details. But yachts should be docking, tennis balls thwocking, in no time. My God: we even have a website (www2.netcom.com/~palmbayb/first.html)! I'll bet Trump Tower can't say that.

Across the Boulevard things are also a little bit better. The Victory Garden, as we call it, has caught on and—while I'm implying no connection here—when the Prince moved away, things seemed to calm down a bit.

But it's a struggle.

Just two examples, because they raise interesting issues (and here is where we get into the area of good intentions but unintended consequences).

The first is simply that one of the worst buildings on one of the worst streets where we have property has been beautifully renovated by a neighbor from the "Bay" side of the Boulevard. Good for her. It's almost finished, and it makes the whole area look better. Good for the neighborhood. The purchase and renovation were made possible by a government subsidy. Good for the government. But here's the rub. Because it was subsidized, the owner can afford to price the apartments as cheap as ours (which were not subsidized). What's to keep all our tenants from moving a couple of doors down into brand-new apartments with brand-new appliances? I would.

So either we'll drop our rents and lose even more money, or maybe get lucky and hold onto our tenants through loyalty and inertia, or lose our tenants but, once the new building is full, attract others in their stead.

I have no answer to this one. I'm delighted to see the block improving; hopeful that the harm the government subsidy does to our unsubsidized business will be canceled out by the good it does the neighborhood, and by extension, my own property. So it's probably a good thing (thank you, taxpayers, for helping out). But it's interesting to think through all the ripples.

My second example is—to me—easier to dope out. It began a couple of months ago, in the midst of my putting together this book. The doorbell rang and instead of being handed a FedEx or UPS, I was served a summons. I was being sued by Legal Services of Greater Miami on behalf of a man I had never met—let's call him Mr. B.

About seven months earlier, Mr. B had rented one of our $300-a-month apartments. He had no furniture, my guys told me, but soon acquired the sorts of things you can pick up walking around a neighborhood—an old chair someone's thrown out, a mattress if you're lucky, a broken TV.

Soon there were problems. Mr. B had fallen behind with the rent. He said he was awaiting a government check and gave us a little handwritten note that he would pay the balance as soon as it came. And there were other problems. Obviously, my manager thought it was important to encourage Mr. B to find another place to live. After all, the last thing he wants to do is lose a good tenant. This is not some tony section of New York or even Miami, for that matter, where apartments are easy to fill with good tenants. Good tenants—even marginal tenants—we do everything we can to hang on to.

Anyway, we apparently went to Mr. B and said, in effect, Look, this isn't working out too well. We'd like to give you $150 so you can check into a motel for a few days and figure out what to do next. Would you be willing to give us back the key for $150?

He said yes and left. Asked if he wanted to take any of his "furniture," he said something about not wanting any of that garbage, took a few personal belongings and left.

That was the last we heard from Mr. B for seven months. Not a call, not a complaint, not a letter, nothing.

And now I was holding this summons. He was suing us for $4,000 in lost furniture, TV and stereo equipment, and for three months' rent—several thousand dollars in all.

As my guys first explained it to me, we had received just $100 from Mr. B and given him $200 to leave, so we he had in effect paid *him* $100 to live in our apartment for six weeks. We had paid for his water (some of our tenants, out of spite, will leave the water running for weeks, knowing that in Miami the water-and-sewer bill can be enormous)—and now we were being sued for it, by a lawyer who had never even called to ask our side of the story, and whose salary my tax dollars helped pay.

Of course, never having met or even heard of Mr. B prior to the lawsuit, I'm going by what my manager, Sal, told me. And in fairness to Mr. B and Legal Services, it appears likely that my guys either screwed up some of the paperwork and/or forgot some of the details in the months and months since all this began.* But on the main point—that Mr. B had agreed to leave voluntarily and had told us he didn't want to take any of the "garbage" in the apartment, which we then put out on the street—their recollection was clear and, to me, believable.

A sane person would simply have handed this matter over to his lawyer, or else to his insurance company. Naturally, I did neither. I called the Legal Services attorney to set up an appointment for Sal and me to come explain what had happened.

The attorney was a nice white guy about my age who clearly means

---

*Mr. B had apparently moved in earlier and paid more than my manager at first remembered. He had paid $1,000 in all for four and a half months—minus $150 in cash we gave him to leave. We had netted $850 instead of $1,350 for those four and a half months, and got back an apartment plastered with hundreds of stickers on the walls. It was no small job readying it for the next tenant.

to do good—and doubtless does some, too. "Equal Justice for People in Poverty" is the slogan on his letterhead.

We went to his office, were buzzed through a series of security doors, and established a rapport. We told him what we've been trying to do in the neighborhood, offered him names of references in the community-policing office who could vouch for us, offered to take him on a tour of the area, showed him the little bit of paperwork we had on Mr. B and his handwritten note.

It was a very low-key, cordial meeting. My overall point was that, like him, we were really trying to be the good guys—we had invested in the slum when no one else would, rather than a few miles away on South Beach. (I was an idiot, frankly, but I try not to dwell on it.) The reason we had come to see him, I explained, was that I just thought it would be nuts to spend a few thousand dollars on my not-poor lawyer that could otherwise go to the Daily Food Bank or to Health Crisis Network or to any of a thousand worthwhile places.

By the end of the meeting the lawyer had given us an extension to reply to the summons, during which time, he said, he would regroup with his client, because this was, of course, quite a different story from the one he had been told.

I could see he would do a little face-saving shuffle, and pretty soon the lawsuit would be dropped.

Instead, when I reached him a couple of weeks later, he said he had spoken with his client, and that his client "significantly disputed" our version of the events. The lawsuit would proceed.

I sent a fax. It shows me at my most annoying, sanctimonious worst:

Dear Mr. ——:

Equal justice for people in poverty? What's equal in a situation where there is absolutely no risk or cost in time or dollars in suing—and complete immunity from being sued, and no practical penalty for lying?* Rich people sure don't have it that good.

---

* Mr. B was charged nothing by Legal Services to pursue this, so far as I know, not even photocopying costs; had no loss of time from work because he was unemployed; and could not be countersued because he had nothing to lose. As for lying, if he was, what was the state going to do: spend thousands of dollars prosecuting him for perjury and then $25,000 a year putting him in jail?

Let's say that, just conceivably, WE are telling the truth. Just for the sake of argument. And that this gentleman, who I presume has no receipts for anything he says he lost, and no copies of any letters to us . . . or anything else . . . has been telling you things that aren't true.

What am I supposed to do? Just pay some middle-class lawyer a few thousand dollars that could have gone to something useful to defend this case? And possibly lose anyway, because if YOU don't believe us, a jury might not either?

Just never again give anyone a place to sleep if he/she doesn't have first, last, security and letters of reference from his/her employer and last landlord? That rules out 99% of the people you are trying to help. Where are they supposed to live?

Mr. B stiffed us, as we often get stiffed. And he certainly got to take with him anything he wanted when he left. The last thing I need is another television set. So that was just routine. We'd been stiffed with no recourse. Happens all the time, and I have no particular bad feeling about it. "There but for the grace of God . . ."

But what IS new is the notion that now you, without even so much as a call to discuss it first, or a letter, are suing me for thousands of dollars.

And the irony of course is that it is my tax dollars that pay for it. I must tell you that, bleeding-heart though I am, it is almost enough to get me to think the Republicans are right about Legal Aid funding. (Not quite, but almost.)

I would *happily* "settle" this matter by giving $1,000 or $2,500 or $5,000 to the Daily Food Bank or Health Crisis Network or some other mutually agreeable group—but only on the express condition that NOT ONE PENNY of that, directly or indirectly, went to Mr. B or to you or to Legal Services of Greater Miami. So where do you want the money to go: some middle-class lawyer or to people in poverty served by one of the groups I've mentioned? Your choice.

I was sanctimonious and annoying. But there's nothing like being sued to bring out the worst in anybody.

The lawyer never responded to my offer of $5,000 to people in poverty, and proceeded with the suit. I finally started the clock and turned it over to a lawyer of my own. The head of Legal Services of Miami, to whom I faxed something similar, made no response either. Depositions begin shortly.

By the time you read this I will have won or lost (to find out, try www.ceres.com and ask), though either way I will have lost, as will the people in poverty whom these same dollars, spent on legal fees, could have helped.

But what strikes me about this is the distinction it draws between a bleeding heart and a jerking knee. To me, a bleeding heart is a nicely functioning body part in absolutely no need of repair—but a jerking knee requires immediate surgery. *Sure,* we should care about people in poverty. *Sure,* we should provide appropriate legal aid for those who need it.

But this? This wasn't about a guy, let alone a pregnant mother, kicked out of his home involuntarily with nowhere to go. This wasn't about helping a poor person evaluate a legal document or fend off creditors, file for bankruptcy or get the electricity turned back on, fight an eviction or file for divorce—none of which would interest a for-profit contingency-fee lawyer. We didn't hear from Legal Services until *months* after the alleged abuse occurred. So this wasn't to protect a poor person from impending homelessness. It was strictly about money. Indeed, it *hurt* the homeless, because it made us less likely to give a homeless person a break the next time. No job? No references? No first-and-last in advance—no dice. As a practical matter, that either leaves potential tenants out in the street or else, unable to scrape together two full months' rent in advance, sleeping in a motel room for $20 a night—$600 a month instead of the $300 we were charging.

Even if Mr. B's story were true, why would Legal Services take this case? Is it so fully funded that this was the most pressing matter it was being asked to handle? Why not simply refer Mr. B to small claims court, or else to a personal injury lawyer? Why is this a matter for the taxpayers to fund?

(In truth, I was relieved it wasn't a personal injury lawyer taking the case, because he or she would then have had a financial stake in getting some money from the case, and might not have cared about our sincerity or credibility. But as it happened, Legal Services didn't seem to weigh these things either.)

And one last question. Why didn't Legal Services begin the process with a phone call or a letter, explaining in simple English its client's grievance, and asking us to make it right? Why proceed straight to a lawsuit? I guess the answer is that it's free to the client, and just a job to the lawyer—the more lawsuits he files, the more wars he starts, the more he's accomplishing.

The problem is that if Mr. B does win some money, and perhaps even if he doesn't, two messages go out. To us: Don't give people like Mr. B the keys. To him and his friends: It's easy to game the system. "Just go tell this nice attorney you've been abused, make it convincing, stick to your story, and you could do real well. They won't check your story, they won't charge you a dime. What's to lose?"

The great majority of poor people are honest and would sneer at such a scheme. But if only a million of America's thirty million poor do sometimes out of desperation or lack of scruples go for the easy buck, that's an awful lot of lawsuits.

### 5—Harvard-1997

Speaking of bleeding hearts and jerking knees, I was back up at Harvard Student Agencies after nearly thirty years, my old hangout— only the hangout had changed. Far from the dingy way-off-campus basement out of which we used to work—leased space I once proudly furnished with a $20 used rug—HSA had just moved into its own newly renovated building in the heart of the Harvard campus (the old "Elsie's" building, to those of you who remember it) at a cost, which they were now raising from alumni, of $4 million.

This is a cause I was pleased to support, not only because I more or less trace my vast fortune back to the young-communist-to-young-capitalist career shift HSA inspired, but also because of the practical good HSA does. To provide $1.4 million a year in student aid from an endowment would require $40 million. (That assumes a conservative distribution each year, with the balance left to keep the endowment growing in pace with inflation in perpetuity.) To provide it via student wages at HSA was going to cost one tenth as much, tops (I'm lobbying for less, with a mortgage), with the added benefit that kids will learn more from jobs at HSA than they do scraping food off trays working in the dining halls.

So there I was, happily inspecting what my contribution had

wrought. Specifically, I was inspecting the impact on this project of the various federal and local regulations designed—with the best of intentions—to provide equal access to the disabled.

And here is where bleeding heart meets jerking knee.

Surely, there is no question that in an ideal world the wheelchair-bound would encounter no barriers whatsoever. It was to move closer to such a world that regulations were adopted pertaining to new and renovated facilities. Keep an old building, and there's no problem. But renovate, as HSA had to do to accommodate the electrical and other needs of its various businesses, and you must conform to the new code.

That makes sense. But should there be room for judgment and waivers and exceptions?

The first thing the four-story building needed was an elevator. Never mind that few of the four-story dorms at Harvard have elevators. Never mind that Harvard students are almost overwhelmingly ambulatory. Or that the primary goal of HSA is not educational, but coldly financial: to provide the most possible student wages. The university could offer me no ready statistics, but the sense was that three or four students out of five thousand undergraduates might at any time be wheelchair-bound. If one of them wanted to work at HSA, he or she should certainly be able to do so. Yet might it have made sense to provide a guaranteed job to any wheelchair-bound student who wanted one—but a job that did not require access to the higher floors? Or even simply to provide the $2,000 a year such a student might have earned, rather than install the elevator?

To accommodate that one possible wheelchair-bound student each year in a higher-floor job—not an unimportant goal, mind you, but not HSA's *only* goal—significant costs were incurred. First, there was $100,000 or more for the elevator itself. Second, there was the space the elevator occupies—the equivalent of four small offices. Finally, there was the cost of the five-inch differential between the floor level of the Tennis & Squash Shop, to which HSA sublets space, and HSA's own ground level. To accommodate wheelchairs, the elevator required an extra stop. (Even though the wheelchair-bound generally do not play tennis or squash, they might reasonably want to buy gifts for friends that do.) However, the elevator's computerized sensors had no idea what to make of a five-inch "story"—even leprechauns require twelve-inch headroom. So in addition to the $15,000 or so it cost HSA to add the extra stop and the extra door (you enter at ground level, go up five inches, then exit through a back door into the Tennis & Squash Shop), the elevator company itself took a bath on the job. They wound up having to build a full-scale simulator in California to figure out how to keep their sensors from becoming confused.

And that was just the elevator. In addition, there were the eight mandated handicapped-accessible bathrooms, two on each floor, which also ate into office space. Might a single such facility have sufficed, given the elevator by which to reach it? And there was the cost of making all the thermostats inaccessible. That's right: *in*accessible. This was necessary because they had been placed at eye level throughout the building—perfect for most people, but too high to read from a wheelchair. They would either have to be moved, it was ruled, or else rendered equally inaccessible to all. The contractor wound up putting locked see-through covers over each thermostat, so only a "key operator" would have access. (HSA management might quietly issue keys to everyone, rather than heat or cool the whole building for the sake of the two students pulling an all-nighter on *Let's Go*. But at least the thermostats would retain the appearance of equal inaccessibility.)

The bleeding heart instinct to provide equal access at any cost is commendable. But before the knee jerks, the head should make some sort of logical analysis of the trade-offs. Might some middle ground have provided greater overall good?*

## 6—California-1997

All told, I had put something north of $250,000 into the auto-insurance crusade (plus another $150,000 loaned interest-free that—to my amazement—I eventually got back). But thinking back on it, I realized that the fight in California hadn't, at root, been between Ralph Nader and me. Neither one of us was personally threatened by the outcome. We're both rich. (Nader may or may not be a millionaire, as I and others suspect; but he is certainly rich

* For numerous other examples of trade-offs not considered, see, among others, Philip Howard's *The Death of Common Sense* and Walter Olson's *The Excuse Factor*.

in the sense he can have essentially anything he wants. If that's not rich, what is?) Rather, it was a battle between victims and lawyers. Ordinary people like Arthur Durone and Jeff and Mylene Reuvekamp.

### The Victim

Arthur Durone, a young underwater demolition specialist from San Gabriel, was riding his bike when he was hit by an uninsured motorist. He smashed into the grill of the car, the front windshield, and then flew over the top of the car as it sped off. The driver was not charged with leaving the scene of the accident because, as it happened, she basically pulled the accident along with her—Mr. Durone's hand had caught in the luggage rack of her Chevy Celebrity. He was dragged four tenths of a mile until the engine, damaged by the impact, conked out.

Amazingly, he lived.

Under today's auto-insurance system, he got nothing beyond the uninsured motorist coverage he had purchased. He lost all his savings. He lost his house. He moved in with his mother.

Under Prop 200's standard policy, he would have had all his medical and rehab covered, plus $30,000-a-year of lost wages, up to a combined limit of $1 million, plus up to $250,000 more in scheduled pain-and-suffering payments. All that for LESS than the cost of auto insurance today.

### The Lawyer

But victims aren't organized or, for the most part, skilled at debate. Lawyers are. As many thousands of trial lawyers as there are in California, that's about how many agents of deception there seemed to me were working against us.

For example, on January 9, 1996, the *San Francisco Chronicle* published a letter from one Jeff Reuvekamp. It was almost word for word from the literature of the lawyers, and it concluded by asking why non-Californians like me were "trying to force no-fault insurance [on the people of California]—*could it be the money?*"

What Mr. Reuvekamp didn't disclose in the letter—and this is what

I'd call the sneaky part—is that while he himself is not a personal injury lawyer, his wife, Mylene, is. So if Prop 200 passed, it wasn't my finances that would have been affected, as he implied—my finances wouldn't have been affected in any way. It was his. *He* was the one with the huge undisclosed stake in this. (The *Chronicle* chose not to reveal this when it was brought to their attention.)

I'm sure the Reuvekamps wish victims like Arthur Durone no harm. Nonetheless, their first concern is protecting their own livelihood, by whatever means it takes.

### The Letters

After we lost the election in March 1996, there were two ways of looking at it. One: that we had been trounced, 65–35. The other: that despite the Big Lie from the other side—your rates would go *up* 40 percent when in fact they'd go down—we got two thirds of the job done. We got two thirds of the votes needed for passage.

My first step toward getting the remaining third, and thus *succeeding* one day, was simply to tell the story of what had happened. To that end, what appears here as Chapter 4 was the October 1996 cover story of *Worth* magazine. There were even photos of Harvey and Ralph standing side by side in Hawaii, with leis around their necks, fighting to protect Hawaii's awful auto-insurance system against the Hawaii legislators, who had voted to fix it. And a photo of Ralph at a press conference with the nurses, who were used as a front in opposition to our proposition, and then paid $190,000 by the trial lawyers a week after the election.

True to form, Ralph did not respond. Debating these issues is beneath him. He told one friend he hadn't read the piece, but that I appeared to be "obsessed" with auto insurance. (Well, of course, he was right.) As if that would explain away the problem that two thirds of the $7 billion Californians pay for lawsuit auto insurance each year goes to lawyers and fraud. Or that those most seriously hurt recoup just 9 percent of their actual losses from that $7 billion pool.

Where were the answers to *those* problems? And why would they not obsess Ralph Nader, of all people, too?

Instead, Harvey Rosenfield wrote a long letter to the editor. Harry Snyder sent a letter, too (Appendix C).

The letter sent directly to *me* came from Harvey's protégé Jamie Court, on Harvey's Prop 103 Enforcement Project letterhead. Lest you dismiss it as coming from some rogue intern, note that when Ralph was asked by the Commerce Committee to present the case against S. 1860 (the bill that had been introduced by Senators Moynihan, Lieberman, Dole and McConnell), Ralph referred the request to Harvey and Harvey sent Jamie to Washington to testify to the United States Senate. So this is a man very directly in the (unofficial) Nader chain of command. In a sense, and by extension from Ralph, he represents the consumer movement.

(He was more than a little startled when—the eternal optimist—I went over at the hearing to introduce myself and shake his hand.)

He wrote:

September 30, 1996

Dear Farmer Andy:

After reading your twenty eight page version of your recent activities, we are convinced that you have become obsessed with no fault. Indeed, the only writing of yours that we can find in which you do ·not discuss no fault is in your book, "The Best Little Boy in the World." Did you use the pseudonym "John Reid" for that book just so no one would be confused about Andy Tobias writing on something other than no fault?

Sincerely,

Jamie Court

P.S. Since your award from the Consumer Federation seems to be your chief claim to consumer fame, we thought we might add a second honor. We have decided to suggest that the Merriam-Webster Dictionary folks consider the creation of a new word. See the attached letter. What do you think?

Before sharing that attached letter, I should explain that *The Best Little Boy in the World* came out in 1973, when books about being gay were much more frequently written under pseudonyms. It struck me as odd to have this raised in the context of a public policy debate over auto-insurance reform, although I am quite proud of that book, now in its seventeenth printing. (I also found his phrase "we are convinced that you have become obsessed" interesting, as the "we" would almost seem to encompass not only Harvey but Ralph, who had struck the same theme.)

Anyway, here is the letter Jamie attached, also on Prop 103 Enforcement Project letterhead:

September 30, 1996

Mr. Frederick C. Mish
Editor-in-Chief
Editorial Department
Merriam Webster, Inc.
PO Box 281
Springfield, Mass 01102-0281

Dear Mr. Mish:

We are writing to suggest a new word for inclusion in the next edition of the dictionary:

*tobiased—(1) to be slandered or to have one's actions falsely described or characterized in a long, obsessively-detailed statement written in a petulant, bordering on hysterical, voice; (2) to be the recipient of a series of twenty-page letters written in carefully-drawn block capital letters by lead pencil in three-point type with no punctuation marks.*

Example (1): "I told that strange old lady next door that she should stop numbering the discarded cans and bottles in my garbage can and the next thing I know she tobiased me in a letter to the local newspaper."

(2) "I got so tobiased by an old boyfriend I changed my address."

Please contact us should you require further information.

Sincerely,

Jamie Court

cc: Members of the United States Senate Commerce Committee
Board of Directors, Consumers Union of America
Board of Directors, Consumer Federation of America
State Insurance Commissioners, National Association of Insurance Commissioners

If they really sent out all those copies, that's a lot of work! ("Twenty-page lead pencil letters with no punctuation?" I can't handwrite three words without getting cramps, and punctuation is my passion.)

But again: Where is the part about how to keep two thirds of California consumers' $7 billion from being eaten up in legal fees and fraud? Where is the part about helping the most seriously injured crash victims to recoup more than just 9 percent of their losses from that $7 billion pool?

October 6, 1996

Dear Jamie:

It was nice meeting you in Washington. Thank you for your letter. I wish the same passion you put into demonizing me could be channeled, instead, into helping the 85 percent of seriously-injured crash victims who get nothing, or next to nothing, from today's expensive auto-insurance system. What are you doing for them? Why are the people in Michigan so stupid for having a system that covers most of their costs? Was *Consumer Reports* really anti-consumer for advocating this from 1962 through 1992? (As you know, CU has long advocated no-fault, and pronounced Michigan's the best auto-insurance system in the country.)

Unlike you, I don't get paid for my work on auto-insurance reform, and I don't get reimbursed for my expenses. If that's obsession, so be it. I'd rather be obsessed with fixing a terrible system than be paid to preserve it . . .

Best wishes,

Andy

To which Jamie responded—and this time on the issues, at least, so that I think you will see he is sincere:

October 17, 1996

Farmer Andy,*

You hardly need demonizing. Any multi-millionaire obsessed with abolishing pain and suffering compensation for even the most seriously injured accident victims demonizes himself.

---

* He refers to me this way not because he knows I . . . had a farm . . . in Iowa . . . but because he's convinced I am a shill for the insurance industry—the evil policyholder/owners of State Farm in particular.

I've spent my adult life fighting for low income people's rights and your twisted crusade to abolish compensation for those with dreams and promise but not much wage loss is antithetical to my values and those of a strong democracy. You front for State Farm in a crusade to take what is not yours. That demands comment.

Most disturbing is that you are very willing to sacrifice that form of compensation only affecting others with an eluvial certainty, an outright arrogance that you are in the best position to discard the rights of others, diminish them to the status of property. Though you can never know their pain and suffering, you make it worthless. It's no wonder, with such little empathy, that you are a second class writer.

You and your special California friend, Mikey Johnson, both have the same high-minded arrogance that seems to stem from the dementia of kids who didn't get enough of their mothers' attention [Geez, Jamie, I was *smothered* (in a nice way) by my mother's attention] and allows you to eliminate compensation for people and pain you will never know just to hear the applause of some group, even if it is State Farm. This narcissism is dangerous to those with little wages but serious injuries caused by the recklessness of another.

You are not so stupid as to believe that no fault has worked any- where [an awful lot of people believe it's worked in Michigan, and that Michigan is the only state that really *has* much of a no- fault law, other than in name] or to not realize that to make a system as draconian as that which you would propose would not come out of the hides of the most seriously injured, low wage accident victims to the advantage of the most profiteering insurers. In Michigan they would never abolish pain and suffering, in fact just a few years ago voters eliminated an insurer ballot bid to limit medical benefits (under Prop 200 insurers had that power to nix medical benefits). Take their compensation, their lawyers, their medical benefits, let welfare pay first . . . Sure sounds like a State Farm fetish to me. [This is not even a remotely fair characterization of Prop 200.]

You clearly have pecuniary ties to the Silicon Valley set. To curry the favor of those who provide great financial windfalls to you in the chip biz [unfortunately I was never in the chip biz, and was out of the software biz by the time Prop 200 rolled around], you've taken on a decades-old corporate crusade to vanquish those without your money and connections from the civil justice system. It's odious, it deserves comment and it will get much more.

Sincerely,

Jamie

PS An item for your therapist. You seem to trust insurers like father figures. Your beloved State Farm, for instance, has three generations of CEOs who are related to each other—does this sound like a policyholder-owned company to you. If you have a fixation on these monarchs, don't make the drivers of the nation pay for it, get some help.

PPS Save your money. You don't have to copy our materials to the poor souls on your mailing list. We are sending copies of all our materials to them—and many others.

There's a great deal there I'd take issue with, but the overriding issue is this: today California consumers pay so much in auto-insurance premiums that many, especially the poor, can't afford them. So clearly the solution is not to *raise* premiums. *Where, then, is better compensation for the most seriously injured to come from?* How do we get that 9 percent average number up closer to 100 percent or even beyond? The additional money can't come from the moon.

My solution: Redirect money that now goes to lawyers and fraud. Assure most people reasonable compensation for medical expenses, rehab, and wage loss, with the option to buy even more coverage, including an inexpensive add-on policy for scheduled pain and suffering.

Is it enough? No. But it's far better than what all but the luckiest few get if seriously injured today. Should the medical reimbursement be unlimited as in Michigan and, as in Michigan, should there be the right to sue in the most egregious cases? That would be fine with me, and if Jamie and Harvey and Ralph were pushing it, I would be applauding them and pushing right along with them. But such a system, with higher benefits and more suing, costs more. Is it fair to price coverage beyond the reach of low-wage people (who in Michigan do not get all these wonderful benefits unless they buy coverage)? I don't think so. And is it possible—realistically—to get voters to pass an auto-insurance reform that doesn't significantly cut premiums? I don't think that, either—especially when you know Ralph Nader and all the trial lawyers will be opposing you.

That's why we made the choices we did. And State Farm (against whom most of Jamie's animus is badly misdirected) did not call the shots or help in any way. I hope they will help the next time. The way I see it, State Farm management has a responsibility to its policy-holder/owners to do so.

Now, I know I'm again reaching the point where I'll be expected to pay you $1,000 for reading so much about my obsession, but lest you think Jamie is the only one in the extended Nader family with a liter-ary flair, let me offer just one more exhibit. *Feel free to skip ahead to the Golf* (page 155).

It is a handout that appeared on the second day of a symposium held in Washington in February 1997 to discuss Senate Bill 1860. Among the speakers at the small, relatively informal gathering were Senators Lieberman and McConnell, two of its sponsors, and a variety of other impressive (to me, anyway) characters from a wide political spectrum. A congenial representative from Ralph Nader's Public Citi-zen was in the room. If this bill *really* would save consumers money, he asked pointedly, why wasn't that guaranteed in the bill itself? (Actually, the bill did have a clause that would keep it from going into effect unless a 30 percent reduction in premiums was forthcoming.) At lunch I made a point of sitting with him. Did he doubt that Cali-fornia consumers paid a fortune for lawyers and fraud? Or that the most serious accident victims don't have millionaires to sue? He said he did not. OK, then: so what the heck was *his* solution?

He said he'd have to think about it, but that he hated to see any restrictions on the right to sue. (He was a lawyer who, though he worked for Public Citizen, described himself as working for Ralph Nader—"it's really about the same thing," he said, surprised, when I asked him about it.) We had a good discussion. Perhaps as one way of showing me he wasn't some radical nut, he told me that Harvey had asked him to distribute a flier that he thought was really . . . well, he refused to do it.

The second day, this fellow was absent, but a young man direct from Ralph Nader's own nerve center, the Center for Responsive Law, came by and left a pile of yellow one-pagers—presumably, the ones the Public Citizen lawyer had declined to distribute. The headline looked like this, only bigger:

Don't Be Fooled by the Academic Veneer—They Are

## PIGS

### AT THE
### INSURANCE INDUSTRY TROUGH

The body text was divided into three sections, the middle one being for me:

## Andrew Tobias

- Business/computer consultant and writer; former executive in National Student Marketing Corp., which collapsed amidst charges of financial wrongdoing.
- Promoter of three business and insurance funded initiatives on March 1996 California ballot to (1) impose no fault (2) prevent victims of financial fraud from suing swindlers (3) limits on plaintiff's lawyers fees. (Initiatives decisively defeated by voter).
- Works closely with State Farm to promote no fault proposals.
- Refuses to release tax return showing his sources of income.

The piece was unsigned. In small type at the bottom: "Sick of insurance hacks? Want more information? Write Insurance Reform, P.O. Box 7160, Santa Monica, CA 90406." Lest I have any doubt this was Harvey, he later faxed a copy to be sure I'd seen it.

To be a pig at the insurance industry trough, it seems to me, one would have to derive at least *some* tiny portion of one's income from that trough. At what point, one wonders, does enthusiastic advocacy cross over into the bounds of "malice" and reckless disregard for the truth? And libel aside, is this really what the consumer movement has come to?

Might it have been fair to point out that National Student

Marketing had collapsed twenty-seven years earlier, when I was twenty-two; that no one had leveled "charges of wrongdoing" at *me*; and that, far from trying to hide this saga, I had written a *book* about it? Does it matter that our initiatives *weren't* insurance-industry-funded, as the public record clearly shows? *I* put in more money than the insurance industry, which put in nothing, except for that one lousy $50,000 contribution from SunAmerica—and SunAmerica sells annuities, not auto insurance. And, no, Prop 201 would *not* have prevented victims of financial fraud from suing swindlers.

Works closely with State Farm? An exaggeration, but yes: I think State Farm's millions of policyholders have a right to expect much better than they're getting, and I'm not remotely embarrassed about working with State Farm to try to get it. What's so evil about mutual insurance companies, anyway? It's a customer-owned structure you'd think consumer advocates might favor. Though any large organization has flaws, State Farm couldn't be *that* horrible—with hundreds of insurance companies to choose from, more drivers choose it than any other, by far.

Refuses to release tax returns? I can't remember ever having been asked. I'd be happy to make not just my tax returns but all my financial records available for audit and responsible scrutiny—at my own expense if it turns out the claims I've made are untrue.

That was the deal I offered Harvey, who declined, and a fifty-three-year-old attorney named David Falvey, who read *Worth* and wrote a long letter demanding his $3.18 back (let us not forget the sales tax). My jaw dropped at the amount of time and effort he had put into this; so while I couldn't imagine he was serious about the $3.18, I scribbled a few comments on his letter and faxed it back. He wouldn't like my comments, I knew, but at least he'd know I had read his letter.

He took my reply and sent it to Ralph. Ralph passed it on to Harvey (in whom Ralph apparently continues to maintain complete trust), and Harvey sent Falvey a letter, which Falvey then faxed to me, along with another long letter of his own (". . . you are hobnobbing with the rich and famous who must be paying you through . . . subterfuge. I don't believe for one minute that you are paying to fight [for] the California initiatives . . .").

## 7—Golfing with Warren Buffett

Well, I *have* done a little hobnobbing in my day, as David Falvey alleges, and I thought I'd just better get this story out in the open before Harvey beats me to it.

A couple of years ago I went golfing with Warren Buffett. Sort of.

I was actually golfing at the invitation of my discount broker. It was the first time in my life I had ever golfed (and the first time in anybody's life to have been taken golfing by a discount broker). But this was a special case, and I learned a few things.

The first thing I learned, I guess, was "never go golfing for the first time in your life." Not that this hadn't occurred to me in advance.

"I never played golf in my life," I explained, when my host, a brokerage operation based in Omaha, as Buffett is, asked why I couldn't come.

"Don't worry! We're all terrible," he said.

He meant they had high handicaps, and this was for charity, the Emmy Gifford Children's Theater, and all in good fun—Warren Buffett's Second Annual Omaha Golf Day—and there'd be a bunch of senators and CEOs there, and everyone would get free golf shoes from Warren, America's second richest man, and it sure was tempting.

"You don't understand," I said. "I mean I have literally never played golf in my life. Other than miniature golf."

I play Scrabble. (So does Warren Buffett. I have never played him directly, but for a while there we were both playing Monty, a computerized game, on which he managed to rack up a 687-point score. I know, because he sent me a Polaroid. To save time, he reported, he'd have his secretary keep starting new games until Monty dealt him a seven-letter word.)

"No problem," my host assured me. And we went back and forth about five times until, against my better judgment and admittedly eager to make the trip, I gave in.

I could tell these were going to be a score of fearsome foursomes assembling in Omaha, in pedigree if not in handicap. Some of them might be lousy golfers, but all, from the sound of it, promised to be heavy hitters. Discount brokers being what they are, I was the heaviest hitter they could get.

"Buy me the most expensive pair of golf pants you can find," I

E-mailed my secretary. (Back then I had a secretary. Ah, how the mighty have fallen.)

"Who IS this?" she E-mailed back. (Little as I am known as a golfer, I am that much less well known to be a big spender. But now was not the time to send her rooting around the aisles of K Mart for golf pants.)

"And a belt and a shirt," I E-mailed back.

Never mind that these items came to $343.27. Green pants do not a golfer make. Though I sure look like a golfer, leaning on my club next to Warren—not only did we get free golf shoes (really handy, I guess, for dancing on your worst enemy's parquet), we got our pictures taken. For those of you who've never heard of Warren Buffett before—and it's interesting how many people have not—he's frequently on the cover of business magazines. Stock in his company has traded on the New York Stock Exchange as high as $48,600 a share. Buffett's a genius, but I've always felt the stock's been a little ahead of itself. I first advised people to buy Berkshire Hathaway—but only after it fell back a bit—when the stock was $300 a share. It never fell back. I advised much the same thing at $3,000 and then at $30,000. Instead of owning, say, twenty-five shares I could have purchased for $7,500, way back when, and having now $750,000 worth, I have a collection of his brilliant annual reports, the Polaroid of his Scrabble game and this framed photo of him and me—duffers.

During the eighteen holes, I asked penetrating questions of my host, the then president of Accutrade, my Omaha-based discount broker (well, *deep* discount broker, if you must know), such as: "Wouldn't it be a lot easier and more efficient if there were just one bag of clubs on the cart for all four of us?" His eyes widened imperceptibly and he pointed out that people come in a variety of different heights.

He was stuck with me, because all this had been his bright idea. But the other two members of the foursome, a former senator and a real estate mogul, had a slightly harder time dealing with me, I think (though not nearly so hard a time as our caddie, who emerged from the afternoon scraped, muddy and exhausted), and I was feeling really lousy—until we hit on the idea of playing for money. For me, this made it fun, and improved my concentration. My host and I played "scrambler"—going to whichever of our shots was the better and playing the next one from there—to their "best ball." If one of them shot a six and the other a five on a particular hole (am I saying this right?), they'd get credit for the five. But sometimes we did better, because usually we just went to my host's ball, but every once in a while he blew one and I actually got us a little farther in the right direction. We had them down $75 at one point.

The real saving grace was that, this event having taken over the entire course for the day, each foursome was quite separate from the others. The only witnesses to my shame were my partners—one of whose fault all this was in the first place—and the caddie. So it was bad, but it could have been worse.

Back in the clubhouse, where all the foursomes converged, everyone was jovially asking everyone else how he had played. The first couple of times I stammered something self-effacing. Then, I figured, screw it.

"How'd you do, young fella?" some billionaire asked me.

"Best damn golf I ever played."

"Really?" he said, a bit taken aback.

"Yep," I said, firmly. "I played the best damn golf of my life."

Well, I did.

(It is also the last damn game of golf I ever played.)

# 6

# YOUR VAST FORTUNE

## (And a Brief History
of the Universe)

### 1—Not the Only Investment Guide
### You'll Ever Need (But Close)

Make a budget, scrimp and save, pay off your credit cards, quit smoking, fully fund your retirement plan and start early—*tomorrow*, if you possibly can—putting away $100 or $500 or $5,000 a month, whatever you can comfortably afford, in two places: short- and intermediate-term Treasury securities, for money you might need in a few years; into no-load, low-expense stock market "index funds," both U.S. and foreign, for everything else. You will do better than 80 percent of your friends and neighbors.*

There's not much more to it than that. (Even so, I'd be deeply grateful if you blew $12 on *The Only Investment Guide You'll Ever Need*. Think of the shoeless Ecuadorian children you'd be helping.) Doing well with money isn't nearly as complicated as many believe. Largely, it's a matter of adopting good spending and saving habits.

---

* You can buy Treasuries through almost any bank or broker or through an excellent program called Treasury Direct—contact any Federal Reserve branch. A good source for index funds is Vanguard (800-662-2739) because it keeps expenses low. In the investment race, it has the lightest jockey.

You can have problems no matter how much money you've got. In fact, the more you've got, the richer your potential mix of problems. A college classmate earning $2 million a year once told me in complete seriousness that he couldn't imagine, frankly, how a family could live nicely in New York on much less.

Here's the trick (if it's too late for you, please write it on some young person's forehead—backward, for easy reading in the mirror): *A luxury once sampled becomes a necessity. Pace yourself!*

You say you don't particularly mind not having a remote-control clicker for your TV? I can state with some assurance, in that case, you've never had one. Touch-tone dialing? Caller ID? Microwave ovens? Seaplanes vaulting Friday-afternoon traffic? Stock markets that only go up 20 percent or 30 percent a year? These are things it's a cinch to be happy without before they've been invented; quite possible to be happy without even after they've been invented; but so awfully hard to be happy without once you've gotten used to them.

Pace yourself! Live a little beneath your means. Don't go into hock buying some whizbang&olufsen sound system right out of college; make do with one of those three-in-one $279 mail-order dealies I still use. Tease yourself with anticipation. Ease the fingers of your aspiration up the inner thigh of your cupidity. Tickle your fancy.

Of *course* money buys happiness. But both will last longer if you remember the importance of foreplay.

## 2—Your New Tailor

It is in this spirit I have to tell you how I discovered my tailor, in the all but certain knowledge he will become your tailor, too.

There we were one recent Sunday evening, men of considerable means, my boyfriend and I, knock wood, walking across Fifty-ninth Street. We were enjoying all the New York things one enjoys—the Plaza, for example—and dodging all the things best dodged.

(I normally dodge the horse-drawn carriages parked around the Plaza. But Charles not only likes horses, he actually *knows one of the coachmen.* Before you could say "Whoa!" we were feeding carrots to a very large horse. He'd just come from Pennsylvania—the horse—

and was now being trained for duty in and around Central Park. Much of the training, apparently, revolves around carrots. You feed the horse fourteen or fifteen bags of carrots at first—the horse can't get enough of them—so that he associates carrots with work and "work is where he wants to be." Then, once you've made your point, the coachman explained, you economize.)

Walking east, Charles and I began to encounter what appeared to be very large orange-vested crossing guards proffering some kind of handout. You see that a lot in the seedier parts of the city—LIVE! NUDE!—and for a moment it occurred to me that, what with the renaissance of Forty-second Street firmly under way, perhaps East Fifty-ninth Street was becoming the new porn district.

I doubted that, though, and I also felt bad for the handout people. After all, they weren't *looking* for a handout, they were attempting to eke out a living *handing things out.* So as Charles passed by, I grabbed one of the fliers and said thanks, fully intending to drop it in the next trash can. But then I started reading.

"Look!" I said.

It was a pink half-sheet for MEN'S SUITS—"Designer Suits at the Lowest Prices"—and I could see Charles begin to roll his eyes. When it comes to clothes, I am known to be a "lowest-prices" kind of guy. Mail-order, mostly. Charles, a big-time designer himself, has been trying to wean me away from that—and yet UPS keeps arriving with more bargains.

Anyway, before he could say anything, we had arrived at the address on the flier—118 East Fifty-ninth Street—and I was already walking up the stairs. (I might not walk a mile for a camel-hair coat, but I will gladly walk up a flight of stairs to save $400.)

There are people who spend $1,200 on suits. Indeed, I'm told it's possible to spend even more.

Not me.

The whole thing took fifteen minutes—two Fioravanti suits, $224 each. Free same-day alterations. Frequent-flier miles from the credit card.

Of course, you can get suits a lot cheaper than $224. But Bill Blass? Perry Ellis? Fioravanti? Ungaro? Thrift shops are an excellent alternative for the up-and-coming, but, being a man with a vast fortune, I speak here of *new* suits.

Even its name is economical: Men's Suits. Like an eatery called, plainly, FOOD. "Open seven days a week. All sizes. Large selection." With a location at 160 Broadway, also.

Here are my fashion tips:

- Bargain a little. (I didn't. I just asked the price. He said: $249, but if you buy two I'll take 10 percent off. So I did.)
- Ask for free alterations. (I didn't. My suits didn't need much work, so he volunteered to throw that in.)

I realize you may not be from New York. But who among us will not find himself (or his son or grandson) near the Plaza Hotel in the not too distant future? Let other tourists take their hansom cab rides at $34 for the first thirty minutes, plus tip. You march right on over and buy yourself a suit!

### 3—A Sigh Not Just a Sigh

And it's not just suits. You've got to learn to enjoy and exploit the difference between frugal and cheap.

Frugal is catching yourself before you say "and a Coke" as you place your order with room service if you notice Cokes in your minibar at a lower price (and not subject to service charge or tip). Frugal (or crazy) is running across the street in the morning to buy a couple of Cokes to restock the minibar before the guy comes to tick off what you've consumed. Frugal, indeed, is avoiding places with minibars in the first place. (If you haven't tried Marriott Residence Inns or Courtyard by Marriott, you don't realize how easy it is to save $60 a night. Not to mention Motel 6.) Frugal is turning off the lights when you leave the room.

Cheap is buying your wife something less nice than she'd like when you can easily afford to make her really happy. Cheap is leaving a 10 percent tip.

Well, just as you must learn to distinguish between frugal and cheap (cheap enters the picture, I think, when other people are involved, not just yourself), so, too, the distinction between negotiation and poor form. It's poor form to bluster or bully, wheedle or whine. It's *not* poor form to hide the depth of your desire, propose creative alternatives, or—I hope—to sigh.

That last tactic I unearthed by accident a long time ago, when my baby cousin was an executive at Pan Am. (Pan Am cratered, but my baby cousin went on to head up marketing for Hyatt, then United Airlines, then to captain a cruise line, and now runs Vail Resorts. His name is Adam Aron. He once turned down a top spot at Ramada Inns when he realized that his name, backward, spelled No Ramada.)

Adam called from Pan Am one day and asked, with the confidence of a man holding three aces: "How would you like a first-class round-trip ticket to Australia, plus a week at a luxury hotel, in return for making a breakfast speech?"

I didn't think of this as a negotiation—this was my baby cousin, whom I love dearly.

"Gee," I said. "I don't *know* anybody in Australia." I wasn't declining, by any means; just mulling over what it would be like to go halfway around the world alone.

"OK," said my cousin before I really had a chance to decide, "how about *two* round-trip first-class tickets?"

"Now you're talking!" I said happily. But it gets even a little better.

As the date of the trip and my breakfast speech approached, Adam called to say my visit was generating enthusiasm. (Either things were *very* dull Down Under, or else they were confusing me with someone else.) He wanted to know whether, on top of the breakfast speech, I'd be willing to have lunch with Pan Am's Sydney station manager and a couple dozen of the airline's best customers.

Obviously, I had to say yes. But . . . well, I'm kind of shy by nature (no, really), and my idea had been to do this one breakfast speech and then go see kangaroos.

Had I said "Yeah, sure" and sighed a bit, that would have been that. Instead, involuntarily and certainly not by design, I sighed a bit *first*. Then, just as the "Yeah, sure" was forming on my lips—the back of my tongue was already touching the roof of my mouth for the "yyy" sound—Adam said, "OK, I'll throw in a first-class round-trip U.S. ticket."

Which goes to show two things. First, Pan Am had a lot of empty seats, so the cost of all this to the airline was maybe $300 in extra fuel and meals. My speeches may not be great, but if George Bush is worth $80,000 on the lecture circuit, I'm worth $300.

Second, the smartest thing you can do in a negotiation, often, is keep your mouth shut. A kiss may be just a kiss, but a sigh—well, a sigh can be worth $2,200.

## 4—Giving It Away

So you have to be frugal (never cheap). You mustn't fear to negotiate (tastefully). You have to pace yourself, living a bit beneath your means to save the difference for a rainy day and a sunny retirement.* Also: buy low, sell high; never shop on an empty stomach; and don't forget your eeps: Sow that ye may reap. Look before you leap. Never make an important investment decision on less than seven hours' sleep.

If your fortune is not already vast, with dynamite advice like that it should be only a matter of weeks.

You're rich.

Which brings me to the topic of giving it away. You know the old line—there are no luggage racks on a hearse. But you may also know Andrew Carnegie's oft-quoted pronouncement: "It is more difficult to give money away intelligently than it is to earn it in the first place."

Carnegie thought giving was hugely important—"Surplus wealth is a sacred trust which its possessor is bound to administer in his lifetime for the good of the community." And yet he knew its limits—"There is no use whatever trying to help people who do not help themselves. You cannot push anyone up a ladder unless he is willing to climb himself."

He also had a few hundred million back in the days when even *one* million made you a millionaire (today: five, and just barely). But what of you and me, who do not have hundreds of millions?

The first thing to say is that no matter how much money you have, *it's your money*. You don't have to give away a penny of it.

The second thing to say is that, interestingly, rich people seem to take that first thing very much to heart.

---

* Yes, Social Security will be there, at least for people who really need it. But you don't want to be one of those people. See Appendix F—How Not to Fix Social Security (and Why We Don't Need a Balanced Budget).

Many are generous—some, like George Soros, magnificently so. But by and large, the rich are different from you and me: on an after-tax basis, as a proportion of their income, *they give less money.*

According to the IRS, the average itemized charitable deduction in 1994 was between $1,200 and $1,800 for itemizers who reported adjusted gross income between $15,000 and $75,000. That's pretty good, considering how tough it is to take care of your own family's needs these days on an AGI of $15,000 to $75,000.

Now go up to the $100,000–$200,000 adjusted gross income range. Yuppies, lawyers, doctors. Their average charitable deduction in 1994 was $3,420—less than 3 percent on average.

Now go up to the $200,000–$500,000 range. Surgeons, law partners, big-time corporate VPs. They averaged $8,372—still barely 3 percent.

Now go up to $500,000–$1,000,000. Small-time CEOs, trial lawyers. (Kidding—but some.) Now you're talking about enough money to pay almost any basic costs of living, so there's really a choice in how you allocate your funds between luxuries for your family and the needs of your community. Plus, you are very likely to be able to do your giving with appreciated securities, which makes it a lot cheaper than for the guy paying cash. They averaged $21,582. *Still* about 3 percent.

The IRS numbers I saw didn't go beyond $1 million, but the trend—a more or less flat 3 percent—hinted at no change as you continued up the scale.

In absolute terms, of course, this means the rich are much more generous than the rest of us—3 percent of $5 million is a heck of a lot more than 3 percent of $35,000. But because the $35,000-a-year family doesn't itemize deductions, that 3 percent is really 3 percent, whereas for a millionaire living in California or New York it is more like 1.6 percent after-tax. And the $35,000 family probably gives cash, whereas the millionaire gives appreciated securities (stock that's gone up, held more than a year), which provides yet more of a tax benefit. So you might say that, on a strict after-tax percentage basis, the rich give only about a third as much as the rest of us.

To be sure, the rich also pay a heck of a lot more in taxes, and many presumably feel that in so doing they've more than done their share. But the presumption here is that giving money, if one could afford to, is naturally something one would want not to do. Yet when you look at all that needs doing, and how tantalizingly close we are as a species to making this thing work (or else having it all blow up in our faces), it turns out that there's nothing some people would rather do than help. (And forgetting all that, look how happy it made Scrooge.)

No one need give a penny if he or she doesn't want to. It's just that those who don't, but could afford to, are missing out on one of wealth's greatest luxuries.

Why don't they give?

"I have often wondered," writes a friend who makes several million dollars a year, "why (some) 'rich' people don't give to charity. Here are my conclusions. Most of these were learned when I solicited funds for the pediatric intensive care unit I largely underwrote. Even with my underwriting, and offering to match two-to-one, this is what I found out." His list:

1. **Most people who are rich don't think they are.** They do not adjust to their new circumstances. If they started out poor, as did many, they are still into saving pennies, and cannot easily change their habits.

2. **Many cannot connect the dots between the giving and results.** They are too busy to do anything but work, and thus give to United Way or some other umbrella organization, and don't feel the connection. Those who have the time start the kinds of project I did. Mine came from a tragedy [the loss of a child], a catalyst I don't wish on anyone.

3. **Taxes.** When taxes approach 50 percent, as they do in some states, people feel they have "given at the office."

4. **Failure to identify.** When I was in eastern Russia, I could not get the money out of my pockets fast enough to give to the blue-eyed, blond children there. When I watch the Rwandan tragedy, I do not feel the same pull on my heartstrings that I do when I see kids who look like my kids. Notwithstanding our pediatric ICU serves mostly minority kids, it took me some time (six months, day to day) to identify with them (their parents never came to see them). While this may sound racist, I feel

there is a lot to it. People often give because ". . . there but for the grace of God . . . ," and they don't identify with [many of the needy].

5. **The rapid pace of change, both technological and societal, makes people anxious, and enhances their perceived need for economic security.** Storing chestnuts away for a long winter—a winter artificially lengthened by biotechnology for the Baby Boomers—may account for the growth in IRAs and mutual funds. They are worried about a life after employment with no government support, or at least none that they would like to think about.

"Good reasons," my friend suggests, surveying his list, "but not good enough."

In a sense I disagree. People don't need to find reasons to justify their not giving. As I say: it's their money. What they need to find is the inspiration to give. (For my lame attempt to supply it, see the Brief History of the Universe, below.)

But first let's take a minute to address the basic philosophical questions a donor has to deal with, as well as some mechanical issues.

*Philosophy*

Here are some of the key questions, it seems to me:

- **How much should I give?** Three percent of your adjusted gross income, like the typical American? Ten percent, as it says in the Bible? Thirty percent, which is ordinarily the IRS cutoff for deductibility (with the balance carried forward up to five years) when you give appreciated securities? Fifty percent (the cutoff if you give cash)? Everyone is different. Not having kids and living in a no-income-tax state—and possessing, after all, a vast fortune—it's easy for me to give a lot more than most. Still, it does seem as if the proportion should rise with income—that those earning big bucks are better able to give a large percentage than those barely scraping by. There is no "should" if giving is voluntary—it's not like tipping, where it's theoretically voluntary but you basically have to leave 15 percent. (You saw the *Seinfeld* where Elaine's dad leaves 4 percent? Ouch!) If you really want someone to tell you how much is enough, I suppose you could do worse than to take a tip from God. God says: 10 percent. Then again, He may not have been figuring FICA into the burden you already have to bear.

- **When?** Warren Buffett's plan is to do most of his giving after he's gone, perhaps on the theory that every dollar he gives now is twenty or forty he won't be able to give later—he surely compounds wealth faster than any charitable foundation could. Yet, ironically, the cause he's singled out for special attention (as have other smart folks like Ted Turner and the late David Packard)—population—has a certain compounding dynamic of its own. It took ten thousand generations (not years, generations) for the human population to reach a billion. Now it swells by an additional billion every dozen years. Not being able to compound my money at anything like the rate Warren Buffett makes look easy, I figure I'd better not wait. I support **Zero Population Growth**, 1616 P St., Washington, DC 20036 (www.zpg.com).

Those who reserve most of their giving for after they're gone, investing wisely in the meantime, are doing two things. They're providing security for themselves on the off chance they need to stretch their fortune way beyond normal—to age a hundred or beyond. And they're providing a sort of discipline in denying the needs of desperate people and urgent causes now, investing instead in the needs and causes of tomorrow. We need both. If everyone gave away everything he had now, and for current needs—you might call it the War on Poverty—it wouldn't necessarily have the desired effect, and would in any event sap strength from tomorrow. If *no one* gave now, there might not *be* a tomorrow.

- **For "now" or endow?** Even if you decide to give a lot of money today, do you provide it for current use or as a contribution to an endowment that will throw off a small sliver each year? Again, the world needs both. The more we put aside for the future, the brighter it will be—but if we care so much about people's future well-being, how can we ignore their well-being, or misery, today?

- **Can we really allocate funds more efficiently than the government?** "Yes!" I hear you cry. But it's an interesting question. Certainly it's more fun to control the money ourselves, and to give it and get a thank-you rather than have it taken away. But as easy (and important) as it is to find examples of government waste, consider that many charities spend 35¢ of each dollar just getting that dollar. The tax authorities spend more like 2¢. And how well do nonprofits spend the rest? Some, very well; others, with good intentions but appalling inefficiency and/or lack of result. The reasons I like **Smokefree Educational Services, Inc.** so much (375 South End Avenue, NY 10280), apart from its mission, are first that it's been so effective getting cigarette ads removed from the New York subways (the city's "school bus") and cigarette vending machines banned (the easiest way for ten-year-olds to buy cigarettes) and New York restaurants to go smokefree, among many other accomplishments; but second that it has almost no overhead. The "staff" both work for free; the "office space" is provided gratis; there are no benefit galas and thus no invitations to print or caterers to pay—kind of like a deep discount broker or a low-expense no-load mutual fund (or a good no-fault auto-insurance system): it keeps its transaction costs low. Almost your entire dollar goes to work doing what you hoped it would.

- **To whom?** Of course, there's no one right asset allocation among nonprofit organizations and "causes" any more than there's a single right asset allocation among investment types or a single right portfolio of stocks. But that's no reason not to try to get the most bang for your social investment buck. In a world of limited resources, tough choices are unavoidable. Even if you don't think you're making them, you are. Money you give to help the elderly is money you don't have available to help the orphanage or the tutoring program. Money you give to help your kid's school put on a play is money you can't give to help it buy new computer equipment.

The two things *I* like to see in a social investment are, as mentioned, low overhead and fund-raising costs. But even more important: *leverage*. For $10,000, you can perhaps supply one person with AIDS the drugs he or she needs for one year. It's something that cries out to be done, and I do try to do some of it; but it provides no leverage. For the same $10,000 to **MESAB**—Medical Education for South African Blacks (120 Albany Street #810, New Brunswick, NJ 08901)—you can provide the funds to train a nurse, or almost half a doctor (six years of medical school in South Africa with room, board and books comes to around $25,000). By now, MESAB's assistance has helped to train something like 10 percent of all the black medical professionals in South Africa. The leverage here, of course, is that each additional young medical professional will impact thousands of lives in his or her community, both in specific illness-curing and lifesaving situations, but also in helping to educate on general issues of health and hygiene. Not to mention helping South Africa, in a tiny way, to build a successful multiracial, tolerant society that one day could be a model for the rest of Africa and beyond.

Just how you allocate your funds between general "asset classes" (to continue with the investment analogy) is the first part of the decision. Education, health, civil rights and auto-insurance reform are my four biggest, but for someone else it might be the church and poverty or the environment and the arts. Then there is the issue of which specific "securities" are the best buys in each class.

Obviously, most people—including me—aren't this methodical in their decision process. They give to their friends when asked; they're true to their school; and they react spontaneously from time to time when they see something particularly poignant in the newspaper or on TV—the equivalent, I suppose, of acting on a hot tip. Some, unfortunately, fall for the phone sales pitches of police organizations and the like, some of which, unfortunately, entail huge commissions to the salesman.

Still, one can "play the market" haphazardly with some of one's money while still attempting to have a rational, effective plan for the rest. For what it's worth by way of example, let me run through the highlights of the civil rights sector of my portfolio, to which I devote maybe 10 percent of the total.

Thirty years ago, that same 10 percent would have been appropriate for the civil rights struggle of blacks. But by now, though a huge racial problem remains, our laws and culture, if not all our hearts, have been transformed. The fundamental work has been done. So today, my favorite black-oriented group is **Xavier University** (New Orleans, LA 70125), which does a great job of targeting mostly African American kids, many of whom go on to teach math and science in inner city schools—leverage.

But if the basic framework of equal rights for most Americans is pretty well established, that's not the case for gays and lesbians—though we've made amazing progress in the last decade. As I write this, employers can still fire you in most parts of America simply because you're gay; and lifelong partners can't necessarily even visit each other in the hospital, because they are not family, let alone married. But all that is changing, and that's where I put most of my civil rights dollars today. In my view, you don't have to be black to support Bob Moses's innovative **Algebra Project** (99 Bishop Richard Allen Dr., Cambridge, MA 02139)—my old high school math teacher is decades back from the struggle in Mississippi, working to improve the math skills of inner city kids. You don't have to be Jewish to support Steven Spielberg's astonishing **Shoah Project** (Box 3168, Los Angeles, CA 90078). And you don't have to be gay or lesbian, or even have gay or lesbian friends or relatives, to support this handful of organizations—all but the last of which provide amazing leverage:

**GLSEN**—The Gay, Lesbian, Straight Education Network (121 West 27 Street #804, New York, NY 10001). Kevin Jennings grew up poor in Appalachia, went to Harvard College on scholarship, taught school for ten years, founded GLSEN in 1994. It now has sixty-two chapters around the country. The idea is to help teachers spread a message of tolerance. Olympic diving gold-medalist Greg Louganis and actress Susan Sarandon are among those on its Board of Advisors. GLSEN's current budget is $950,000, much of it in tiny amounts from teachers around the country. The leverage here is clear: if you can reach thousands of teachers, and thereby hundreds of thousands of high school kids, you can affect their attitudes for the rest of their lives, and the attitudes they pass on to their kids. The "agenda": tolerance and mutual respect.

**IGLHRC**—International Gay & Lesbian Human Rights Commission (1360 Mission St. #200, San Francisco, CA 94103). This organization is run by Julie Dorf, a wonderfully cheerful, dedicated, bright young woman. I was turned on to it by Barney Frank's partner Herb Moses, one of its founders, and have supported it enthusiastically ever since our trip to Russia to try to strike down Stalin's awful Rule 121. It attempts to project America's example of tolerance and freedom to countries throughout the world; to nurture nascent civil rights movements in other countries; and to focus attention and pressure on emergency situations. Again, with about a $500,000 budget, the leverage is huge. And with E-mail and the Internet and so forth, the ability to make that money stretch around the globe is a lot greater than it could have been even ten years ago. When you think about it, something on the order of 5 percent of the world's population is probably gay or lesbian—perhaps 300 million people, most of them living in fear and repression.

**Lambda Legal Defense Fund** (666 Broadway, New York, NY 10012) and the **ACLU Lesbian & Gay Rights Project** (132 West 43 St., New York, NY 10036). The leverage with these is twofold. First, representing individual gays and lesbians in civil rights cases affects the rights of everyone else. (In Dr. King's words: "Injustice anywhere is a threat to justice everywhere.") Second, both benefit from a great deal of volunteer legal work. As large as Lambda's budget is—a little over $3 million—it would be several times larger if all the pro bono legal time it organizes had to be paid for.

**HRC**—The Human Rights Campaign (1101 14th St., NW #200, Washington, DC 20005). This is the basic and wonderfully successful gay and lesbian rights group that's emerged under the strong leadership of Elizabeth Birch, who used to be Apple Computer's senior litigation counsel. She has ramped it up from a hundred thousand members to two hundred thousand on its way to a million, straight folk as well as gay, just as civil rights organizations have traditionally included a lot of white people as well as black. It's HRC that is spearheading the effort for ENDA, the "Employment Nondiscrimation Act" that forty-nine senators have endorsed. Right now, in most parts of America, you can be fired simply for being gay. ENDA says: No, you can't. If you haven't done anything wrong, your sexual orientation is irrelevant. HRC's budget is large—$10 million—but the $20 it costs to join is a way of basically signing on to the issue.

If you're horrified by all this, and even if you're not, let me be very clear: I'm not suggesting that you contribute to any or all these groups. I'm just sharing some "stock tips." Like most tips, you will and should ignore them, pursuing, instead, your own investment goals.

### Mechanics*

Whatever you choose to support, if anything, there are a few things to keep in mind. Most important, if you give money in sizable chunks: you'll save a lot in taxes by giving appreciated securities instead of cash. Not only do you get the tax deduction for the gift, you avoid the capital gains tax that otherwise would have been due. In the case of a stock you bought for $1,000 that's now worth $10,000 (oh, happy day), you'd save $2,520—28 percent federal tax on the $9,000 gain— and possibly some local tax as well. (The savings will be less great, of course, if the capital gains tax rate is cut, as at this writing seems likely.) But be careful:

- Be certain to have your broker transfer the stock to the charity *before* she sells it. If the stock is held in your name when it's sold, you pay the tax.

- Be certain you've held the shares (or the building or the painting) *at least a year and a day,* or the IRS will allow you to deduct only your original cost—you'd *lose* a big chunk of your charitable deduction.

Of course, this doesn't make sense for small gifts. Apart from the hassle, the commission a charity would have to pay to sell $250 or $500 worth of Microsoft could easily eat up 10 percent or 15 percent of the gift. But if you're someone who likes to give $250 or $500 a year to several different charities, there's a solution. Open an account

* Apologies to readers of *The Only Investment Guide You'll Ever Need,* from which this is lifted.

with the **Fidelity Investments Charitable Gift Fund** (800-682-4438). Transfer your $10,000 worth of stock to that account, for which you get an immediate charitable deduction, just as if you'd given it to the Red Cross. Then, from time to time, mail or fax instructions to Fidelity. They'll send out checks on your behalf as small as $250, investing the balance in the meantime in your choice of four different kinds of funds—so you may have even more to give away than you planned.

This is the poor man's way to set up a charitable foundation—the Ford Foundation, the Rockefeller Foundation, and now *Your* Foundation. Almost.

Fidelity's Gift Fund is also handy if you should get a windfall. Say you exercised the last of your Microsoft stock options this year and reaped $400,000, of which you'd like to give $100,000 to charity. The Charitable Gift Fund could be perfect. After all, there you are, a young receptionist who just happened to be with Microsoft from the beginning. If you gave all $100,000 to your favorite charities this year, you'd be showered with love and appreciation—and *deluged* with requests next year. But what could you give next year? You're still a receptionist, albeit a darned good one, and you make $26,000 a year. But suddenly the people you gave $5,000 to last year are expecting $6,000 this year . . . and you were thinking more along the lines of $50, which for a guy or gal making $26,000 is a very nice gift. They'll hate you!

With $100,000 in the Gift Fund, you might decide to distribute $5,000 a year—out of the growth in the fund itself, with any luck, perhaps never dipping into the $100,000 at all. That way, you are perceived as a very generous person indeed—how many receptionists make $5,000 a year in donations?—and can enjoy and refine your giving over the years without undue stress.

### *Charitable Fine Points*

- If you've given $250 or more to a charity, you'll need a receipt—not just your canceled check. Most charities send them automatically, but it's your responsibility to get them and keep them if you're ever audited. It's not good enough to get them a year or two later, when the audit notice comes—the receipts must be dated no later than the date you file the tax return claiming them as deductions.

- Receipts are supposed to make clear that you received nothing of significant value in return for your contribution, or else disclose the fair value of what you did receive—e.g., $60 of your $150 benefit ticket went for food and entertainment. You get to deduct only $90 even if you have witnesses who will swear you ate just *one dinner roll* the whole night and fell asleep three words into the after-dinner speech.

- If you give something other than cash, the charity is expected to provide only a description of the goods, not an estimate of their value. That's your job. Back when he was governor, President Clinton valued a pair of old shoes at $80. Your old shoes might not have the same cachet, and will almost surely be smaller, so you might value them at somewhat less.

- If you're giving something (other than marketable securities) valued above $5,000, an appraisal is usually required. Testimony from your aunt who knows antiques ("GAWgeous!") will not do it.

- If you go to a charity auction and buy a Warhol print, or the actual Bic used by Paul Simon to pen "Bridge Over Troubled Water," you are entitled to deduct only that portion of your check, if any, that exceeds the fair market value of what you purchased. So if the estimate in the auction catalog is $1,500 and you snag it for $900, you get no charitable deduction.

- If you're planning to leave some money to charity when you die, and if you have an IRA, consider naming that charity as the beneficiary of your IRA. That will save the income tax your heirs would otherwise have to pay on it. Give your heirs "regular" money from outside your IRA instead—money on which income tax has *already* been paid. To the charity it won't make any difference (charities don't pay taxes); but to your heirs it will.*

---

* One small drawback: with a charity as the beneficiary, you might be required by IRS regulations to withdraw money from the IRA faster, once you turn seventy and a half, than if, say, your spouse were the beneficiary, thus exposing more of it to taxation.

- If you have a ton of dough and are planning to leave some of it to charity, there are tax advantages, once you're in your later years, to giving it while you're still alive. You give the cash (or the appreciated property) now, but arrange to receive all the income from it as long as you live. In the meantime, you get a tax deduction—now—for the "present value" of your gift. If you're eighty-five, the present value is nearly as high as the gift itself, because the IRS doesn't realize you're one of those feisty old codgers who're going to play tennis for another twenty years. If you're fifty, there's no point bothering with this, because the present value of your gift will be very small. But you might want to mention it to your folks. Almost any large charity will eagerly walk you through the basics of this. And then you might want to discuss it with your accountant and the attorney who prepared your will.

- For reports on specific charities, call the Council of Better Business Bureaus (703-276-0100) or send them $2 and a self-addressed envelope for a free copy of *Give but Give Wisely*, which rates charities across twenty-two parameters (4200 Wilson Blvd., #800, Arlington, VA 22203). Or write the National Charities Information Bureau for its free *Wise Giving Guide* (19 Union Square West, New York, NY 10003).

### 5—Socially Responsible Investing

Forget it. By and large, I've always been fairly cold-blooded about this—the notion of shunning investments in companies that have subsidiaries in South Africa (back before the fall of apartheid) or that make cigarettes or bombs. I think I'm as antiapartheid, antitobacco, and antibomb as most, but that limiting my investment choices will ordinarily do no good at all (except maybe to make *me* feel good), while reducing the returns I can earn and then contribute to fight apartheid, tobacco or bombs.

What's more, if you do buy shares in a company doing something you find objectionable, you can vote against management if and when a shareholder resolution is presented to stop it. Not that these ever win, but sometimes management does notice.

I would never buy a new issue of stock or bonds from a tobacco company, because that might in some small way help raise the money needed to build a new cigarette factory. But the tobacco companies (to continue with this example) are awash in cash, so my buying their securities in the secondary market will in no practical way help them—while the considerable profit I once made speculating on R. J. Reynolds zero-coupon bonds, bought at a huge discount long after they had been issued, was a dandy source of funds to finance anti-tobacco activities. (While it's hard to know which dollars are which, in my mind it was those particular dollars that paid for a full-page ad in *The New York Times* and *The Washington Post* headlined: MEET FIVE OF AMERICA'S BIGGEST DRUG PUSHERS. It pictured well-known multibillionaires—magazine magnates and tobacco titans—who make a fortune selling an addictive drug that is the nation's leading cause of preventable death. My favorite part of the ad was in the style of a Surgeon General's warning box at the bottom: "What do all five of these men have in common?" it asked. "Like most drug pushers, they're smart enough not to use the product they sell. Not one of them smokes cigarettes.")

So you can see I have been something of a skeptic when it comes to clearly well-intentioned but, in my view, merely "feel good" mutual funds that promise to shun the bad guys. Collectively, they have so little clout as to be infinitesimal.

That said, some of them have done rather well. While one can see little logical advantage in limiting the range of investment opportunities, many of the companies considered most socially responsible often seem to be the most forward-thinking—e.g., the high-tech companies—and have been among the best to invest in. So at least lately, screening on the basis of social responsibility may not be a handicap at all. It could be a plus.

The plus could in some small measure be because good social policy improves morale or attracts more of the best people. (For example, IBM recently extended spousal benefits to same-sex couples. That could encourage a brilliant gay man or lesbian to join or stay with IBM. It would be less likely to cause someone outstanding to quit or fail to apply. So in that sense, IBM improves its position in the competition for talent.) Good social policy could also suggest a wider vision and a greater motivation. Or fewer regulatory actions and liability suits down the road.

Then again, if your competition is packing more chickens into the coop, to their discomfort but your lower costs; or using live bunny rabbits to test something quickly that you test in a more humane, roundabout way; or you subcontract to Chinese prison labor in order to get your costs down—in these and countless other ways, the less "socially responsible" company might be able to bring goods to market faster or cheaper than the competition, and thereby reward its shareholders with higher profits.

So it's not at all clear that past success achieved by social screening equals future success. But it's possible. And worst case, with a universe of choices this broad—many hundreds of companies in a great many industries usually qualify—it's unlikely you'd be sacrificing much.

And there are other potential ironies. Is a company that produces life-saving drugs, but sells them much cheaper abroad than in the U.S., gouging its richer U.S. customers, or practicing a sort of Marxian strategy of "from each [nation] according to its ability [to pay] to each according to its need?" Or what of George Washington's dictum that "to be prepared for war is one of the most effectual means of preserving peace"? If true, might our top military defense contractors not be the best antiwar bet of all?

Finding the moral high ground ain't always simple.

## 6—A Brief History of the Universe

People with money are stewards of capital. We either spend it, invest it or give it away. It's ours, so whatever we do with it is our business. But then again, few of us could have amassed surplus wealth, whether it be $20,000 or $20 million (or $20 billion, in a couple of cases), all by ourselves, simply by the sweat of our brow or our transcendent brilliance. Robinson Crusoe did pretty well by himself even before Friday turned up, but he was no millionaire. Like it or not, we are all part of an economic fabric without which appreciable wealth would be impossible.

The people I admire feel a responsibility to spend, invest and donate wisely. Sure, the occasional whim seasons the stew—and if you have a billion dollars, then a million here and a million there is a not unreasonable whim. But by and large, it's painful to see money wasted, because waste—whether it involves leaving the TV on when no one's watching or digging holes only to fill them up again—impoverishes us all.

This matters because we happen to be alive at the most extraordinary time in human history. Consider: the universe exploded into existence twenty billion years ago, or so they say. I find this hard to believe, in part for all the obvious reasons (could Bill Gates really have $1.75 for every year since the beginning of the universe?) not to mention the logical headaches (where did it come from?), but I am one of the millions of readers who stopped understanding Stephen Hawking's *A Brief History of Time* midway through Chapter 4, so let's just assume it's true.

For the first fifteen billion years, nothing happened.

Then—they say—the Earth was formed. That was about five billion years ago, give or take.

Now, to put this in a scale we can more or less comprehend, imagine that one century equals an inch. A hundred years—an inch. On that scale, the Earth was formed 789 miles ago. *Milwaukee*, if you live in New York. *Denver*, if you live in L.A. *New Orleans*, if you live in Chicago.

And every hundred years, since the Earth was formed, you moved one inch closer to today.

I know this sounds like the story of the bird that lives on the cliff above the beach. (Every hundred years, it flies down from its perch and eats one grain of sand from the beach. When the bird . . . [pause for effect] . . . has eaten all the sand on the beach . . . [pause and then intone solemnly] . . . *one second of eternity shall have elapsed.*) I love that story.

The difference is, *this* story is real, as best we know. One century, one inch, 789 miles, give or take, since the Earth began.

The first four billion and some years nothing happened. Oceans, mountains, DNA maybe—don't hold me to exact dates. But it was really, really slow. One inch a century. That brought you to around Scranton or Death Valley or Indianapolis.

Oh, sure, life was evolving, but it would be another eight hundred million years or so before you got your dinosaurs, and a hundred forty million years more till they disappeared—which brings us, sixty million years ago, just nine miles or so from today.

And in the 59.9 million years after that, bringing us up to a hundred thousand years ago, and eighty-three feet from where you're sitting, *still* nothing much happened. Early man had evolved and, I don't know, maybe he had invented primitive language, maybe fire, maybe the wheel.

Finally, inching along, century by century, about half a foot away, we came up with printing, and a few inches later, steam.

But my point is this: in the last inch and a half—the last one hundred fifty years—we have invented *everything*. Electricity, automobiles, radios, television, computers, faxes, airplanes, lasers, microwaves, Velcro—everything. And it's only accelerating. As with any unimaginably complex jigsaw puzzle, the first pieces take forever to link. But as more pieces fit, the faster and faster it takes shape. We are mapping the human *genome*. (Decades ago, don't forget, with by now ancient technology, humans *walked on the moon*.) We are cloning living beings; freezing others, with the prospect, one day, of bringing them back to life.

None of this makes any sense whatever to me as a layman, except in one very obvious overall way. Namely, that we are either at the beginning or the end of the human species, for all practical purposes—we will in the next inch or so either screw it all up, *à la* nuclear winter or the release of some plague to end all plagues, or else we will launch ourselves into the dawn of an entirely new era (and even one day get enough human consciousnesses off this physical globe so that, should some comet bopp into us one day, all will not be lost).

This huge long journey that began with the formation of our planet 789 miles ago, proceeding century-long inch . . . after inch . . . now has reached what really appears to be the climax.

So?

So what we do matters.

There are dozens of persuasive political and economic philosophies, and I certainly don't pretend to know for sure which is best. But I know this: whatever your politics or ideology—or even your religion—waste is bad. Waste impoverishes us all.

Thus, without being slavish or ridiculous about it, a good starting point for anyone in stewarding his or her money, it seems to me, is to try to spend, invest, and donate wisely. At worst, it will do no good (I think it will do lots of good). But where's the harm?

Just a few words here to note that waste is not all of a single kind or severity. For example, if I get a parking ticket I've learned not to let it bother me. So long as I wasn't blocking traffic or creating a hazard, what difference does it make? Instead of feeding a quarter in the meter, I send the city $35. The money doesn't disappear, and given what I already pay in taxes, another $35 is so trivial as not to be worth a second thought. No appreciable resources have been wasted, no appreciable human effort misdirected. (Yes, there's the meter maid, but it's unrealistic to think that a change in my behavior will obviate the need for meter maids—more likely they'll soon invent some sort of "wand" that can be quickly passed over the meter and your license plate, automatically printing and mailing you a ticket, and perhaps debiting your checking account.)

But compare that with the time my car was parked eighteen inches too close to a fire hydrant (but I *swear* there was still plenty of room—honest!). Instead of a ticket, my car was towed, and damaged in the process. The $125 ticket and $75 in towing fees and all that weren't the waste. It was damaging a perfectly good car that was a waste; and all the time (and a bit of fuel) involved in towing the car and then my having to go and retrieve it, and the paperwork, and . . . it wasn't the stuff of an NBC special report. But *this* was what I mean by waste.

Leaving a tool outside to rust is a waste.

Burning fuel into the air to power a Sea-Doo is a waste—but it's so damn much fun, it's one of those trade-offs that's not so simple. Part of the trick may be to build the "externalities"—the awful racket Sea-Doos make, the pollution they cause, the cost of disposing of them when they're eventually junked and wash up on some seashore—into the price of driving them.

Long brisk walks are less wasteful than unused treadmills and Exercycles. (If you use yours, that's different. But most of the exercise machines I've bought over the years become tie racks.)

Spending money on a fancy dinner isn't a waste, in the sense that you're simply transferring most of it to other people—you're satisfying one another's needs. (In this country, given our resources, capital and technology, we'd need relatively few people just to feed, clothe and house us. The rest of the jobs, so long as we enjoy or profit from the products and services they create—in which group I would not include the services of a lawyer when you're bleeding after a car crash—are valuable too. Man does not live by bread alone.)

Digging for gold is a waste. After all, gold's value lies largely in its scarcity. (We have more than enough already for our industrial and decorative needs.) Digging up more only makes it less scarce.

Building casinos may add some measure of happiness to the lives of those who enjoy gambling, but would seem to be a lot less productive then building a factory or a school or a research lab.

And so on. You get the idea. And your judgment in assessing wastefulness is just as valid as mine—and we may differ. But it's an assessment we six billion Earthly denizens should perhaps routinely make. To me, spending $5 billion a year in the U.S. to *promote* the leading cause of preventable death is a waste. Bulldozing a clubhouse and filling in a perfectly fine pool—only to one day rebuild it—is a waste. And you already know past all patience what I think about that *other* obsession of mine. With luck, one day there will be a postscript. In America, anything is possible.

$$$$$$$$$$$$$$$$$$$$$$$$$$$$$$$$$$$$$$$$$$$$$$$$$$$$$$$$$$$$$$$$$$$$$$$$$$$$$$$$$$$$$$$$$$$$$$$$$$$$$$$$$$

# APPENDICES

APPENDIX A

# Props 201 and 202

### Prop 201—The "Strike Suit" Initiative

A stock drops sharply on bad news, and virtually the next morning the company is hit with a class action suit alleging securities fraud—a so-called "strike suit."

Typically, the suit isn't filed because an angry shareholder calls a lawyer. Quite the opposite. Most are initiated by a small group of lawyers who keep a Rolodex of small shareholders they can use as "named plaintiffs." One such shareholder has reportedly been a named plaintiff in thirty-eight different suits. According to the American Electronics Association, *every one of the top ten public companies in Silicon Valley has been hit with one of these suits* (though neither Tom Proulx nor Intuit). Is the whole high-tech community a bunch of crooks?

Once hit, the targeted company has a choice: It can fight and probably win (but you can never tell what a jury will do)—which costs millions and takes a tremendous amount of time. Or it can just pay a few million dollars to make it go away. Bet the company and go to war or just pay the lawyers' toll. Almost everyone grits his teeth and pays. And while this actually winds up *hurting* shareholders, it's a *phenomenal* business for a small group of lawyers.

There's plenty of real securities fraud out there, and lawsuits are an important way not just to compensate its victims (if there's anything left with which to do so) but also to deter securities fraud in the first place. It's important to keep that threat real. (It's also important to put the occasional swindler behind bars for a while.) The trick is to discourage the extortionate "strike suits" without shutting off the legitimate ones. Prop 201 would have done this for California by requiring the loser to pay the winner's legal fees—but only in this very limited niche of the law, and with safeguards. (It required the judge to waive "loser pays" when there were reasonable grounds for bringing the suit even though it lost. And the "little guy" wouldn't have to join the suit and risk a dime to get his full 100 percent pro rata share of any settlement.) Prop 201 lost.

Congress's strike-suit bill, which addressed the problem at the federal, but not the state, level, passed over the howls of some of the Democratic party's largest contributors (like strike-suit king Bill Lerach, whom Common Cause singles out as having given $382,500* and being "a White House regular"). When the bill got to President Clinton's desk, he halfheartedly vetoed it—and, for the first and only time in his presidency, was overridden. So the strike-suit problem is now less severe at the federal level, with more of these suits brought in state court instead.

## Prop 202—The Lawyer-Fee Limit on Early Settlements

With Prop 202, when an acceptable settlement offer was forthcoming from the defendant within sixty days of receiving an initial "demand letter," the lawyer couldn't take more than a 15 percent slice. If there was no early offer, then the lawyer's compensation would not be limited in any way. Nothing would change from today.

Interestingly, if there was a *low-ball* early offer—as there often is today—under Prop 202 lawyers would be far less tempted to urge acceptance and grab a quick fee. They'd get only 15 percent, versus today's typical 33 percent. But because they could charge 33 percent, 40 percent, even 50 percent on anything *extra* they won by rejecting the low-ball offer and fighting for more, they'd have exactly as much

* That was to the federal effort. His firm gave more than $1.9 million to fight Prop 201.

incentive as today to fight hard for their clients. Same incremental effort; same incremental reward.

Not only might this scheme net victims more money, faster; it could even help a bit to unclog our courts.

Yet what struck me about this idea, when I first saw it on the front page of *The New York Times*, February 11, 1994, was not just how smart it was, but the remarkable diversity of the people endorsing it. Conservatives like Robert Bork, but also two former Harvard Law School deans (Derek Bok and the late Erwin Griswold, LBJ's solicitor general), former Brandeis University president Morris Abram, former ACLU president Norman Dorsen, and even a former president of the American College of Trial Lawyers, Leon Silverman. This idea seemed to be *so* good (like Props 200 and 201, I felt), it cut across ideological lines.

The 15 percent cap wasn't a control on what lawyers could *earn*—they could still earn millions—but rather a control on the "contingency fee" they could *charge* when there was an early offer and little real "contingency." After all, if a lawyer will typically take a case all the way through trial, risking tremendous amounts of time and even his own cash for 33 percent or 40 percent, isn't 15 percent more than adequate for doing the basic work of finding out the plaintiff's grievance and preparing a really strong demand letter? The California State Bar's own canon of ethics requires lawyers, in setting fees, to take account of eleven factors—mainly, how much work they had to do and how much risk they took. Yet—and isn't this remarkable?—the fee almost always seems to come out to 33 percent.

Prop 202 was less "wage controls" than a sort of "usury law" for lawyers.

(When someone—often unsophisticated, sometimes desperate—goes to borrow money, there's a power imbalance. The lender holds most of the cards. Hence the usury laws. It is very much the same—but without benefit of any analogous laws—when someone has been hurt or defrauded and needs a lawyer. He or she is often unsophisticated, sometimes desperate—sometimes on massive painkillers or other judgment-altering drugs. The lawyer holds the keys to the judicial system. "Everybody knows" 33 percent is standard—sign here. I'm not a big fan of government regulation, but I think usury laws are a reasonable trade-off for the social good.)

APPENDIX B

# Michigan: The Exception

Michigan's no-fault, adopted in 1973, is widely regarded as the nation's strongest and best plan. It provides unlimited medical and rehabilitation benefits as well as substantial coverage for wage loss. Yet premiums in Michigan today are significantly *lower* than in California—about $350 versus $500 on average for the "damage to people" portion of the insurance premium. This is possible primarily because Michigan also has the nation's strongest "threshold." You can sue for pain and suffering only in cases of "death, serious impairment of body function or permanent serious disfigurement."

(Until 1986 judges decided when that threshold had been met. Then the trial lawyers succeeded in getting the Michigan Supreme Court to rule that, because the law had not specified otherwise, this was a "question of fact" for a jury to decide rather than a "question of law" for the judge. The result was rising costs—which the trial lawyers gleefully cite as an argument against no-fault—as more and more cases went to jury trials, expensive to the system even when no money is awarded. Recently, some balance was restored by the Michigan legislature that should at least partly rein in the lawsuits, and thus the costs, once again.)

Some thoughtful people felt Prop 200 should have allowed more lawsuits and unlimited benefits like Michigan. Fair enough. But lawsuits and unlimited benefits are expensive. How will low-income families pay the bill? We chose a middle ground.

APPENDIX C

# Letters to the Editor

### Harry's Letter

Tobias states twice that Consumers Union did not provide an analysis of the ballot initiatives he promoted. Not true. We provided Tobias, the media, and the public with a statement of our analysis of all three measures on October 4, 1995; it was even quoted in the ballot argument sent to all California voters. Tobias's statement that we did not review Prop 200 is also untrue. I have a letter from Mike Johnson, the campaign consultant/manager, in which he thanks me for my help in previewing the proposal, and an E-mail message from Tobias that shows I previewed the proposal. His claim that CU is "tightly bound" with trial lawyers is spurious. For 60 years, CU has been an independent voice for consumers and beholden to no commercial interests. On occasion we have publicly and specifically differed with trial lawyers, who certainly do not share our position on no-fault. Tobias's adventure in California politics resulted in an overwhelming loss and, unfortunately, set back the goal of enacting a consumer-supported no-fault insurance measure, the kind Consumers Union has urged.

*Harry Snyder*
*Consumers Union*
*San Francisco, California*

The October 4 "analysis" Harry speaks of did not compare Prop 200's proposed system of auto insurance with the current system. Yet that comparison is exactly what voters would have needed to make an intelligent choice—and exactly what consumers look to Consumers Union to do. As for the letter from Mike Johnson, surely Harry knows, or should have known, that it was sarcastic.

## Harvey's Letter

Andrew Tobias's novella about the defeat of three anti-tort propositions on the California ballot last March is fiction. Far from the noble venture he wishes to portray, Tobias's role in backing the measures bears more resemblance to that of Captain Ahab obsessively hunting Moby Dick— only this time the quarry is the fundamental American right to go to court.

Tobias asserts that I somehow tricked every citizen group in California, Ralph Nader (everyone knows how easy it is to fool *him*), and three million voters into rejecting the proposals. Here's the truth: California voters opposed the measures because they were designed to enrich insurance, tobacco, oil, and high-tech companies and other big-business sponsors. For the first time in the nation, the corporate rampage against consumer-protection laws, known as tort "reform," was presented directly to voters and, despite a $15 million campaign budget, decisively rejected.

The proclaimed targets of the March initiatives were greedy trial lawyers and frivolous lawsuits, but it is public access to the judicial branch that the corporations want to crush. The civil justice system is far from perfect. But it is the only remaining branch of government in which an average American can take on the wealthy and the powerful and where truth and justice still have a fair chance over money and influence. Like all tort "reform," the propositions would have left consumers more vulnerable than ever to rip-offs, layoffs, and irresponsible conduct.

The strategy of the Alliance to Revitalize California—the consortium of Silicon Valley corporations, Wall Street investment firms, and wealthy CEOs that backed the three initiatives—was to depict Proposition 200 (the no-fault initiative) as a populist measure. It was a Trojan horse, necessary to sneak the two other initiatives past the voters in a screw-the-lawyers political orgy.

Yet no-fault was a solution in search of a problem in California, where, contrary to Tobias's assertions, a 1988 ballot measure regulating the insurance industry's outlandish waste and inefficiency succeeded in lowering auto-insurance premiums by 4.5 percent between 1989 and 1994 (the rest of the nation saw premiums rise an average of 30 percent), saving drivers an estimated $12 billion. [As noted, *Auto Insurance Report* estimates Prop 103 actually *cost* consumers $4 billion.]

No-fault, by contrast, is an inherently more costly system because it pays the guilty as well as the innocent people involved in a car accident. The average auto-insurance premium rose 45.6 percent between 1989 and 1994 in no-fault states—33 percent more than in liability states. Besides California, the states with the lowest rates of premium growth since 1989 are Georgia, New Jersey, and Pennsylvania. They all repealed their mandatory no-fault systems. Connecticut repealed its no-fault law in January 1994; premiums fell 10 percent that year. [Harvey insists on calling all the lawyer-sabotaged no-fault states "no-fault," when in fact—he's right—they were a disaster. Michigan is the state to compare California with.]

Prop 200 would have cut policy benefits to the bone [just a paltry million dollars per person?] and, at the same time, completely blocked the right of injured car-accident victims to seek compensation in the courts. Here's how it would have worked: Say a reckless driver blows through a stop sign and seriously injures you and your family. Once the minimum benefits of the no-fault policy ($50,000 to cover medical bills and lost wages) are exhausted, you're in big trouble. You're forbidden from going after the driver in court—no matter how serious your injuries, how negligent the motorist, how wealthy he is, or how large his insurance policy.

In its effort to reduce costs, the plan exacerbated no-fault's other congenital defect: its profound departure from the American tradition of individual accountability. Conceptually, no-fault treats good drivers and bad drivers the same. [No, bad drivers pay more and are liable for any property damage they cause.] This is not an endearing quality in California, where the automobile is an integral part of everyday life, nor is it congruent with the state's contemporary politics of "personal responsibility." No-fault means your fault when it comes to your insurance company.

Tobias has never acknowledged the cruel, and ultimately fatal, expediency of eliminating the right of consumers to go to court against a reckless driver. Nor has he been held to account for his actions in Hawaii in the spring of 1995. At the time, State Farm, the nation's largest auto insurance company, was promoting "pure no-fault" legislation with an expensive public-relations campaign across the state. Lured by the limelight, Tobias was squired around Honolulu by State Farm's public-relations people in support of the bill. He even made an appearance in the insurer's newspaper ads, arguing there would be a 45 percent rate reduction if the bill passed. (The reduction was fraudulent; independent experts concluded that the bill was drafted in a way that would allow insurers to avoid reducing rates by even one penny [Oh, nonsense, Harvey].) Governor Ben Cayetano subsequently vetoed the legislation.

In California, Tobias's most inexcusable capitulation involved packaging no-fault with two other proposals that would have severely eroded the rights of injured or defrauded consumers. Proposition 201 was the prize for the Wall Street and Silicon Valley CEOs, speculators, and high-tech moguls who financed the three initiatives. It would have forced consumers who had been swindled out of their savings, pensions, or IRAs to post a bond to cover the thief's legal fees before filing a lawsuit against him. [It is the multimillionaire investors, equally swindled, who would have posted the bond—or the rich law firms that stand to gain so much from well-founded suits. Small shareholders would risk nothing, yet be entitled to 100 percent of their pro rata share of any settlement.] Worse, if the investor lost the case—or won, but got less from the jury than the defendant had offered to pay—the investor would then forfeit the bond and pay all the defendant's legal expenses. The obvious effect: to prevent people from pursuing justice.

Proposition 202 was even more insidious. The proposition would have cut lawyers' fees by up to 50 percent. But whose lawyers? Not the lawyers for insurance companies like Transamerica, a heavy contributor to the initiatives. Not lawyers for Intel; the company and its chairman, Gordon Moore, kicked in more than $1 million. Instead, it limited the fees of lawyers who work on a contingency. These attorneys represent consumers who can't afford to pay $300 an hour for legal help. They are, in effect, the private cops of our legal system. Cutting their fees in half was designed to discourage them from taking cases against wealthy defendants. [No, it was designed—and endorsed by legal scholars across the political spectrum—to save consumers money and encourage early settlements.]

When it comes to promoting the destruction of tort laws, big business prefers to rely on its multimillion-dollar "sales force": think tanks like the Manhattan Institute; academicians like University of Virginia law professor Jeffrey O'Connell, who has been paid to consult with no-fault supporters; and Tobias. But California voters are too savvy to be fooled by trickery. So the proposition sponsors created a "virtual consumer group" populated by PR strategists and other flacks.

A political fund-raising company, incongruously named Progressive Campaigns, was paid $5.3 million by the tort deformers for its "grass-roots" work on behalf of the initiatives. Bill Zimmerman, a onetime liberal political consultant, claimed to be a consumer advocate in support of the measures; his political consulting firm was paid $766,000 by corporate sponsors in the last 12 weeks of the campaign—pretty good for a "consumer advocate." [Harvey's Prop 103 Enforcement Project has been paid about $2 million for its efforts over the years.]

Tobias also adopted a new identity as a "consumer advocate" in a constant stream of letters, telephone calls, and E-mail to citizen leaders who had come out against the three propositions, urging that they recant. But most dismissed him, perhaps because they agree with me that he's a kook. Defeated, he now mocks Nader's opposition to the initiatives, concluding his article with a sniveling of praise.

A few more corrections: First, I was not, as Tobias asserts, forced to resign from the organization known as Voter Revolt. Second, the fees and expenses obtained by our nonprofit organization for successfully challenging unjustified-rate cases are returned to our organization. I do not, as Tobias implies, keep any of this money. [Except perhaps for the matter of his salary, the size of which he does not disclose.]

Apparently, Tobias just can't comprehend the commitment Nader and I share to defending and advancing the civil-justice system that protects Americans injured by the misbehavior of others. When lawyers agree with our positions, we welcome their support. When lawyers compromise consumers' interests in a strong legal system, or when they propose settlements in airline or automobile class-action lawsuits that give consumers too little, Nader intervenes in opposition. When insurance companies jack up rates without justification or sponsor proposals like Prop 200 to enrich themselves at the expense of injured motorists, Nader can be counted on to stand up for the average person. For 35 years, Ralph Nader has been America's public citizen for the consumer's health, safety, and economic well-being. He has never benefited personally from any of his work, which is why so many rightly consider him an American hero.

*Harvey Rosenfield*
*Los Angeles, California*

Harvey thinks no-fault was "a solution in search of a problem in California." Wow. Rates are so high in California that nearly 30 percent of the drivers on the road (and perhaps 50 percent of the accident causers) are uninsured—so high that many of those who are insured buy the legal minimum $15,000 coverage. No problem, says

Harvey. Yet if you are hurt by one of these drivers—or by a hit-and-run driver or in a one-car crash or in a crash where you can't prove the other driver was at fault—you get nothing, or next to nothing, from your right to sue.

Under Prop 200, by contrast, the standard policy—which the Rand Corporation estimated would cost people less than they pay today—would have provided up to $1 million in medical, rehab and lost wages in all those cases. And even more to pedestrians and kids on skateboards. (And automatic bare-minimum $50,000 coverage to every child in California, no matter what.) Harvey sees no virtue in that. He is untroubled that $2.5 billion of the auto-insurance premiums Californians pay each year goes to lawyers—more than to doctors, hospitals, rehabilitation specialists and chiropractors combined. Untroubled that drivers in California are more than three times as likely to fake "soft tissue" injuries as drivers in Michigan (the one state with close to true no-fault) and that honest consumers wind up paying the tab.

Much the same is true in Hawaii, where—Harvey is right—I did join State Farm (a mutual company, owned by its policyholders) in supporting a bill the Hawaii legislature had passed by a wide margin. It would have slashed insurance premiums by cutting out most of the legal expense and fraud. The governor, a former trial lawyer, vetoed it, and I flew out to Hawaii to urge override. Let me offer you the same Hawaii deal I got: an all-expenses-paid vacation. That is, you have to pay all your own expenses; you have to go in late June and wear a suit and tie the whole time; and you have to spend that time, unpaid, talking about auto-insurance reform. But, yes, you do get to be driven to appointments by a PR guy in a sedan. Any takers?

$$$$$$$$$$$$$$$$$$$$$$$$$$$$$$$$$$$$$$$$$$$$$$$$$$$$$$$$$$$$$$$$$$$$$$$$$$$$$$$$$$$$$$$$$$$$$$$$$$$

APPENDIX D

# A Sampling of Historic Document Dealers— No Endorsement Implied!

ADS Autographs
Box 8006
Webster, NY 14580

Walter Burks
Box 23097
Stanley, KS 66223

Gary Hendershott
Box 22520
Little Rock, AR 72221

Lionheart Autographs
470 Park Avenue South PH
New York, NY 10016

Profiles in History
345 N. Maple Drive #202
Beverly Hills, CA 90210

Max Rambod
9903 Santa Monica Blvd.
Beverly Hills, CA 90212

Remember When Auctions
Box 1829
Wells, ME 04090

Joseph Rubinfine
505 S. Flagler Dr.
West Palm Beach, FL 33401

Scott Winslow Associates
Box 10240
Bedford, NH 03110

APPENDIX E

# How Not to Fix Social Security (and Why We Don't Need a Balanced Budget)

The most frequently proposed Social Security reform—to gradually privatize the system, with people managing their own retirement accounts—has great surface appeal but big problems:

- While you're making the transition, one generation has to shoulder the nearly impossible burden of *two* systems—saving for themselves *and* providing benefits to today's older generations.

- What do you do if a person invests poorly? You'd still need a safety net.

- Won't this leave an awful lot of unsophisticated people prey to slick pitches, high commissions and transaction costs?

- But mainly (to my mind): why should everyone have to save—and live, once retired—as if he or she will last to age hundred and ten? Social Security is not just a "pact between generations," though it is that, with each generation pledging to assist the previous one. It is also a pact among citizens of the *same* generation. We all pay in more or less equally (given equal incomes), knowing that those who die first will have wound up subsidizing those who outlive them. Yet this seems a reasonable deal, because it keeps us from *all* having to live like paupers at age sixty-five in case we have to stretch our funds to last thirty-five or forty years. (So there's another reason we'd still need a taxpayer-financed safety net: would we allow ninety-two-year-olds whose cash has run out to freeze and starve?)

There's a reasonable case for going partway. With enough warning, you could eliminate benefits to those who don't need them and cut back somewhat on benefits even to those who do. The savings from this would be used to fund the individual investment accounts people are talking about. But why? Why take that extra step, in effect penalizing people who live longer than average, as tens of millions will?

After all, there's still plenty of variety in retirement lifestyles. It's not as if America becomes a homogenized, socialized society even with today's rather modest benefit levels. Some retire in splendor; others manage on Social Security alone. If the "safety net" is indeed a bit above bare subsistence—well, why not? For one thing, it's a relatively small concession to a sort of national neighborliness. A social compact that binds us together. We're the only advanced country in the world without universal health insurance, and we no longer have the common experience of the draft or of Walter Cronkite every night. Maybe we should keep Social Security.

The good news is that Social Security is finally salting away some money as "reserves" for the looming baby boom generation. That money—roughly $75 billion in 1997 alone—is invested in "special" Treasury securities of varying maturities that are actually special only in one important respect: the trust fund can redeem them "at par"—100¢ on the dollar—anytime it wants, should it need the money before the bonds mature. (That's a nice feature. If you or I wanted to cash in long-term bonds at a time when interest rates had risen, we'd lose money. They'd be trading at a discount.) The average interest being earned on the accumulated reserve is about 7.5 percent.

I know that in a world of huge increases in the stock market each year this must seem paltry, but actually—historically—it ain't hay. The more typical, long-term return that can be expected from the stock market (dividends plus price appreciation) is around 9 percent or 10 percent, and there have been long periods when it's been lower. (Did you know, for example, that the market was no higher in 1978 than it had been fourteen years earlier?)

The bad news is that what you may have heard is true: when politicians talk about "balancing the budget" in 2002 (or whenever), they are including as "revenue" the excess Social Security taxes being set aside as reserves for the future. In other words, that money is being double-counted. In 2002, if the budget does indeed "balance," as Democrats and Republicans are using the term, it will still be in deficit by a projected $96 billion. (That's the excess Social Security expects to collect in 2002 to augment its reserve.) So it won't be balanced at all.

You can certainly get a bit hot under the collar at the lack of candor on this issue. I'm frankly surprised more hasn't been made of it, except that I guess neither party feels it can convincingly blame the other for sweeping this under the rug.

The good news about the bad news is that, impossibly large as these numbers are, viewed in context they're not so bad.

Let's say we pretend to have a balanced budget but that, in fact, after being honest about Social Security, we're actually running a $100 billion deficit—and adding that much, year after relentless year, to the overall national debt. Sounds awful, no?

But let's say, also, that as this is happening the economy is growing 5 percent a year—2.5 percent inflation plus 2.5 percent real growth. What does that mean?

Well, it means that our national debt, $5.25 trillion or so now, would be growing by just under 2 percent a year ($100 billion is 2 percent of $5 trillion) while the economy as a whole would be growing at 5 percent.

Imagine a home you had bought for $100,000 appreciating in value at 5 percent a year while the $80,000 mortgage you had taken to buy it grew at 2 percent. After twenty years the home would be worth $265,000, while the mortgage would have grown to $119,000.

Naturally, it would be nice to have a house with no mortgage at all. But really, when you think about it, so long as the debt is growing slower than the economy as a whole, *it is shrinking* relative to the economy as a whole. It's a lot less nerve-racking to have a $119,000 mortgage on a $265,000 home, I should think, than an $80,000 mortgage on a $100,000 home.

Run this out yet another twenty years and the home's value is up to $703,000, while the mortgage is $177,000. A century later (just for the fun of it—and one can imagine the U.S. economy really might be around a century from now, growing 5 percent a year, just as it was a century ago), this hypothetical house would have grown in value to an astonishing $92 million and change, while the mortgage would be barely $1 million.

At the end of World War II, the national debt was well over twice as large as the gross national product. Then it got down as low as 45 percent. Today it's climbed back toward 70 percent—which is actually a fairly low ratio compared to most other nations. But the main thing is this: until recently, the annual budget deficit was so large, especially when reported honestly, without double-counting the money to be set aside for the Social Security trust fund, that the national debt was actually growing *faster* than the economy as a whole. Big trouble. Lately, and going forward, and even after admitting that the Social Security "reserves" should really not be counted as "revenue," the national debt has been growing *slower* than the economy as a whole. So we've begun the long, gradual process of shrinking the debt again.

That's good.

Is it important to be "leaning against the wind" and, in all but recession years, have the debt gradually shrink relative to the size of the overall economy? I think so. Must it ever be paid off in full? Not really. Lots of healthy enterprises have some debt.

It's reasonable to be concerned and vigilant, but the sky is not falling. And yes, although it won't be much, and it may not go to people who don't need it, and it may even be called something else, there will be Social Security. But you won't be a happy camper if it's all you have to fall back on.

# Index

Abram, Morris, 187
accounting, creative, 11
Accutrade, 156
Acheson, Dean, 129–30
ACLU Lesbian & Gay Rights Project, 171
*Actuarial Review,* 74
Adams, Samuel, 130
advertising, 7, 59, 72
    auto insurance and, 92–93, 107, 111–12
    for Proposition 202, 107
    TV, 57, 60–66, 68, 69, 107, 111–12
AIDS, 65, 101–2
AIG, 92
airplanes, 126–27
alcohol, 45, 65
Alexei (Tobias's Russian partner), 65–68
Algebra Project, 170
Allen, Woody, 20
Alliance to Revitalize California, 100, 190
Allstate, 92
American Electronics Association, 185
American Trial Lawyers Association (ATLA),
    104, 109, 110
Anthony, Michael, 15
anti-Semitism, 129
antiwar movement, 6, 7
apartments:
    appraisal of, 22
    co-ops vs. condominiums, 21
    painting and maintenance of, 23
    purchase of, 18–23, 39–43, 46–68, 117

Apple III, 33
appraisals, 22, 23, 123
Aron, Adam, 162
Arthur, Chester A., 132
Article 121, 60–61
Atari, 33, 34
Atkins, Chet, 107
ATMs, 25, 26
Australia trip, 162–63
Auto Choice Reform Bill, 114
auto insurance, 74–115, 144–55, 185–201
    facts about, 83–85
    in Hawaii, 91–94, 146, 191–92, 194
    liability, 84
    in Michigan, 74, 83, 84, 85, 99, 100, 150,
        151–52, 188, 191
    NICO study of, 76–77
    no-fault, 71, 72, 77–83, 85–115, 144–48,
        151, 188–91, 194
    pay-at-the-pump, 77–78, 100
    Proposition 103 and, 75–76, 79–80, 81*n,*
        97, 190
    Proulx's strategy for reform of, 88–90
    *see also* Proposition 200; Proposition 201;
        Proposition 202
*Auto Insurance Alert!* (Tobias), 77
*Auto Insurance Report,* 190
averaging down, 47

Mr. B, lawsuit of, 137–42
Bailey, F. Lee, 71–72, 95, 106

Bankers Trust, 24
Bedford Village, N.Y., 119
beefalo, 30
being with money, 3, 68
Belle Meade Studios, 49
bench warrants, 48
Berendt, John, 27n
Berkshire Hathaway, 37, 136
*Best Little Boy in the World, The* (Tobias),
    147, 148
best-sellers, 18, 26–27, 73
bills, unpaid, 49, 54–55
Biscayne Boulevard, 46, 49
blue jeans, sale of, 57, 58
boats, 126
Bob (Tobias's partner), 44, 46, 48–49, 52,
    53, 55
Bogart, Humphrey, 128
Bok, Derek, 187
bonds, municipal, 15
Bork, Robert, 187
Bradshaw, John, 14
Brando (Jimmy's German shepherd), 54
*Brief History of Time, A* (Hawking), 178
budget, balancing of, 198–99
Buffett, Warren, 37, 155–57, 167
Bush, George, 163
Butyrka prison, 61
Buyer, Liz, 112

cabdrivers, Russian-born, 59
California, 70
    auto insurance in, 74–91, 94–115,
        144–55, 185–87, 189–201
    Insurance Department of, 80, 88
    Proposition 103 in, 75–76, 79–80, 81n
    Senate insurance committee in, 77–78
Californians to Save Our Economy, 83
California Nurses Association, 95n
California State Bar, 187
California Trial Lawyers Association, 90
Cambridge Trust Company, 24
capital gains tax, 172
Carnegie, Andrew, 163
cars:
    insurance for, *see* auto insurance
    purchase of, 126
Carson, Rachel, 72
Carter administration, 21
Catherine the Great, Czarina of Russia, 61
cattle-breeding shelters, 29–30
Cayetano, Ben, 92, 93, 192
Center for Responsive Law, 153
Chamber of Commerce, California, 83, 85,
    86
charitable giving, 163–75
    fine points of, 173–75
    mechanics of, 172–73
    philosophy for, 166–72

Charles (Tobias's boyfriend), 159–60
cheap vs. frugal, 161, 163
checking accounts, 24–26
Cherner, Joe, 107
Chernobyl, 118
Chernomyrdin, Viktor, 65
Child, Julia, 34
Childreach, 128
*Chorus Line, A,* 28
Christie's 132
Citibank, 24–26
Citicorp, 16–17, 25
Citizens Against Phony Initiatives, 91, 94
*Civil Action, A* (Harr), 115
civil rights movement, 6, 170
Claybrook, Joan, 104
Clinton, Bill, 106, 186
closings, 22
clothes, 126, 127–28, 156, 159–61
cocaine, 41, 45, 48
Cold War, 59, 60
commercials, TV, 57, 60–66, 68, 69, 107,
    111–12
Common Cause, 186
communism, 7, 61
computer graphics, 65–66, 68
computers, 33–38, 68, 127
computer software, 33–38, 46
    Wavefront, 65, 66
condominiums:
    co-ops vs., 21
    in Florida, 39–43, 46–48, 136
Congress, U.S., 89, 112, 114, 147, 186
Connecticut, auto insurance in, 191
Consumer Attorneys Issues Political Action
    Committee, 106n
Consumer Attorneys of California (CACA),
    90–91
consumer movement, 72
*Consumer Reports,* 99–100, 109n, 149
"Consumers and Their Attorneys Against
    Proposition 200, 201 & 202," 95n, 111
Consumers Union (CU), 72, 83, 85, 93,
    99–100, 101, 104, 109–11, 149, 189
"contingent fee" initiative (Proposition 202),
    89–90, 95n, 97, 105, 112–13, 186–87,
    192
Cook, Scott, 87
co-ops:
    boards of, 22
    condominiums vs., 21
corn, 120, 121
Costco, 127
Council of Better Business Bureaus, 175
Court, Jamie, 94, 147–52
C-Saw, 34
Czechoslovakia, 58

Dakota, 19–20

Darrow, Clarence, 128
Davis, Joe, 39
*Death of Common Sense, The* (Howard), 144*n*
DeLaurentiis, Semena, 125
Democrats, Democratic party, 78, 107, 186, 205
disabled, equal access for, 143–44
disability insurance, 84
discount brokers, 122*n*, 155–57
Dmitri (Tobias's Russian partner), 65–68
Dole, Robert, 114, 147
*Don't Bother to Knock* (film), 130
Dorf, Julie, 171
Dorsen, Norman, 187
drug dealers, 50, 51
drugs, 41, 45, 46, 48–50, 52–55, 137
drug treatment, 46, 50, 53
Durone, Arthur, 145, 146

Einstein, Albert, 129, 131, 132
Employment Nondiscrimination Act (ENDA), 171–72
Erhard, Werner, 3
*Esquire*, 12, 14–17
*Excuse Factor, The* (Olson), 144*n*

Falvey, David, 154–55
fantasy sex hangings, 74
farmhouses, sale of, 121–23
farm managers, 119, 122–23
farms, purchase of, 117–23
"Fearless Forecast," 16–17
Federal Reserve banks, 158*n*
Feinstein, Dianne, 89
Felker, Clay, 12, 13
Fellmeth, Bob, 102–3, 105
Fidelity Investments Charitable Gift Fund, 173
*Fire and Ice* (Tobias), 18, 19, 31
fire-safety violations, 49
Fixx, Jim, 33–34
Florida, real estate in, 39–56, 136–42
*Forbes*, 96–97
Forbes, Malcolm, 127
Forbes Building, 132
Ford, Henry, 129
Ford Motor Company, 118, 129*n*
*Fortune*, 34*n*, 74
Foster Parents Plan, 10
Fox, 131
Frank, Barney, 60–61, 107, 171
Franklin, Benjamin, 118*n*, 130
Franklin group of funds, 117
fraud, auto insurance and, 74, 84, 92, 146
Freedley (merchant), 123
From, Al, 107
*From the President's Pen* (Manuscript Society), 132

frugal vs. cheap, 161, 163
*Funny Money Game, The* (Tobias), 12

Gamboa, John, 83
Garamendi, John, 78, 79
Garfield, James A., 132
Gates, Bill, 79
Gay, Lesbian, Straight Teachers Network (GLSTN), 170–71
GEICO, 92
General Dynamics, 4–5
General Motors (GM), 4–5, 72, 89*n*, 104
Georgia, auto insurance in, 191
Gibbons, Bob, 96
*Give but Give Wisely*, 175
Goethe, Johann Wolfgang von, xiii
Goggin, Danny, 125
golf, 155–57
*Good Morning America* (TV show), 76
Greenberg, Maurice, 92
Greenlining Coalition, 83
Griffin, Merv, 37
Griswold, Erwin, 187
Gubarev, Vladimir, 63, 64

Häagen-Dazs, 52, 54
Hafif, Herb, 97
hair-gel stock, 123
H&R Block, 38
Harcourt Brace, 27
Harr, Jonathan, 115
Harvard Business School, 11, 17
Harvard Student Agencies (HSA), 7–10, 59, 142–44
Harvard University, 5, 7, 59
Hawaii, auto insurance in, 91–94, 146, 191–92, 194
Hawking, Stephen, 178
Hayes-Raitt, Kelly, 91, 94, 95
health insurance, 74, 75, 84
*Henry Ford and the Jews* (Lee), 129*n*
Herzog, Werner, 61
Heston, Charlton, 107
historic documents, collecting of, 128–33
Hitler, Adolf, 129, 131
hockey team, as tax shelter, 32–33
homeowner's insurance, 84
homosexuality, 60–61, 107
hostile takeovers, 13–14, 18
hotels, 161
houses:
    sale of, 121–23
    Tobias's purchase of, 42–44
Howard, Philip, 144*n*
Human Rights Campaign (HRC), 171–72
Hunter, Bob, 76–77, 104

IBM, 34, 37, 176
Ilya (Tobias's Russian partner), 65–68

index funds, 158
Indiana, real estate in, 121–23
inflation, 28, 51, 198
insurance, 71–100, 119
  auto, *see* auto insurance
  health, 74, 75, 84
  homeowner's, 84
  life, 74
Insurance Reform, 153
Intel, 192
Internal Revenue Service (IRS), 164, 166, 172, 174n
Intuit, 87–88, 185
investment:
  beating the system and, 15
  guide to, 26–28
  *see also specific investments*
*Invisible Bankers, The* (Tobias), 73–77, 103
Iowa, farmland in, 117–21
IRAs (individual retirement accounts), 14, 117, 166, 174
*Izvestiya*, 68

Jennings, Kevin, 170
Jimmy (Tobias's building manager), 44–46, 48–55
  brokerage firm job of, 44
  death of, 52, 54–55
  in monastery, 45
  properties managed by, 46, 48–55
  safe of, 54
Jobs, Steve, 33
Johnson, Mike, 79–81, 86–87, 91, 97–98, 104, 150, 189
Johnson & Johnson, 33
Julie (real estate agent), 47

Kaiser, Herb, 107
Kaiser, Joy, 107
Karpatkin, Rhoda, 93, 109
Katz, Michael, 68–69
Keating, Charles, 111, 112
Kennedy, Edward (Ted), 89
Kennedy, John F., 129
KGB, 57, 58
*Kids Say Don't Smoke* (Tobias), 62, 63–64
Kirkwood, James, 28
Klein, Robert, 108
Koscot Interplanetary, 70–71
Kosinski, Jerzy, 27n
Kroll Associates, 67

Lambda Legal Defense Fund, 171
landlords, problems of, 51, 137–42
Latino Issues Forum, 83
Latvia, 66, 67
lawyers, 22, 39, 40–41, 48, 71
  auto insurance and, 74, 78, 83, 90–97, 106n, 107–13, 145–46, 186–87

Lee, Albert, 129n
Lefrak, Samuel Jonathan, 13
Legal Services of Greater Miami, 137–42
Lerach, Bill, 186
*Let's Go*, 8–9
leverage, social investment and, 169, 170–71
Levin, Fred, 96
Lieberman, Joseph I., 114, 147, 152
life insurance, 74
Lightner, Candace, 106n
Lincoln, Abraham, 131, 132
Lipsen, Linda, 110
Listyev, Vladimir, 65, 66
Little Building No. 2, 44, 46, 48–49, 55
Los Angeles *Daily News*, 94
*Los Angeles Times*, 79, 85
Los Angeles Trial Lawyers Association, 95
loss aversion, 127–28
lottery tickets, 124
Louganis, Greg, 170
Lowenstein, Al, 6
Luce, Claire, 129
Luce, Clare Boothe, 129

McCaw, Craig, 79
McConnell, Mitch, 114, 147, 152
McGovern, George, 115
Macon Whoopees, 32–33
Madison Avenue Bookshop, 18
Madonna, 131
Maloney, Pat, 97
*Managing Your Money* (software), 33–38, 46, 87
  version 12 of, 37–38
Manhattan Institute, 192
Mann, Valerie Papaya, 101–2
Manuscript Society, 132
Mary (Tobias's assistant), 53, 54
Massachusetts, auto insurance in, 87, 99
May, Elaine, 19, 20–21
MECA, 33–38, 87
Media Arts, 66–68, 133
Medical Education for South African Blacks (MESAB) 169
Metcalf, Wayne, 93
Miami, Fla., real estate in, 39–56
Miami Beach, Fla., 44, 46
Michigan, auto insurance in, 74, 83, 84, 85, 99, 100, 150, 151–52, 188, 191
*Midnight in the Garden of Good and Evil* (Berendt), 27
*Mikey and Nicky* (movie), 19
Mikulski, Barbara, 89
*Millionaire, The* (TV show), 15
Mish, Frederick C., 148
monasteries, 45
money:
  being with, 3, 68
  doing well with, 158–59

keeping score with, 4
*Money,* 81
*Money Show, The,* 29
Monroe, Marilyn, 130–31
Monty (computerized game), 155
Moore, Gordon, 90, 192
Moore, Mary Tyler, 20
Moore, Michael, 104$n$
mortgages, 19, 20, 21$n$, 118, 120, 198–99
Moses, Robert, 6, 170
Mothers Against Drunk Driving, 106$n$
movies, 18, 19, 20, 104, 129$n$
Moynihan, Patrick, 114, 147
Murdoch, Rupert, 14, 131
mutual funds, 14, 117, 122$n$, 133, 135, 166
Mutual Shares, 14, 117

Nader, Ralph, 7
  auto insurance and, 70, 71–72, 74, 75–76,
    79–80, 83, 85, 86, 91–98, 100–110,
    112, 114–15, 145–48, 152–54, 190,
    193
  Tobias's correspondence with, 103–4
Ralph Nader Congress Project, 72
National Charities Information Bureau,
  175
national debt, 198, 199
National Insurance Consumer Organization
  (NICO), 76–77, 81
National Press Club, 77
National Student Marketing Corp. (NSMC),
  9–11, 34, 70, 153, 154
negotiation, poor form vs., 161–63
Network Project (Proposition 103
  Enforcement Project), 80, 94–96, 147,
  148, 193
net worth, 36–37, 38
New Jersey, auto insurance in, 191
News Corp., 131
*Newsweek,* 74
*New York,* 12–14, 18, 28–29
New York, N.Y.:
  apartments in, 18–23, 42, 43
  Finance Department of, 43
  finances of, 21
  taxes in, 18, 43
New York State Lottery, 14
*New York Times,* 18, 19, 72, 74, 96, 176,
  187
*New York Times Magazine,* 43, 79
no-fault auto-insurance initiative
  (Proposition 200), 88–89, 90, 95$n$,
  100, 102, 105, 107–11, 113, 145, 151,
  188–91, 194
*Nunsense,* 124–26

O'Connell, Jeffrey, 102, 192
oil-and-gas tax shelters, 30–31
Olson, Walter, 144$n$

*Only Investment Guide You'll Ever Need, The*
  (Tobias), 26–28, 31, 158
*Opportunities for Industry and the Safe
  Investment of Capital—or—1,000
  Chances to Make Money* (Freedley),
  123
Orwell, George, 108
ostrich burgers, 127

Packard, David, 90, 167
*Painted Bird, The* (Kosinski), 27$n$
painting, 23
Palm Bay Club, 39–43, 46–48, 56, 136
Pan Am, 162
*Parade,* 109
Paramount, 19
password, forget-proof, 35
PBS, 45, 46, 127
Peat, Marwick, Mitchell, 11
Pennsylvania, auto insurance in, 191
*Pennsylvania Gazette,* 130
Philip Morris, 57, 68
Poland, 59
poor form, negotiation vs., 161–63
Price, Michael, 14, 117
Prince, the, 51–52, 54, 136
prisoners, Soviet, 60–61
Progressive Campaigns, 192
property taxes, 81$n$
Proposition 103, 75–76, 79–80, 81$n$, 97,
  190
Proposition 103 Enforcement Project
  (Network Project), 80, 94–96, 147,
  148, 193
Proposition 106, 97
Proposition 200 (no-fault auto-insurance
  initiative), 88–89, 90, 95$n$, 100, 102,
  105, 107–11, 113, 145, 151, 188–91,
  194
Proposition 201 ("strike suit" initiative), 89,
  90, 95$n$, 105, 111–14, 185–86
Proposition 202 ("contingent fee" initiative),
  89–90, 95$n$, 97, 105, 112–13, 186–87,
  192
Proulx, Tom, 87–91, 185
*P.S. Your Cat Is Dead* (Kirkwood), 28–29,
  125
Public Citizen, 7, 72, 79, 96–97, 115, 152

Quicken, 38, 87
Quinn, Jane Bryant, 77, 108

Raftery, Mary, 102
Randall, Cortes Wesley, 11, 70
RAND Corporation, 88, 107, 108, 194
  Institute for Civil Justice of, 84
real estate, 30
  in Florida, 39–56, 136–42
  stock compared with, 44

Tobias's purchase of, 18–23, 39–56, 117–23
*see also* apartments; condominiums; co-ops; mortgages
real estate agents, 19–22, 39–40, 47
real estate investment trusts, 56, 117
recession, 80
Reeves, Richard, 81*n*
refrigerators, dorm-room, 10–11
rents, 137
for farmhouses, 122–23
for farmland, 119, 120
Republicans, Republican party, 107, 115, 205
research and development partnership, as tax shelter, 33
retirement savings, 13, 14
*see also* IRAs
Reuvekamp, Jeff, 145–46
Reuvekamp, Mylene, 146
Revlon, 18
Revson, Charles, 18
Rickles, Don, 37
risk, 15, 124
RJR, 57
*Roger and Me* (film), 104
Rose, Billy, 118*n*
Rosenfield, Harvey, 76, 80, 83, 85–86, 90, 91, 92, 94–96, 100, 101, 112, 146–48, 152–55, 190–94
Rostelekom, 134–35
Rubin, Jerry, 34
Rukeyser, Louis, 34
Russia, 60–69, 165
stock in, 133–35
Tobias in, 60–62, 64
TV commercials in, 57, 60–65
Russian language, 6, 58, 59, 62, 64

*Sacramento Bee*, 78, 94, 96
Sal (Tobias's building manager), 55–56
*San Francisco Chronicle*, 145–46
*San Jose Mercury News*, 112
San Remo, 20–21
Sarandon, Susan, 170
savings, 4, 13, 158–59
interest on, 4
retirement, 13, 14; *see also* IRAs
*Schindler's List* (film), 129*n*
Scorpio Entertainment, 126*n*
Seagate Technology, 111–12
Security National Bank, 119
Senate Bill 1860, 152
Shernoff, Bill, 95*n*
Shoah Project, 170
Shugart, Al, 111–12
*Signatures*, 12
Silverman, Leon, 187
Silvers, Sid, 26

Simon, John, 28–29
Simon & Schuster, 73
Simpson, O. J., 95, 101, 106
Slater, Mark, 61, 62, 63, 65, 133
Sloate, Laura, 118
Smith, Roger, 104
Smith, Wesley, 85, 91, 95
Smith Barney, 42
Smokefree Educational Services, 168
smoking, 57, 60–65, 68, 133
Snyder, Harry, 83, 100, 109, 110–11, 147, 189
socialism, 6–7, 59
socially responsible investing, 175–77
Social Security, 163*n*, 196–99
Social Security tax, 101, 205
Social Venture Network conference, 104–5
Soros, George, 164
Sotheby's, 132
South Africa, 6, 169, 175
South Beach, Fla., 43, 44, 56
Soviet Union, 57–60
Tobias in, 6, 7, 58
*see also* Russia
speech making, 43, 162–63
Spielberg, Steven, 170
Stalin, Joseph, 60
State Farm, 92–93, 150–54, 191, 194
stock, 4–5, 28, 204–5
of Berkshire Hathaway, 37, 156
of Citicorp, 25
of Ford, 118
hair-gel, 123
of NSMC, 9, 10, 11
real estate compared with, 44
Russian, 133–35
stock brokers, 122, 123, 155–57
stock options, 9, 10, 11, 34
Stoddard, Tom, 107
Streisand, Barbra, 105
"strike suit" initiative (Proposition 201), 89, 90, 95*n*, 105, 111–14, 185–86
subsidies, government, 137
Sullivan, Brian, 80
SunAmerica, 154

Tabankin, Margery, 105–6
Talese, Gay, 73
Talese, Nan, 73
Tass, 63
*Taxcut* (software), 34
taxes, 16–19
charitable giving and, 164, 172–74
cut in, 101
income, 16, 17–18, 164, 165
payroll, 55
real estate and, 19, 81*n*, 119
Social Security, 101, 205
taxis, 59

tax shelters, 28–33, 124–26
Taylor, Cornelius, 101, 103
Taylor, Zachary, 132
television, 45
  in Russia, 57, 60–66, 68, 69
  Tobias's appearances on, 9, 37, 64, 76, 93
Templeton Russia Fund (TRF), 135
Teresa, Mother, 129
Thaler, Dick, 127
theatrical tax shelter, 28–29, 124–26
Thoreson, Dick, 119, 121
*Thy Neighbor's Wife* (Talese), 73
Tillinghast & Co., 81
*Time*, 7, 39, 76, 77
tobacco, 57, 60–65, 68, 107, 133, 175–76
Tobias, Andrew (author):
  allowance of, 3–4
  anti-smoking activities of, 57, 60–65, 68
  arrest of, 57, 58
  article writing of, 12, 19, 21–22, 76, 77
  award of, 17
  book writing of, 12, 18, 26–28, 31, 71–77
  checking account of, 24–26
  computer software development and, 33–38
  education of, 5–9, 11, 17, 58, 59
  as entrepreneur, 8–12
  *Esquire* column of, 14–17
  family background of, 3–6
  at Harvard Student Agencies, 7–10
  Legal Services lawsuit of, 137–42
  as neurotic, 116
  at *New York*, 12–14, 18
  at NSMC, 9–11, 34, 153, 154
  real estate purchases of, 18–23, 39–56, 117–23
  retirement savings of, 13, 14
  Russian language skills of, 6, 58, 59, 62, 64
  Russian partners of, 65–68
  socialism of, 6–7, 59
  speeches of, 43, 162–63
  stock of, 4–5
  stock options of, 9, 10, 11, 34
  taxes of, 16–19, 43
  tax return of, 153, 154
  tax shelters of, 28–33
  $10,000 investment money of, 14–18
  as treasurer, 4, 8
  TV appearances of, 9, 37, 64, 76, 93
  warrant received by, 48
  *see also specific topics*
Tobias, Audrey J. (mother), 4, 7, 11, 42, 121–22

Tobias, Seth D. (father), 3, 7, 11, 59, 72, 103
*Today* show, 9
Torres, Art, 78
Transamerica, 192
Treasury Direct, 158*n*
Treasury securities, 158, 197
Trella's, 3–4
Trial Lawyers for Public Justice, 104
"Trouble in Paradise," 39
T. Rowe Price, 112
Truman, Harry, 129–30
Turner, Glenn Wesley, 70–71, 72, 106
Turner, Ted, 167
Twain, Mark, 118*n*

Ukraine, 117–18
Unincorporated Business Tax, 43
Union of Concerned Scientists, 83
universe, brief history of, 177–81
*Unsafe at Any Speed*, (Nader), 72
USAA, 92, 93

Vanguard, 158*n*
Velez, Eloy, 10
venture capitalists, 124
Victory Garden, 136
Voter Revolt, 76, 79, 83, 90

*Wall Street Journal*, 57, 60, 61, 69, 78, 111
Washington, George, 177
*Washington Post*, 176
Wavefront software, 65, 66
Webb, Clifton, 128
Wertmuller, Lina, 61
Westchester Farm Management, 121
"Whatever Happened to No-Fault?," 99–100
wheelchairs, accommodating, 143–44
*Wise Giving Guide*, 175
Workers' Compensation, 98
World Smoke-Out Day, 64, 68
*Worth*, 146, 154
Wright, Steven, xiii
Wriston, Walter, 16, 17

Xavier University, 170

Yablans, Frank, 13
Yeltsin, Boris, 64–65

Zalaznick, Sheldon, 12, 13
Zanuck, Darryl, 130–31
Zero Population Growth, 167
Zimmerman, Bill, 105, 192–93

You can reach
Andrew Tobias via his daily
comment at www.ceres.com.